NIH READINGS ON THE PROTECTION OF HUMAN SUBJECTS IN BEHAVIORAL AND SOCIAL SCIENCE RESEARCH

Conference Proceedings and Background Papers

NIH READINGS ON THE PROTECTION OF HUMAN SUBJECTS IN BEHAVIORAL AND SOCIAL SCIENCE RESEARCH

Conference Proceedings and Background Papers

Edited by
Joan E. Sieber

University Publications of America

44 North Market Street, Frederick, Maryland 21701

Library of Congress Cataloging in Publication Data

NIH Conference/Workshop (1983: Dallas, Tex.)
NIH Conference/Workshop proceedings and background papers.

1. Social sciences—Research—Moral and ethical aspects—Congresses. 2. Research—Moral and ethical aspects—Congresses. 3. Confidential communications—Congresses. 4. Privacy, Right of—Congresses. 5. Human experimentation in psychology—Congresses. I. Sieber, Joan E. II. Title. III. Title: Protection of human subjects in behavioral and social research.
H62.A3N54 1983 174'.90901 84-7563
ISBN 0-89093-557-2

Printed in the United States of America.

CONTENTS

1. Preface and Overview 1
2. Conference Speakers and Discussants 5

PART 1. OPENING REMARKS

3. Introduction: The IRB and Social and Behavioral Research
Charles R. McCarthy 8
4. Institutional Review Boards and Social Research: A Disruptive, Subjective Perspective, Retrospective and Prospective
Edward L. Pattullo 10
5. A Response to Pattullo
Sue Kier Hoppe 18
6. The IRB Review Process: Applicability, Exemption, Expedited Review
Philippe V. Cardon 23

PART 2. INFORMED CONSENT

7. HHS Regulations on Informed Consent and Their Impact on Behavioral and Social Research
Philippe V. Cardon 28
8. Informed Consent—Always Full Disclosure?
Paul S. Appelbaum 32
9. Informed Consent and the Therapeutic Misconception
Paul S. Appelbaum 36
10. Informed Consent and Deception
Joan E. Sieber 39

PART 3. RESEARCH DESIGN AND EQUITY

11. Equity and Randomized Experiments
Robert F. Boruch 78
12. Some Issues in IRB Considerations of Randomization
Charles R. MacKay 83

PART 4. PRIVACY AND CONFIDENTIALITY
13. Methods for Assuring Individual Privacy and Confidentiality of Information in Social and Behavioral Research
Robert F. Boruch 86
14. The Use of Video Tapes and Issues of Privacy and Confidentiality
Deborah Lowe Vandell 89
15. Some Special Confidentiality Protections for Research on Deviant Behavior
Lorraine B. Torres 95

PART 5. MANAGEMENT OF IRB DATA
16. The Need for a Common Data Base for Human Subjects in Biomedical Research Studies
Robert E. Krebs 99
17. Recent Modifications in the Computerized Data Systems to Track Grant Applications Involving Human Subjects
Joan P. Porter 109

PART 6. IRBS AS MONITORS OF RESEARCH
18. The Perceived and Actual Role of the IRB in Monitoring Research
Joel Cooper 114
19. The IRB's Role in Monitoring Research
Charles R. MacKay 117
20. The Potential Legal Liability of IRBs—A Legal Perspective
Roger Reinsch 120

PART 7. ETHICAL CONSIDERATIONS IN SOCIAL AND BEHAVIORAL RESEARCH
21. The Modern Evolution of Human Experimentation
Stanley J. Reiser 146
22. Emerging Ethical Issues in Social and Behavioral Research
Joan E. Sieber 148
23. Ethical Considerations in Protection of Human Subjects in Social and Behavioral Research
Eleanor S. Kohn 160
24. Animal Welfare Issues
Perrie M. Adams 167

PART 8. FEDERAL REGULATIONS
25. Flexibility for Behavioral and Social Research in Revised HHS Human Subjects Research
Michele W. Applegate 171

26. Flexible Regulation: A Boon to Scientific Freedom and Responsibility
Joel Cooper 175
27. Government Regulations: Do They Facilitate or Hinder Social and Behavioral Research?
Richard T. Louttit 179
28. Research with Vulnerable Populations: Ethical Considerations and Federal Regulations
Natalie Reatig 182

PART 9. FOSTERING INTEGRITY IN RESEARCH

29. Fostering Integrity in Research: A Collective Responsibility
Thomas E. Malone 186
30. The Risks of Government Action and University Inaction
Joel Cooper 191
31. A University Perspective on "Fostering Integrity in Research"
Herman S. Wigodsky 194
32. A Federal Perspective on "Fostering Integrity in Research"
Michele W. Applegate 200
33. Fostering Integrity in Research—NIH Response
Mary L. Miers 203

1. PREFACE AND OVERVIEW

On April 18–19, 1983, the NIH Office for Protection from Research Risks, in collaboration with the University of Texas at Dallas, conducted the first NIH workshop/conference designed solely to address ethical and legal issues that arise in *social and behavioral research.* Other NIH/OPRR workshops have focused on ethical and legal issues in biomedical research, but provided little guidance for IRBs in the area of social and behavioral research. It was therefore decided that the proceedings of this conference should be published, and thus made available to a wider audience. This monograph, which was funded in part by the National Institutes of Health, is the result. The substance and organization of its contents are altered but slightly from that of the conference, to enhance readability.

Special thanks are due to those who made this effort possible. This project began in Washington, D.C. where Charles R. McCarthy, Director, Office for Protection from Research Risks, and Charles R. MacKay, Deputy Director of that Office, created the framework within which this special conference could occur. At the University of Texas at Dallas, John A. Rodman, Director, Office of Sponsored Projects, organized the conference and facilitated the production of this monograph. The staff of the Center for Continuing Education at the University of Texas at Dallas capably administered both the conference and the production of this monograph. Acknowledgement is also due to the Faculty Planning Committee of this workshop/conference: John Rodman (Chair), Perrie Adams, Douglas Glascock, Robert E. Krebs, Stanley J. Reiser, Joan E. Sieber, and Deborah L. Vandell.

This conference and proceedings were designed to stimulate examination of perspectives on the protection of human subjects. Since prudent protection of human subjects involves balancing such powerful competing interests as the autonomy of individuals, social welfare, and the autonomy of science and scientists, differing perspectives abound on this topic! And fortunately, since the individuals representing these perspectives are excellent problem solvers, approaches to resolving conflicts and aligning competing interests also abound. We hope the reader enjoys and profits from the diversity, both of perspectives and of approaches to problem solving, presented here.

Part 1 provides an overview of the new regulations governing social and behavioral research and of the political context in which they were developed. Chapter 3, by Charles R. McCarthy, gives an historical perspective and rationale for the current regulations. This is followed, in Chapter 4, by opinions and brickbats from the loyal opposition, Edward L. "Pat" Pattullo, who has criticized since its inception the federal regulation of social and behavioral research, *and* who has worked unstintingly within that system, as chairperson of an IRB and member of the editorial board of the journal, *IRB.* In Chapter 5, Sue Kier Hoppe, rebuts Pattullo's contention that the regulation of social research raises problems that outweigh its benefits. She then raises other problems based on her experience as a social scientist and IRB chairperson in a medical center. In Chapter 6, Philippe V. Cardon summarizes the actual and intended (as opposed to the perceived) requirements of the new regulations.

Part 2 considers some current issues of informed consent. In Chapter 7, Philippe V. Cardon discusses the flexibility that the new regulations lend to the formulation of informed consent. In Chapter 8, Paul S. Appelbaum analyzes what is meant by full disclosure, and why it may be neither possible nor desirable to attain full disclosure in informed consent. In Chapter 9, Appelbaum discusses the "therapeutic misconception"—subjects' misconception in treatment programs that the researcher necessarily acts only in the subject's best interests. In Chapter 10, Joan E. Sieber considers four issues that arise in research where deception is employed: (l) the kinds of deception that may be employed (e.g., self-deception, deception by a third party, deception with consent to deceive, deception without consent, etc.), (2) possible moral wrongs connected with each kind of deception, (3) possible harms connected with each kind of deception, and (4) the nature and limits of debriefing (dehoaxing and desensitizing). This taxonomy is designed to aid the investigator and the IRB member in choosing the least harmful form of deception that will accomplish the desired scientific objective.

Part 3 is devoted to problems of random assignment in social and behavioral research. In Chapter 11, Robert F. Boruch considers legal, social, methodological and ethical issues connected with random assignment of subjects to conditions in experimental research. He shows that the issues are not necessarily as they appear on the surface, and that a variety of approaches are available to the experimentally oriented investigator. In Chapter 12, Charles R. MacKay discusses the role of procedural justice in resolving these methodological and ethical problems so that the ends of good science and social justice are served.

Part 4 considers various methods and procedures for assuring privacy and confidentiality. In Chapter 13, Robert F. Boruch presents an ingenius array of statistical, legal and procedural tools for protecting the privacy of persons and the confidentiality of data. In Chapter 14, Deborah Lowe Vandell discusses ethical and methodological solutions to problems that arise when data are collected on video tape. And in Chapter 15, Lorraine B. Torres discusses special problems of confidentiality that arise in research on deviant behavior, and legal shields currently available to investigators.

Part 5 considers solutions to problems of managing IRB data. In Chapter 16, Robert E. Krebs presents a computerized IRB data management system that is currently used at the Health Sciences Center, University of Illinois at Chicago. And, in Chapter 17, Joan P. Porter describes the computerized data system that is used at NIH to track grant applications involving human subjects.

Part 6 considers the legal and logistical problems connected with the conception of the IRB as a monitor of research. In Chapter 18, Joel Cooper points out that much attention is given to review of the proposal, which may be vague about the design of certain parts of the study, while little or no attention is given to observing how the design or procedure is carried out or altered in the course of the research. He raises questions concerning the legal liability of IRB members given that they do not monitor the research at all stages. In Chapter 19, Charles R. MacKay addresses the question of legal liability and monitoring, pointing out that the federal regulations do not call for monitoring and that IRB members would not be legally liable unless they chose to disregard or subvert their own procedures, as by failing to respond to reports of noncompliance or harm to subjects. In Chapter 20, Roger W. Reinsch raises some speculative issues about potential liability of IRB members. However, these issues have yet to be raised either in the actual activities of IRBs or in the courts. The views expressed by Charles MacKay give us an alternative perspective on the actual level of concern in these matters.

Part 7 considers a range of ethical considerations that remain outside of the federal regulations. In Chapter 21, Stanley J. Reiser discusses the evolution of human experimentation and its consequences for current conceptions of human research and research regulation. In Chapter 22, Joan E. Sieber discusses a range of ethical issues that are emerging as important issues in social science—issues of epistemology (how we conceive of human social behavior and learn about it) and issues of dissemination and use of knowledge about human social behavior. In Chapter 23, Eleanor S. Kohn examines concerns about the protection of human subjects of social and behavioral research in the context of current social, economic and political crises and warns that the protection of human subjects is not a *fait accompli.* In Chapter 24, Perrie Adams discusses problems that arise in connection with social and behavioral research on animals.

Part 8 discusses the new federal regulations. The main theme of these papers is whether the new regulations help or hinder social and behavioral research. In Chapter 25, Michele W. Applegate discusses the elements of flexibility in the new regulations. In Chapter 26, Joel Cooper attests to the ways in which this flexibility promotes scientific freedom and responsibility. In Chapter 27, Richard T. Louttit discusses problems that arise in the process of IRB interpretation of the new regulations. In Chapter 28, Natalie Reatig discusses ways in which the new regulations do and do not provide protection for vulnerable populations.

Part 9 considers the way in which the federal government and research institutions respond to questionable research activities. In response to social and scientific concern about research fraud, the federal government has recently sought to develop equitable procedures for investigating alleged research fraud or misconduct. In Chapter 29, Thomas E. Malone outlines the policies of NIH for handling these problems. In Chapter 30, Joel Cooper considers possible roles of the university in precipitating and in responding constructively to research fraud. In Chapter 31, Herman S. Wigodsky presents a university perspective on the new NIH policies for handling allegations of research fraud or misconduct. In Chapter 32, Michele W. Applegate presents a federal perspective on the application of these new policies. In Chapter 33, Mary L. Miers summarizes NIH's response to the policies and procedures that have been developed.

2. CONFERENCE SPEAKERS AND DISCUSSANTS

Perrie Adams
Department of Psychiatry & Behavioral Science
University of Texas Medical Branch
Galveston, Texas

Paul S. Appelbaum
Department of Psychiatry
University of Pittsburgh
Pittsburgh, Pennsylvania

Michele W. Applegate
Deputy Associate Administrator for Extramural Programs
Alcohol, Drug Abuse & Mental Health Administration
Washington, D.C.

Robert Boruch
Department of Psychology
Northwestern University
Evanston, Illinois

Philippe V. Cardon
Educational Consultant
National Institutes of Health
Bethesda, Maryland

Eleanor Cohn
National Mental Association
Washington, D.C.

Joel Cooper
Department of Psychology
Princeton University
Princeton, New Jersey

Sue Keir Hoppe
Department of Psychiatry
University of Texas Health Science Center
San Antonio, Texas

Robert E. Krebs
Graduate College
University of Illinois Medical Center
Chicago, Illinois

Richard T. Louttit
Division Director
Behavioral & Neural Sciences
National Science Foundation
Washington, D.C.

Charles R. MacKay
Deputy Director
Office for Protection from Research Risks
National Institutes of Health
Washington, D.C.

Thomas E. Malone
Deputy Director
National Institutes of Health
Bethesda, Maryland

Charles McCarthy
Director, Office for Protection from Research Risks
National Institutes of Health
Bethesda, Maryland

Mary Miers
Office of Extramural Research and Training
National Institutes of Health
Bethesda, Maryland

Edward L. (Pat) Pattullo
Director, Center for the Behavioral Sciences
Harvard University
Cambridge, Massachusetts

Joan P. Porter
Office for Protection from Research Risks
National Institutes of Health
Bethesda, Maryland

Natalie Reatig
Pharmacologic and Somatic Treatments Research Branch
Division of Extramural Research Programs
National Institutes of Health
Bethesda, Maryland

Roger W. Reinsch
Department of Business Law
Emporia State University
Emporia, Kansas

Stanley J. Reiser
Director, Humanities & Technology
University of Texas Health Science Center
Houston, Texas

John A. Rodman
Director, Office of Sponsored Projects
University of Texas at Dallas
Dallas, Texas

Joan E. Sieber
Department of Psychology
California State University, Hayward
Hayward, California

Lorraine B. Torres
National Institute of Mental Health
Washington, D.C.

Deborah Lowe Vandell
Department of Psychology
University of Texas at Dallas
Dallas, Texas

Herman S. Wigodsky
Department of Pathology
University of Texas Health Science Center
San Antonio, Texas

PART 1
OPENING REMARKS

3. INTRODUCTION: THE IRB AND SOCIAL AND BEHAVIORAL RESEARCH

Charles R. McCarthy

In 1979, after issuance of controversial proposals concerning social and behavioral research, HHS (HEW) and particularly my quiet corner of HHS, OPRR, was buffeted by strident criticism. Threats and epithets were hurled at us from many sides. These comments can be summarized as follows: "Social and behavioral research is essentially harmless to individuals and benign to society. If you do not accept this view of the social and behavioral sciences, we will organize ourselves to see that you and your misguided staff are drawn and quartered." The charges were led by Ithiel de Sola Pool, who insisted that OPRR had developed a regulatory fulcrum with which to topple the pillars of law and order, and that our four pages of fine print in the *Federal Register* were about to lay waste to the First Amendment of the Constitution. We even began to receive what my office calls "Son of Sam" letters threatening our integrity. Because we are lacking in heroics, we looked about quickly for an ally, and we discovered that Pat Pattullo of Harvard was taking a position similar to that of Dr. Pool and his friends, but presenting it with such good humor and grace that it actually sounded reasonable to us. So we began to listen to him. Pat Pattullo, John Dearden of Johns Hopkins, Joel Cooper of Princeton, Dick Louttit of the National Science Foundation, and a few other friendly champions of social and behavioral sciences showed us how to back away from our unpopular positions while continuing to offer what we felt were reasonable protections for the dignity and rights of subjects involved in social and behavioral research—to say nothing of saving the face and the jobs of OPRR staff.

What were the indignities to subjects that we felt needed attention? The Wichita jury bugging case, the tearoom trade research, the decision of a Georgia court concerning Medicaid co-payment experiments—and our own unpleasant memories of Psychology 101 and Sociology 202, when we felt we had better humor our professors (hungry for material they could publish), so we "volunteered" as research subjects rather than risk grade discrimination!

We discovered that we could write exemptions for broad categories of social and behavioral research—categories in which subjects' behavior seemed to us little different than the commerce of daily life. It has been estimated that up to 80% of social and behavioral research funded by our Department is now exempt. For the rest, we thought it not unreasonable to concern Institutional Review Boards with matters of privacy and confidentiality, and with efforts to protect unsuspecting and vulnerable subjects.

We have some evidence that we have been successful. Generally, the research community has found our rules to be reasonable. We have not had reports of problems like the controversial Milgram "authority" experiments.

But perhaps the strongest defense of the rules can be made in terms of their pedagogical impact. They require investigators to consider the rights of subjects when they are designing research. They require institutions to look at the human dignity questions associated with research. Finally, they provide some degree of evidence to the public that pays the bills that the research carried out on behalf of all is, after all, respectful of our rights as citizens and our dignity as human beings.

We have learned a few things as a result of the uproar over the 1979 regulations. The following aphorisms summarize what we have learned. I offer them to you for your consideration and evaluation:

1. Sound ethics in research must finally be applied at the point of interaction between the research investigator and the subjects of research.
2. The sensitivity of investigators to the dignity and rights of subjects can be heightened in positive ways by the wise application of reasonable regulations communicated through structured deliberations of scientific colleagues and concerned nonscientists.
3. Administrators, department heads, IRBs and colleagues establish a research environment. If the environment is a positive one, subjects will be respected. If the environment is negative, subjects will bear the burden.
4. In a society like ours, the advance of human knowledge should never be achieved at the expense of human dignity.
5. Without adequate comprehension, the formality and technicality of the regulatory format will be a nuisance rather than a foundation for protection of human dignity.
6. Regulations are the beginning, not the embodiment, of sound ethics in research.

4. INSTITUTIONAL REVIEW BOARDS AND SOCIAL RESEARCH: A DISRUPTIVE, SUBJECTIVE PERSPECTIVE, RETROSPECTIVE AND PROSPECTIVE

E.L. Pattullo

In late January, when Charles MacKay called, asking me to speak at this meeting, the news was rife with re-assessment of Reaganomics and other aspects of the current Administration. The new budget had just reached the Hill. The Year of the Bible had been proclaimed. Political pundits of all persuasions were analyzing, anatomizing, satirizing, summarizing, excoriating and enucleating left, right and center. What has the revolution-of-the-right wrought? How goes this presidency? Will he "stay the course"? Is it time for a "mid-term correction"? What has been gained and lost? None but Mr. Reagan himself and Speaker O'Neill seemed certain as to how the scales would finally—you'll excuse the pun!—tip.

All of which suggested to me it would be appropriate to use this occasion to similarly assess the results of federal intervention intended to assure the protection of human research subjects. It has now been seventeen years since the U.S. Surgeon General first issued regulations governing the use of subjects in studies supported by the National Institutes of Health (NIH). The Office for Protection from Research Risks (OPRR) has been around quite a while. The Charleses, McCarthy and MacKay, laughing boys when we first met them, light of heart, fresh of face, full of hope, are now long of tooth, large of girth, and sage of mien. I, myself, though still uncertain what I'll be when I grow up, have been chairman of our Institutional Review Board (IRB) for twelve years. If we all pounce on Presidents, weighing results after two years, it's scarcely too soon to lean back and assess the modest enterprise in which we ourselves engage.

Perceiving that there are some amongst us who may not know there was life before 45 CFR 46, let me first provide a thumbnail sketch of where we came from and how we got here. During the decade from the mid-fifties to the mid-sixties, four widely reported incidents gave the public and the professions reason to wonder if research subjects were being mistreated.

In 1965, in New York, Dr. Chester Southam, a renowned cancer specialist, later to become President of the American Association for Cancer Research, was put on probation for a year by the Board of Regents for injecting "live cancer cells" into elderly patients, many of whom plainly were not in a position to give free and informed consent. In 1954, Edward Levy, the Dean of the University of Chicago Law School and, more recently, U. S. Attorney General, was one of the principals in a project that involved the bugging of federal jury rooms in Wichita, Kansas without the knowledge of the jurors. This procedure led to a tumultuous congressional investigation, which resulted in legislation that now makes such action felonious. At my own institution, in 1961, two young instructors, Tim Leary (who would subsequently serve time in San Quentin) and Dick Alpert (who now pursues spiritual salvation as Baba Ram Dass) put the cat amongst the chickens by generously distributing sugar cubes laced with psilocybin and LSD to Harvard students, young and old. Their interest focused on the behavioral effects of ingesting such substances in a "normal social setting"; they insisted that the necessary research design was inconsistent with following the rigid, sterile protocols previously characteristic of such studies. Finally, in 1964, a junior member of Yale's faculty, Stanley Milgram, was conducting the studies of "obedience to authority" that would make him famous, and infamous, within and without the psychological profession. He was a man ill-served by possession of a considerable literary talent. His graphic descriptions of the stress suffered by subjects, fooled into believing they were administering dangerous electric shocks to others, succeeded only in persuading many readers that the subjects were being inexcusably abused.

Meanwhile, though not publicized until the early seventies, the Public Health Service, itself, was quietly slogging along with the longitudinal study, begun in the thirties, of several hundred poor, Black, syphilitic Alabama males—a study that James Jones has recently excoriated in his book, *Bad Blood.*

Still vivid today, memories of Nazi atrocities were fresh, indeed, twenty years ago. Even more important, however, at just about that time America's long love affair with science (like all grand passions) was beginning to cool. Having given herself with reckless abandon, the country was awakening, slightly hungover, and eyeing her bedfellow balefully with stirrings of remorse. What might follow from so wanton an orgy? That science was potent and capable of giving great satisfaction had been amply demonstrated; that it was also a demanding lover was becoming apparent. The fiscal bills were mounting and growing suspicion that there might be other costs would soon prove well founded. Sociologists and political scientists seemed intent on producing reams of unpersuasive yet discomfiting data that upset the comfortable stand-off achieved by familiar antagonists in many an age-old disputation. Economists, when not quarreling amongst themselves, kept proposing nostrums, each purportedly "scientific," and all smelling of snake-oil when uncorked. Chemists produced silk purses from sows' ears and, while nylons clearly did things for female leg that cotton lisles failed to do, the shade of Love Canal was beginning to be glimpsed. Even the medical sciences were losing their resemblance to Romeo. Doctors were bossy and male; the American Medical Association made the UAW-CIO seem selflessly public spirited; and, then, there were these disturbing, occasional reports of people being treated like guinea pigs—to say nothing of the unease felt about guinea pigs being treated like guinea pigs!

It was at this juncture, with prescience of gathering storms, that U.S. Surgeon General Dr. William H. Stewart first issued orders that plans for using human subjects in external studies funded by NIH be reviewed in advance by third parties, as was the practice for NIH in-house research. Re-reading his notice of 8 February 1966, one is struck by its completeness. That is, all the principal matters which concern us now are contained therein. "Informed consent" is the linchpin; the review group is to weigh the "risks and benefits"; the purpose is to protect "the rights and welfare" of the subjects. As striking is the fact that he spoke, initially, only of "clinical research and investigation," clearly perseverating on the avoidance of physical harm. It was not until December, obviously in response to skeptics, that Dr. Stewart made unambiguous his intention that behavioral and social, as well as biomedical studies be reviewed. The spirit of Stewart's words, as I recall them, was that of an afterthought: "Well, sure, there are a few circumstances in which problems might arise with social research, too. Informed consent is always important and, of course, confidentiality matters when you're looking at behavior. Anyway, there aren't many such studies. Let's treat 'em all just like the biomedical stuff."

By the early seventies, the stormy weather foreseen by the Surgeon General was upon us, reaching gale force with the issuance, by the Department of Health, Education and Welfare (DHEW), of the "yellow book" of 1971, codifying the regulations. Hurricane warnings were hoisted, in 1974, with the publication of 45 CFR 46 and congressional passage of the National Research Act. These two acts combined to extend federal regulation far beyond research funded by NIH to all research conducted at institutions that received any DHEW research support. The hurricane took on the dimensions of a natural disaster in August 1979 when DHEW published its scandalous "proposed regulations" that would have made almost all systematic study of human activity subject to veto by third parties. For eighteen months the nation was threatened with the possibility that scholarly free inquiry would become a thing of the past. Not until January 1981 did the Department of Health and Human Services (DHHS) disperse the clouds, leaving scientists and subjects alike to bask in the relatively balmy climate provided by the "final regulations" issued that month.

Which brings us up to the present and back to the original question: Have science and society gained more than they have lost by government intervention to ensure the protection of research subjects? My judgment is a disappointing equivocation: "Yes," so far as clinical research is concerned; "No," for the area I know best, the behavioral and social sciences.

Seeing you prepare to jump all over me, I will immediately start backpeddling! First, my judgment about the largest and most important part of the enterprise is informed by little first-hand knowledge. That is, neither I nor my colleagues do much work that involves the use of patients as subjects, or requires physical interventions. I imagine, as do most laypeople, that such research often carries risks of harm the laity is incompetent to assess. In that circumstance, subjects neither lose dignity nor are scientists denied legitimate freedom if someone intervenes between the subject and the scientist to judge the risks of the research. If protective regulation has been over-extended in the medical area, with social costs exceeding social benefits, I depend on those in the relevant professions to make the case. I believe that few wish to do so, having the impression that most in bio-medicine now agree that the IRB system, despite occasional lapses, has worked to net advantage.

Considering social and behavioral studies, alone, I reluctantly conclude that the risks of federal intervention outweigh any benefits achieved or foreseeable. I have already referred to the principal one in describing as 'scandalous' and 'threatening' the proposed DHEW regulation of August 1979. I take little comfort in the fact that disaster was then narrowly averted. It is happenstance that the political dice rolled as they did in 1980 and that wise men like MacKay and McCarthy presided at OPRR. As they will be the first to attest, individuals come and go but the bureaucracy remains, ever ready and conscientiously struggling to extend its reach. With the IRB system firmly established and worthwhile for clinical research, but applied also to social science, there remains an ineradicable threat to academic freedom, small but real, that is unjustified by the benefits the system brings to social science.

Beyond that, as you are beginning to sense, the rationale for my judgment is as namby-pamby as the conclusion itself. It is simply not the kind of argument that sets the blood racing. On the one hand, and on the other!

Assessment of the IRB system is boring because there was not much of a problem to begin with. Despite the handful of horror stories, the record of the professions in protecting their human subjects is remarkably good, in all fields, I believe, though I now address just the behavioral and social sciences. If one includes survey research, millions upon millions of subjects have been "used" in this century. Despite intense inquiry (some conducted by individuals whose concern for subjects seems a surrogate for worries about unrelated problems of modern society), it appears the actual harm done by this vast enterprise is negligible. Thus, any margin of additional protection that the IRBs provide represents an inconsequential gain.

A single, minor harm, of course, is one harm too many, which prompts the thought that our efforts may be worthwhile if they provide assurance none will occur. Is there an IRB member so bold as to assert that? Can any knowledgeable person doubt there will be cases of subject abuse in the future? If these are no more frequent and no more serious than in the past, those of us involved know enough to thank good fortune rather than our own efficiency. Realizing that, it is reasonable to doubt that the game is worth the candle. Seeking to make it so, a few bioethicists, in recent years, have begun insisting on our duty to ensure not only against "harm" but against "wrong." The reference here is to moral wrong, which, in the absence of harm, is both intangible and highly arguable. Yielding to no one in strength of conviction that it is a Good Thing to raise moral and ethical standards, I still stoutly deny that IRBs, or other agencies invested with quasi-governmental power, should set themselves as arbiters, let alone enforcers, of moral precepts. In adopting Article I of the United States Constitution two hundred years ago, we decided that, failing a showing of actual harm, present or potential, the state should not attempt to impose a common morality. Any IRB so foolish as to accept such a role, undertakes an impossible, as well as improper, task. I urge that the challenge be spurned. None can be adequate to it.

My certainty on that score stems both from political theory and from empirical observation of the modest results after twenty years of attempting to persuade working scientists to be more analytical about the relatively simple ethical questions raised by risks of tangible harm. Yet even now, few investigators attend OPRR conferences. (I have suggested to Dr. McCarthy they be held in Hawaii, with costs chargeable to NIH grants and contracts, assuring him that attendance will soar.) Few more greet new issues of the *Hastings Center Report*, *IRB*, and other such journals with glad cries of joy, eager to peruse the contents. (In my own field, the *Worm-Runners' Digest* sets more pulses pounding.) Most grant-swingers remain, today, only vaguely aware of the IRB as another hurdle to be jumped en route to a well-funded future. Seventeen years after Dr. Stewart initiated third-party review of plans for using human subjects, most scientists continue to apply to their research the ethical standards that guide them in their daily lives. Most, fortunately, are guided by reasonably high standards.

Perhaps I can best make my point by telling you more about the Harvard Drug Case, which I earlier invoked as one of the scandals prompting government intervention. I choose it because I was personally, if marginally, involved. Then Assistant Dean of the Faculty, I was teaching an experimental Freshman Seminar, trying to engage students' minds and souls in a way seldom achieved by lectures. We focused on the concept of "cultural relativity," thinking it would provide opportunities to relate distant social phenomena to students' own experience. (Little did we then know the fate that would befall Margaret Mead these many years hence!) One result was the exchange of unusually intimate information amongst members of the seminar and, as the term progressed, several Freshmen came to me with tales of marvelous sugar cubes freely made available to adventurous souls by Messrs. Leary and Alpert and cohort. "Come on, Pat," they teased (we were on easy, first name terms), "Don't be a stick-in-the-mud. If you think 'Coming of Age in Samoa' gives a titillating glimpse of other ways of life, just try these little suckers." Well, I WAS a stick-in-the-mud, having been brought up on J. Edgar Hoover, reefer madness, and the horror of becoming a drug-crazed sex fiend. (Then still youthful, I knew myself to be in sufficient danger without drugs!) I made inquiries, only to be told by the project directors to back off; this was RESEARCH; Deans (Assistant or other) should mind their own business and leave science to scientists. (Here, you will recognize that progress has been made. Today it would be an unusually naive investigator who questioned the right of a Dean, however humble, to inquire about how subjects were being used.)

More striking, however, is how little else has changed. Though my first, timorous inquiry was rebuffed, it turned out that fellow-scientists were concerned about the project, also. Within the Department of Social Relations, questions similar to mine were being raised and it took members only about one uproarious meeting to hoot down Leary and Alpert's feeble appeals to academic freedom. The situation being unprecedented, there was some backing and hauling before an interim resolution was imposed, but no great amount of time was wasted. The *public* scandal followed upon the pair's deliberate flouting of the procedures agreed upon, even as it would today. (By then, both Leary and Alpert had given up all pretense to research and, quite consciously, were promoting a social gospel based on LSD being the road to personal salvation.)

I give you all this detail to make a point that is probably obvious long since. In twenty years, there has been no change in the ethical standards by which we judge a notorious case of subject abuse, and only insignificant change in the administrative measures available to deal with it. The project was condemned then as it is condemned now. It was no great trick in 1961, prior to government regulation, for the investigators' colleagues to impose on them procedures similar to those we would now require. When the investigators chose to defy those requirements, then as now, they were summarily dismissed and each departed the scientific profession. In sum, so far as the rare case of a patently risky project is concerned, the vast panoply of IRBs, backed by the muscle of the U.S. government, has added little to our defense arsenal.

I see you wondering if I've travelled from Cambridge simply to bite the benevolent OPRR hand that feeds me. That is certainly not my intention, nor do I wish to sound grudging in acknowledging the real benefits of regulation, even though I judge them to be outweighed by the risks in the social sciences. Substantial numbers of subjects have been spared unnecessary affront in recent years because IRBs, looking over the investigator's shoulder, have discerned the possibility of such and have been able to suggest acceptable alternatives that would obviate it. In my bailiwick, at least, the frequency of deceptive research has decreased markedly. This may have to do as much with substantive changes in the relevant fields as with regulation, but the decline is closely correlated with increased IRB activity. That our Board would be much less active than it is, in the absence of 45 CFR 46, none will dispute. Further, the pointless replication, for training purposes, of the ingenious, interesting and ethically problematic studies associated, especially with social psychology, has become a thing of the past. I credit the regulations. Such experiments were excellent teaching devices, seizing students' imagination. Many of them were, also, landmarks in the discipline and only arguably unethical; I doubt they would have been abandoned without outside pressure. (I have in mind the various "bystander" studies, versions of Milgram, the Asch experiment, et cetera.)

Finally, the DHHS regulations issued in January 1981, under which we now function, are reasonable, workable, and fair, if imperfect. They mirror the democratic process that produced them. Wisely and conscientiously administered they can serve subjects, scientists, and society well. The research enterprise is too complex to be managed by rote from afar, and 45 CFR 46, as it now stands, provides a useful compass to guide those of us close to the scene in applying common sense to the problems of protecting research subjects. It responds to public demand (that scientists underestimate) for assurance of some protection from unwonted danger, without cheating the same public of needed knowledge and without infringing on legitimate liberties. That is the intention. IRBs have the authority needed to intervene before damage is done and to resist those who would tempt them to misuse their power to impose ethical standards on research that are alien both to science and to the larger society. And, OPRR has the power (just in case!) to move in on any of us who abuse our discretion in either direction.

Fortunately, perhaps, the instruments of social and behavioral science remain primitive, seldom capable of inflicting serious harm except by means ordinary adults can understand, anticipate, and defend against if need be. As IRB members, it is our task to master, as best we can, the details of the sensible rules now imposed by federal regulation and to resist, by reasoned argument, rules proposed by government or others that do not make sense. Though necessarily complex, the process of protecting human research subjects from risks of harm they would not knowingly accept is not mysterious, nor is there anything arcane about the dangers against which IRBs should mount defenses. Most IRBs, in most institutions, and all IRBs, under HHS regulations, are given comfortable latitude for carrying out their duties; duties that can be responsibly discharged by anyone generally familiar with the rules and endowed with a healthy degree of common sense.

5. A RESPONSE TO PATTULLO

Sue Kier Hoppe

I would like to respond to the question of whether the regulations facilitate or hinder social and behavioral research by focusing on particular ways in which the regulations have been applied to such research when it is conducted in a biomedical setting. A 1974-75 study of IRB practices conducted for the National Commission estimated that social and behavioral science projects accounted for about 16 percent of all research conducted in the medical schools surveyed (Cooke and Gray, 1977); in 1982, the proportion of social and behavioral research reviewed by our IRB was slightly less. My remarks derive from two perspectives: one, as the chair of an Institutional Review Board in a health science center, and two, as a sociologist and researcher.

Before describing the impact of the regulations on social and behavioral research conducted in a biomedical setting, let me respond to some of Dr. Pattullo's remarks. He raised the question, "Have science and society gained more than they have lost by government intervention to ensure the protection of subjects in social and behavioral research?" Dr. Pattullo answered "No" seemingly for two reasons:

1. The harm done in the course of social and behavioral research is negligible; thus, any margin of protection that an IRB provides is an inconsequential gain; and
2. IRBs are a small but real threat to academic freedom, unjustified by any benefits the system brings.

Dr. Pattullo did not deny that the regulations have brought benefits, but he argued that the gains have been insignificant. Among the gains which he attributed to the regulations are a decrease in deceptive research and meaningless replication by students of unethical social psychology experiments. These do not appear to be inconsequential gains in themselves but, as Dr. Pattullo implied, they are perhaps inconsequential compared to the gains that have accrued from the regulation of biomedical research.

Let's examine each of the reasons for Dr. Pattullo's answer. He asserted that the actual harm to subjects who take part in social and behavioral research is negligible. I think few social or behavioral scientists would want to disagree with this. However, it is more accurate to say that the risks to individuals involved in such research are not easily recognized or defined. The nature and extent of risks are still empirical questions. For example, the frequency with which such widely-acknowledged risks as embarrassment or other psychological discomfort are experienced by subjects has not been quantified. We need research, not necessarily independent studies of risks, but systematic methodologic components of on-going research projects, to help us to learn more about the risks inherent in social and behavioral research.

Recently, for example, McCrae (1982) examined the effect of a personality test and an inventory of recent stressful life events on a sample of community residents taking part in a longitudinal study of stress and coping in aging. One-half of the subjects were asked to complete the Profile of Mood States (POMS) before the study questionnaire; the other half were asked to complete it last. When the POMS scores of the two groups were compared, there was no evidence to suggest that emotional distress was associated with taking the questionnaires, either among "well-adjusted" subjects or among those high in neuroticism or high in stressful life events. Without more work like McCrae's, there is the possibility that IRBs—and investigators—will err in the assessment of risks involved in social and behavioral research in two directions: on the one hand, being complacent about and underestimating harm to subjects involved in such research; on the other hand, imagining risks that have little if any empirical foundation. I will return to the latter point as it pertains to the review of social and behavioral research by a biomedical IRB.

I must confess that I have never really understood the argument that the regulations and IRBs are a threat to academic freedom. I have been studying and observing the professional socialization of medical students for a number of years and am familiar with the presumed tendency of physicians to be more concerned about protecting their own interests than about meeting the needs of patients. When I hear social and behavioral scientists argue against the regulation of research on the basis of academic freedom or similar rights, I find it peculiarly close to the professional protectionism that is attributed to the medical profession. As Judith Swazey (1980) has noted, it is a "specious argument to equate IRB review of a protocol with censorship or prior restraint of free speech, one that distorts the objectives of an IRB and shows little concern with maintaining the rights of subjects..." The regulations do not seek to restrict our right to choice of research goals or topics by virtue of the First Amendment: they seek to improve research methods, like the *manner* of conventional forms of speech is limited, when every attempt is not made by an investigator to minimize threats to the safety and rights of subjects (Robertson, 1978). Although our expertise lies in the study of human behavior, we have been slow to recognize that the "seminal problem in social and behavioral research is that not all investigators respect their subject-participants as persons or appreciate their contributions to the research endeavor" (Baumrind, 1979).

There is, of course, nothing new in what I say, so let me return to the question of the effect of the regulations on research. Like Dr. Pattullo and others, I think the regulations are reasonable as they pertain to social and behavioral research, but I feel that when such research is reviewed by an IRB in a biomedical setting, it may receive an overly-critical evaluation. Levine (1980) has asserted that the conservatism of an IRB is correlated with experience, inexperienced boards tending to act more conservatively than others. Perhaps this partly explains the uneven way in which social and behavioral science and biomedical research tend to be reviewed at our health science center. Many biomedical scientists are "inexperienced" with respect to the research norms of the social and behavioral sciences. In my view, this inexperience has primarily hindered two types of social and behavioral research: descriptive surveys and exploratory studies.

There is little awareness among many biomedical scientists of some of the basic differences involved in the conduct of descriptive as compared to explanatory or experimental research. The critical importance of the response rate in terms of validity, reliability, and error estimation is an example. Balancing the need to achieve a high response rate and the protection of the right to refuse to take part in a study is an issue our board has dealt with on several occasions. We have also considered the need for written consent in studies that involve personal interviews, especially door-to-door surveys, about sensitive topics. Interviewers in such studies increasingly report that subjects are willing to be interviewed but "don't want to sign anything." Once an interviewer has introduced him- or herself, explained the purpose of the study, enumerated a household, selected an eligible individual, and is in the door, most survey researchers assume that consent has been given. Kelsey (1981) has noted that written consent in many epidemiological studies tends to decrease participation rates without any compensating advantages. Often, the requirement of written consent grows out of the feeling of biomedical scientists that respondents have no defense against sensitive questions, an assumption which has been challenged by social and behavioral scientists (cf., e.g., Suskind and Vandergrift, 1982).

In addition to methodologic issues involved in the conduct of descriptive surveys, "problems of conceptualization" in descriptive research are often identified by the IRB. Some social and behavioral research is admittedly poorly conceptualized, but I suspect that this shortcoming is no more prevalent in the social and behavioral sciences than in biomedical research. I had always assumed that the difficulties in conceptualization in social and behavioral research (due to complexity of the phenomena under study, etc.) were widely recognized, but the highly specialized fields in which biomedical scientists work and their day to day isolation from colleagues in other disciplines apparently works to keep that recognition out of awareness.

Exploratory research is evaluated similarly. The descriptive survey, in one sense, represents a formalized exploratory study because it is often the initial stage of formulating an explanatory study. But, we would be fooling ourselves if we didn't admit that the growth of social scientific knowledge stands in contrast to the advancement of biomedical science in that the former often proceeds in a more fortuitous, seemingly less systematic manner. IRBs should not approve mere "fishing expeditions," but sensitivity to the fact that much exploratory research in the social and behavioral sciences fails strict methodologic criteria needs to be fostered.

A nagging problem for our IRB is the review of student research, most of which can be considered exploratory, even at the doctoral level. Most commonly, complaints about the obstructiveness of the IRB come from social and behavioral science students whose research is being undertaken to satisfy degree requirements at another institution. The students typically have not contacted the IRB at their institution, either because they are not aware that one exists or that there is a need to do so. This situation highlights the lack of uniformity with which the regulations are applied, not only within an institution but, perhaps more importantly, among them. While students (and faculty) from institutions outside the health science center complain about the hoops through which our IRB makes them jump, few social and behavioral scientists who are members of our faculty have expressed to me that the regulations or the IRB are a serious impediment to their research. The extent to which IRBs are seen as an obstruction or hindrance is not reflective of the regulations, *per se*, but of the particular local interpretation of them.

I've pointed to ways in which I see some social and behavioral research conducted in a medical setting being "hindered" by the background and training of some biomedical members of an IRB. My opinions are based on experience with only one IRB. I hope that I have not been overly-critical of the overly-critical reviews of social and behavioral research rendered by some of my biomedical colleagues. Those of you who have spent your professional lives in a medical school likely share my frustration that social and behavioral research is not a politically neutral topic in that setting and that it is often seen as a pedestrian pursuit.

On occasion, it has been suggested that social and behavioral research conducted at the health science center be reviewed by a subcommittee of the full board, the members of which would be more "technically competent" to review such protocols, i.e., they would be primarily social and behavioral scientists or would be individuals familiar with the canons and methods of these disciplines. A similar suggestion has been made with respect to the review of oncology group protocols, for example. I reject the notion of separate review. For one, as our experience with the regulations has increased, we have tended to apply them with greater uniformity to different kinds of research. Second, social and behavioral scientists at our institution *want* their research reviewed in the same manner as the research of their biomedical colleagues. Third, separate review is inconsistent with my interpretation of the regulations which stipulate interdisciplinary review of research through the mechanism of categories of board membership. The intent of the regulations is clearly to foster the kinds of interchange that occurs when social and behavioral science and biomedical researchers together consider the protection of human subjects in research.

REFERENCES

Baumrind, D. IRBs and social science research: The costs of deception. *IRB: A Review of Human Subjects Research*, 1979, *1*, 1-4.

Cooke, R.A., and Gray, B. *A survey of institutional review boards and research involving human subjects: A report to the National Commission for the Protection of Human Subjects of Biomedical and Behavioral Research.* Ann Arbor: Survey Research Center, Institute for Social Research, The University of Michigan, November 1, 1977.

Kelsey, J.L. Privacy and confidentiality in epidemiologic research involving patients. *IRB: A Review of Human Subjects Research*, 1981, *3*, 1-4.

Levine, R.J. Address. In K.S. Culver and J. Rachlin (Eds.), *Behavioral and social science research and the protection of human subjects: A symposium sponsored by Public Responsibility in Medicine and Research.* Boston: PRIM&R, 1980.

Robertson, J.A. The scientist's right to research: A constitutional analysis. *Southern California Law Review*, 1978, *51*, 1203-1279.

Susskind, L., and Vandergrift, L. IRBs and the regulation of social science research. In R.A. Greenwalk, M.K. Ryan, and J.E. Mulvihill (Eds.), *Human subjects research: A handbook for institutional review boards.* New York: Plenum, 1982.

Swazey, J.P. Professional protectionism rides again: A commentary on exempted research and responses to DHEW's proposed regulations. *IRB: A Review of Human Subjects Research*, 1980, *2*, 4-6.

6. THE IRB REVIEW PROCESS: APPLICABILITY, EXEMPTION, EXPEDITED REVIEW

Philippe V. Cardon

As previous speakers have pointed out, the scope of the HHS regulations and earlier policy was always intended to include behavioral and social research. Among some of the more celebrated incidents, which historically are referred to in recounting the evolution of the modern concern for human subjects, are some involving behavioral research, as Drs. McCarthy and Pattullo have explained. And the famous *Crane vs. Matthews* case demonstrates the applicability, as interpreted by the courts, of the Department's regulations to social research. Yet there is continued sentiment among behavioral and social researchers that IRB review may constitute some form of censorship or prior restraint or abridgement of academic freedom.

This last contention was addressed in hearings and deliberations of the National Commission for the Protection of Human Subjects in Biomedical *and* Behavioral Research. In fact, the Commission also "commissioned" a study by legal experts to help determine whether protections of the sort presented by the federal regulations, and which it was prepared to reaffirm, actually did infringe on First Amendment rights of researchers. The legal experts and the Commission, which included two lawyers, one of whom was a distinguished constitutional lawyer, concluded that the regulations did not interfere with academic freedom or the right of free inquiry in a way that was inconsistent with the need for appropriate protections for human subjects. A study by the Department of Health and Human Services (HHS) legal counsel reached a similar conclusion.

Nevertheless, there is so much of social and behavioral research which involves little or no risk to subjects or to the dignity of subjects—although sometimes it may make us indignant or in the view of some, undignified—that it would seem not to be necessary or wise to introduce an unwieldy apparatus to contain it. "Shotguns after mosquitos," so to speak. Thus, the drafters of the current regulations tried to make a "scaling" to allow fairly innocuous, yet important, research to be carried out without the need for review or extensive review.

The matter was complicated by another factor as well—the extent to which research not funded by the federal government, or at least not by HHS, was covered by the regulations. Following PL 93-348, which established the National Commission, the Department had, in keeping with the wording of the law, requested institutions to extend coverage of the requirement for IRB review of all biomedical *and* behavioral research, regardless of the source of funding. However, when the revised regulations were under consideration in 1980 and the issue was raised regarding the applicability of *all* behavioral research, regardless of the source of funding, the HHS legal counsel took a slightly different view than earlier. The result was that the revised regulations don't require IRB review of research not funded by the Department but do require a statement in the assurance about the ethical principles and what procedures apply to research that is not Department funded. Furthermore, regarding research that falls in exempt categories, the institution is not required to include in its assurance to the HHS any statement about the principles which govern exempt and non-Department funded research.

Let us sum up the question of applicability so far:

1. The regulations apply to all HHS funded research, unless the research is exempt.
2. The ethical principles requirement applies to research, not in the exempt categories, even when no Department funds are involved.
3. When the research does not involve Department funds and is exempt, then the requirement for a statement of ethical principles does not apply, even if common sense indicates that ethical norms will be applied.

In fact, however, over 90% of all institutions in their assurances include all research, except exempt, in the requirement for IRB review. It just doesn't make sense, in their minds, to differentiate on the basis of source of funding; it isn't relevant ethically whose money it is—unless, as in the case of some behavioral research, it might be CIA money.

How are the institutions handling exempt research? It isn't easy to state it simply and generally. Over 85% of institutions require some type of oversight—administrative or even expedited review. But not all institutions have faculty engaged in all types of research in the exempt categories—for example, medical schools have little educational research, and liberal arts schools don't do much with pathological and diagnostic specimens. So the generalization masks some variation in the way "applicability" is applied.

There are other steps in the "scaling" to be considered. So far, we have looked basically at the funding source and the matter of exempt research, without attempting to elaborate on what the details of the exemptions are. Even prior to the question of exemption, there is the matter of whether human subjects are involved. Thus, the definition of human subjects requires that there be "interaction" or "intervention" by the researcher or that the researcher obtain "identifiable private information" about the subject. Many questionnaires are anonymous. It is doubtful whether, in the ordinary sense, a mailed anonymous questionnaire constitutes interaction. But if it is so determined, then human subjects are involved, but the research would be exempt. More commonly, a great deal of statistical aggregate data is available about people, perhaps even in individualized form. But there may be no identifiers attached to it—census data, for example. Thus, according to the definition in the regulations, no human subjects are involved, because there is no identifiable private information.

Given all these provisions, then, which are incorporated into the 1981 revised regulations, it is easy to see that the drafters of the regulations made special efforts to avoid extending the regulations into areas where regulatory protections for human subjects seemed inappropriate. Even in types of research in which IRB review would seem appropriate, the regulations offered the possibility of expedited review. Most of the list of expedited review procedures focus on the more typically biomedical procedures of very little or no risk—such as collection of urine, blood samples, or EKG. But some focus on specific types of epidemiologic research and on behavioral research. In addition, a couple of the medical procedures are often used in behavioral research (e.g., collection of urine or blood samples), and the category of expedited review relating to the recording of data may often figure prominently in behavioral research. I suppose it is not stretching the matter too far to see even taking a medical history as a "noninvasive procedure routinely employed in clinical research." Consequently, while one might not be entirely comfortable in considering an "interview" exempt, when it was as thorough and sensitive as a medical history done solely for research or as part of a research activity, yet one might stop short of requiring full board review for this procedure.

As you realize, the expedited review procedure requires that two conditions be met. One is that the procedure or category be on the list published by the Secretary. The other is just as important, and sometimes seems more important in that it can be overlooked: the research must involve no more than minimal risk. If there is a doubt on the part of the chairperson or other IRB member designated by the chairperson to perform the review, then, of course, it is to be referred to the entire board for review. This may prove trickier in applying the concept of expedited review to behavioral research than it first appears. Why? Well, quite often the risks of behavioral research are not so much in the actual procedures employed, which may be fairly innocuous. The risks arise from the possibility that confidential information about individuals may be revealed with damaging consequences.

Hence, a pen and paper screening test, if reliable and sensitive and specific enough, might yield information about behavioral disorders or problems which, if known outside the research, could cause serious harm through labeling, loss of employment, or severe stress. This aspect might escape the researchers' notice and even that of the IRB reviewer, if either fails to appreciate the nature of the risks.

This point illustrates well the reason why there exists in our society a good deal of uneasiness about social and behavioral research. Such research purports to be as harmless as answering a question. Yet, it has the potential to cause serious harm, objectively (e.g., economically) or subjectively (e.g., through stress and worry). The examples of harms or abuses that have resulted from behavioral research demonstrate why the federal regulations have always tried to encompass behavioral research; and under the current revised regulations, there has been an attempt to deal with it in a more satisfactory fashion.

What I have been explaining is the intent and scope of the regulations with regard to behavioral and social research. By limiting the impact of the regulations to the area of widest consensus on the need for regulatory and ethical protection of human subjects, the drafters of the regulations sought to be responsive to the issues raised by such research. There are possible harms to subjects in behavioral and social research. Furthermore, the privacy rights of individuals and their autonomy—both deriving from the principle of respect for persons—certainly need to be recognized by any system of protections. On the other hand, it makes little sense to require extensive procedural protections when the research methods are well understood and agreed to by subject participants who are capable of making decisions on their own about how much of their privacy or autonomy may be threatened by answering a few questions. Within the academic and research community, there is a tradition of independent scholarship and academic freedom. It is arguable, of course, whether IRB review has any adverse impact on this tradition as is sometimes claimed. However, one of the more successful aspects of the revised regulations has been limiting anything that might be called "federal intrusiveness" to a minimum.

There are two new specific issues that call for comment regarding the applicability of the HHS regulations in areas of social and behavioral research. The first relates to the new exemption promulgated about a month ago in social research which is intended to evaluate certain programs under the Social Security Act or other public benefit programs. This new exemption, known as "Exemption Six" on the list, is aimed at the earlier issue arising from the *Crane vs. Matthews* case. It allows the Administration and the Congress some flexibility in revising and experimenting with tax-supported service and benefit programs. Thus, IRB review and approval and the other protections in the regulations are not required in this type of broad national policy research because it is considered to have been thoroughly reviewed in a more public forum by elected representatives and government officials. Furthermore, most of the evaluation is in direct response to specific Congressional mandates to improve the effectiveness and efficiency of these public benefit programs. It is not reasonable to expect IRBs to become involved in public policy evaluation since their task is already complicated enough.

The second matter also relates to exemptions. Specifically, how are the exemptions to be applied in the case of children? The new Subpart D, the so-called "Children's Regulations," was published on March 8, 1983. Most of the exemptions apply to research involving children. However, there are two important differences. First, Exemption 3, the exemption for survey and interview research, does not apply if the subjects are legal minors. The reason is that the assumption, valid for adults, that the subject can judge for him- or herself whether to answer questions, is not considered true for children. They are normally not in a position to appreciate whether the interviewer should be told what is asked. In addition, children might, without realizing its significance, reveal information about others in the family that ought to be kept private. Hence, all survey and interview research involving children (legal minors) is to be reviewed by the IRB.

Second, Exemption 4, observation research, applies to research involving children with an important qualification. When the observation research involves participant observers, then the IRB must review the research. The reason is that it is not easy for children to recognize how their behavior may be under the influence of the participant observer, when actual manipulations are involved. Hence, to protect the children against the natural disadvantage they have because of their immaturity and inexperience, IRB review and approval are required.

There are some remaining questions and dilemmas about research on older minors—adolescents, for example—and the need for parental consent. But those will be addressed in the sessions on informed consent and vulnerable populations.

PART 2
INFORMED CONSENT

7. HHS REGULATIONS ON INFORMED CONSENT AND THEIR IMPACT ON SOCIAL AND BEHAVIORAL RESEARCH

Philippe V. Cardon

Unquestionably, the most studied topic of ethical relevance is informed consent. Legal, psychological, sociological and linguistic studies in the empirical field, in addition to philosophical and theoretical discussions, make up a large portion of the literature of bioethics. So, it isn't surprising how complete the HHS regulations are on the topic of informed consent. However, because most of the development of this topic has occurred in the medical field, some of what comes through in the HHS regulations seems not to apply readily to the models of research usually employed by social and behavioral researchers. For example, we have all heard the stories of elaborate written consent forms that are reputed to have been required to accompany mailed questionnaires when it is clear that individuals wishing to decline can just toss out the questionnaire, and if they return the completed questionnaire, a signed consent form seems redundant. Of course, in cases of sensitive, private information, protections of subjects are necessary.

The point is that the model of juridico-medical signed documentation may not be appropriate in social and behavioral research. Still, there is no reason to suppose that the subjects of this kind of research have any fewer rights or are any less desirous of being fully informed about what will be involved in the research. Some have tried to argue that, since there is little or no risk, consent is not important, that the integrity of the researcher is guarantee that nothing harmful will happen to the subject. These views, I believe, are not widely shared or at least are not often publicly espoused. However, in my remarks I want not to join the basic ethical issues of informed consent, but to address some key points of the HHS regulations that seem to accommodate the models in behavioral and social research. These are points for investigators and IRBs to keep in mind as they plan or consider such research.

First of all, within the basic elements of informed consent listed in 46.116(a) of the regulations, two elements in particular are qualified by the note of "not always uniformly required." What am I referring to? First is the matter of alternative procedures. Obviously, in much social and behavioral research there isn't a sensible alternative. If one wants to know what someone's opinion is, or what their life style entails, or what their experience has been, one has to ask them. All too often, the untested assumptions and prejudices of conventional thought or unthinking people are used as a basis for decisions or actions that turn out to be dead wrong. So it is obvious that in order to make reliable assertions about people's views or experiences, one must begin by asking them. There aren't really any alternatives to this method. Thus, IRBs should not require investigators to identify alternatives or to invent them. Nor should they stipulate that there be some statement that, "No alternative methods exist," or even that declining to participate in the research is a so-called "alternative procedure."

The second point to be made concerning the basic elements regards the requirement to disclose what "compensation and medical treatment" is available in the event of injury. The revised regulations specify that when the research is "more than minimal risk," then it is necessary to include a statement about compensation and medical treatment in the event of injury. In one way, this accommodates most behavioral and social research because a great deal of it presumably is less than minimal risk. But keep in mind that there can be some significant risk in behavioral research—as evidenced by some of the more notorious incidents recounted in the historical background of the current regulations. Therefore, when behavioral or social research entails more than minimal risk, then it is appropriate to explain to the subject whether or not compensation and medical treatment will be provided and of what they consist. Let me add, however, that it is the IRB that determines whether or not the risk is minimal based on several factors: the magnitude, the probability, and what is encountered ordinarily in the daily life of subjects or in routine physical or psychological examinations and tests. Hence, one ought not automatically to conclude that a risk of great magnitude—say loss of a job—is necessarily more than minimal. It may be so remote in probability that it is hard even to imagine how it could occur because, for example, the identifiers will be coded and the code sent to a Swiss bank. It may also be that the risk—e.g., legal liabililty—is one the subject faces in ordinary life—e.g., as a burglar. The IRB must consider and weigh a variety of factors, including safeguards that make the risk remote or highly improbable.

Let us now turn to the question of the waiver of informed consent which is described under 46.116(d). Under this provision, it is possible for the IRB to modify some or all of the elements of informed consent or to waive the requirement completely under certain conditions: 1) minimal risks; 2) rights and welfare protected in other ways; 3) research could not practicably be carried out without the waiver; or 4) where appropriate, inform the subjects after participation. This waiver provision applies to biomedical and behavioral research, but it was prompted principally by the concern that a rigid and absolute requirement for informed consent might not allow some forms of behavioral research in which the purpose of the research, for example, needs to be kept from the subject in order to obtain valid results. Or, in another example, the participation of a "non-naive confederate" is necessary to ensure that the subject reacts as if some real event were actually occurring and this feature of the research is not disclosed to the subject in advance. Perhaps in a more creative fashion, the type of interaction that a field anthropologist might use in winning acceptance and becoming a part of the life and activities of a primitive tribe or an isolated group exemplifies how the concept of the "regulatory waiver" takes shape in actual research. An IRB might choose to waive the conventional consent procedures because there are more imaginative and effective methods of accomplishing the same objective.

At the same time, it is important to remember that the regulations offer another sort of flexibility to social and behavioral researchers in connection with informed consent. This is the feature that permits the IRB to waive the documentation of informed consent in certain circumstances. Whenever the signed consent form would be the only link of the subject to the research and the principal risk entailed is the risk of breach of confidentiality, then the IRB may waive the requirement of documenting the consent. In addition, the IRB may also waive the documentation requirement when the research involves no more than minimal risk and no procedure for which written consent is normally required outside of the research context. Both of these provisions may readily accommodate the types of research which behavioral and social researchers carry out. For example, the procedures used outside of the research context by such researchers ordinarily do not require written consent.

Whether the IRB is requested to waive or modify the consent procedures or whether the request is only for a waiver of documentation—or for use of a short form—the investigator must provide a summary to the Board of what actually is to be told the subject. When the documentation requirement is waived, the IRB may require that the investigator provide a written summary to the subject.

The provisions for waiver of consent and for waiver of documentation have been specifically adopted in the case of parental permission for minors in the newly published Subpart D, Research Involving Children. Additionally, the IRB may waive the requirement for assent of children and for the documentation of assent. Subpart D also provides another waiver circumstance. Whenever the IRB determines that a research protocol is designed for conditions, or for a subject population, for which parental or guardian permission is not a reasonable requirement to protect the subjects, the IRB may waive the consent requirements. In this instance, there must be the substitution of some appropriate mechanism to protect the subjects. Of course, the waiver must also be consistent with federal, state or local law. This provision of the regulations may well be useful in assuring that older minors are not put in the position of having to disclose to their parents their participation in research which may relate to activities in which older minors have legitimate privacy interests, such as their sexual behavior, pregnancy, drug or alcohol use, or other. Such undesired disclosure might be the result if it were necessary to obtain parental permission, for example, to participate in research interviews or questionnaires related to the older minors' seeking or obtaining services or assistance regarding these sensitive matters.

8. INFORMED CONSENT—ALWAYS FULL DISCLOSURE?

Paul S. Appelbaum

The title of this workshop is based on two implicit assumptions about informed consent: first, that "full disclosure" with subject comprehension is possible in human subjects research; and second, that full disclosure is (at least *prima facie*) desirable. In the absence of data that would prove or disprove these assumptions conclusively, I would like to suggest some reasons why these propositions might be open to doubt. In this argument, I will make reference to a number of empirical studies of informed consent, while recognizing that most studies in this area are subject to challenge on methodological grounds (Meisel & Roth, 1981).

An initial definition of terms is necessary. By "full disclosure" I will presume that we are referring to all those elements enumerated in the current HHS regulations governing informed consent. I will further presume that "full disclosure" implies that a thorough and wholehearted, rather than a superficial and insincere, attempt will be made to convey the requisite information to potential subjects.

I see three problems with "full disclosure" as so envisioned. First, we have reason to believe that the more concise and more simply written the informed consent form, the greater the level of subject understanding. In a classic study, badly in need of replication, Epstein and Lasagna (1969) presented three consent forms of varying length and detail to three groups of subjects. The forms described a hypothetical study designed to test the efficacy of a new drug—which in reality was aspirin. The investigators found that both comprehension and frequency of consent for participation were inversely related to the length of the forms.

HHS regulations, however, have failed to heed the note of caution sounded in this study, requiring that ever-increasing amounts of information be presented to potential research subjects. A more recent study by Grundner (1980) pointed to the results of such tendencies in the treatment area, which has been subjected to similar pressures. Grundner used two readability scales to analyze the comprehensibility of five surgical consent forms. On one scale, all forms were rated at the advanced undergraduate or graduate level; on the second scale, four were found as comprehensible as a professional scientific journal, with the fifth at the level of an academically-oriented magazine.

Now it might be argued that Grundner demonstrated only that current forms are overly complex, not that they necessarily need to be that way, and in any event, that his study dealt with consent to treatment and not to research. I doubt, however, based on a study my colleagues and I are currently undertaking of informed consent to psychiatric research, that most research consent forms are any more readable that those Grundner analyzed. Further, I believe a major cause of that state is the current HHS requirements for "full disclosure." Given the extent of disclosure required, the nature of the material involved (often reflecting complex scientific concepts), the exponential growth in length that accompanies attempts at simplification, and the inherent limitations of those involved in the consent process (many of whom have lost whatever ability they once had to communicate intelligibly to lay people), consent forms and oral disclosures are not unlikely to be unassimilable by research subjects. As my home IRB interprets the HHS regulations, for example, it is impossible to construct a consent form limited to a single page, and most forms require at least three single-spaced, typed pages.

Research that has examined informed consent from the perspective of the research subject, rather than the consent form, has pointed to another set of limitations on full disclosure. Cassileth, *et al.*, looking at consent to cancer chemotherapy, found that one day after consent only 60% of 200 patients understood the nature and purpose of the treatment and only 55% could list one risk or possible complication (Cassileth, Zupkis, Sutton-Smith, *et al.*, 1982). This performance was directly related to level of education, as Grundner's data suggests it should be. The data of Roth, *et al.* derived from a study of severely depressed psychiatric patients, confirms the importance of education in determining both level of understanding and degree of educability of patients (Roth, Lidz, Meisel, *et al.*, 1982). In most research projects, of course, extent of education is distributed rather broadly; if we are demanding that research subjects comprehend "full disclosure," and if the limits I referred to earlier on the extent of simplification possible actually exist, it may be inevitable that we will be disappointed in the majority of cases.

A further reason to doubt the possibility of subject understanding of full disclosure is the tendency of subjects not to hear certain kinds of information. McCollum & Schwartz (1969) found that less than half of the parents who had admitted their children to nontherapeutic research projects in fact comprehended the true nature of the protocol. A recent report from our research group at the University of Pittsburgh emphasized the barriers to acceptance by research subjects of the fact that experimentation taking place in a hospital or other "therapeutic" setting may have goals other than simply providing maximal therapeutic benefit for the patient/subject (Appelbaum, Roth & Lidz, 1982).

None of this, of course, proves that full disclosure with full comprehension is unattainable. For those who see a symbolic value in provision of information, regardless of whether subjects actually comprehend the disclosure, nothing here challenges their beliefs. But for those with a more pragmatic orientation, who advocated full disclosure because of its putative advantages for subjects' decision making, this brief survey should raise some doubts about the current tendency to cram ever more information into consent forms.

There is an alternative, although I suspect it is a controversial one. We could reject "full disclosure" as empty symbolism and embark on a reasoned appraisal of which information is genuinely crucial to the decision making of most subjects. It may be, as I have suggested elsewhere, that some of this information may not even be included in the current disclosure requirements (Appelbaum, Roth & Lidz, 1982). Anything not likely to be understood by a high school graduate could be discarded, and consent forms could be limited to a single page. Subjects could then be given an opportunity to request whatever additional information they deemed relevant. If we embarked on this course, we would have to overcome our obsessive fears that we might be omitting some information that might be relevant to some subjects; it would probably be useful in that regard to recall that the more information we present, the less likely subjects are to understand any of it. Have we sufficient mettle for such a process, or are we too rooted in the false security of telling all?

REFERENCES

Appelbaum, P.S., Roth, L.H., and Lidz, C.L. The therapeutic misconception: Informed consent in psychiatric research. *International Journal of Law and Psychiatry*, 1982, *5*, 319-329.

Cassileth, B.R., Zupkis, R.V., Sutton-Smith, K., *et al.* Informed consent— why are its goals imperfectly realized? *New England Journal of Medicine*, 1980, *302*, 896-900.

Epstein, L.C., and Lasagna, L. Obtaining informed consent—form or substance? *Archives of Internal Medicine*, 1969, *123*, 682-688.

Grundner, T.M. On the readability of surgical consent forms. *New England Journal of Medicine*, 1980, *302*, 900-902.

Meisel, A., and Roth, L.H. What we do and do not know about informed consent. *Journal of the American Medical Association*, 1981, *246*, 2473-2477.

McCollum, A.T., and Schwartz, A.H. Pediatric research hospitalization: Its meaning to parents. *Pediatric Research*, 1969, *3*, 199-204.

Roth, L.H., Lidz, C.W., Meisel, A., *et al.* Competency to decide about treatment or research: An overview of some empirical data. *International Journal of Law and Psychiatry*, 1982, *5*, 29-50.

U.S. Department of Health and Human Services. Final regulations amending basic HHS policy for the protection of human research subjects. *Federal Register* (January 26, 1981) *46*(16), 8366–8392.

9. INFORMED CONSENT AND THE THERAPEUTIC MISCONCEPTION

Paul S. Appelbaum

The most important characteristic that differentiates research from treatment is the absence in the former of what Fried (1974) calls "personal care." That is, the care that research subjects receive "is not chosen exclusively out of a concern for their individual well-being, but with regard to the success of the experimental design."

In many types of research, the absence of personal care is of little consequence. Most social science research and much behavioral research is designed to offer no therapeutic benefit to participants, but that is rarely problematic because it accords with the expectations of both researchers and subjects. In biomedical research, however, the converse is true. Patient subjects generally approach the research setting with the expectation, although it is often unconscious, that some benefit will result, or at least, that they will receive personal care. I have elsewhere referred to this mind set as "the therapeutic misconception" (Appelbaum, Roth & Lidz, 1982).

It may not be immediately obvious why the therapeutic misconception ought to be a matter of concern. I will suggest, however, that patient subjects who anticipate personal care in biomedical research are likely to have difficulty in assessing accurately the risk-benefit ratio of their participation.

How is the therapeutic misconception evidenced? In the medical setting there is a tendency for patients to assume, unless told otherwise, that everything that is being done is performed with their best interests at heart. In a research project, however, that is rarely true. Subjects often assume, for example, that the choice of experimental therapies is being made on the basis of their needs; most often, of course, such assignment is random. Although, in theory, for the group of subjects in a well-designed project, the treatments are equally likely to be effective, in the individual case this is often untrue. Subjects may have had previous experience with one of the treatments or may have particular difficulties with a given set of side effects (e.g., a heavy equipment operator may need to avoid sedation). To the extent that subjects fail to recognize that the therapy is not being chosen for their benefit, they ignore a potentially important set of risks.

Similar considerations apply to other aspects of research methodology including the use of placebos if subjects are convinced that they will receive active treatment; the use of double-blind procedures which again means that treatment is being administered in disregard of subjects' idiosyncratic needs; and the presence of a fixed protocol which limits investigators' abilities to adjust dosage, change medication, add adjunctive treatments that might ease patient discomfort (e.g., sleeping medication) or otherwise respond to changes in patient subjects' conditions. Subjects who are unaware of the methodological issues are unlikely to grasp the real risks of participating in a research project.

Surprisingly, given this, current HHS informed consent requirements do not require that these methodological aspects of research projects be discussed with the potential subjects (U.S. Department of Health and Human Services, 1981). Systematic interviews with investigators carried out by our group at the University of Pittsburgh as part of a larger study of informed consent in psychiatric research have revealed that most investigators (even those committed to the idea of informed consent) avoid discussing these aspects of methodology with potential subjects (Appelbaum & Roth, in press). Most often these investigators maintained that the reason for this was a fear of frightening off potential subjects with unnecessary details. A moment's reflection will testify to the accuracy of their fears, but not to their explanation for them.

For the investigator to discuss in a genuine manner the various aspects of methodology that preclude "personal care," he or she must, in effect, disabuse subjects of the notion that they can trust the investigator to act in their best interests. Although this could comport with reality (and there need be no pejorative connotations to this—it simply reflects an inherent element of research), it is an extraordinarily difficult task to ask investigators to undertake. The entire consent process is usually structured to develop precisely the sense of trust that must here be undermined.

But the issue is even more complex. So deeply rooted are many subjects' therapeutic misconceptions that subjects may unconsciously resist hearing the information that would tend to undermine their beliefs. Our own research with psychiatric patients, including many on the healthier end of the spectrum, revealed many instances in which patient subjects questioned immediately after consent, denied or (more commonly) distorted the data they had just received to preserve the idea that everything was being done with their best interests in mind. This may account for the studies that have demonstrated that a significant percentage of subjects were unaware even that they had consented to research (McCollum &

Schwartz, 1969; Gray, 1975). Thus, even to require an expansion of already too-lengthy consent forms might not completely solve the problem.

Nonetheless, it is clear that unless the therapeutic misconception is dispelled, research subjects, particularly in biomedical research, will not be given the opportunity for a genuine informed consent. We must begin to explore approaches to this problem.

REFERENCES

Appelbaum, P.S., and Roth, L.L. The structure of informed consent in psychiatric research. *Behavioral sciences and law* (in press).

Appelbaum, P.S., Roth, L.H., and Lidz, C.L. The therapeutic misconception: Informed consent in psychiatric research. *International Journal of Law and Psychiatry*, 1982, *5*, 314-329.

Fried, C. *Medical experimentation: Personal integrity and social policy.* New York: American Elsevier Publishing Co., 1974.

Gray, B.H. *Human subjects in medical experimentation: A sociological study of the conduct and regulation of clinical research.* New York: John Wiley & Sons, 1975.

McCollum, A.T., and Schwartz, A.H. Pediatric research hospitalization: Its meaning to patients. *Pediatric Research*, 1969, *3*, 199-204.

10. INFORMED CONSENT AND DECEPTION*

Joan E. Sieber

Probably most IRB members have memorized the elements of informed consent that were published in the *Federal Register* on January 26, 1981, and every reflective IRB member knows that fulfilling the *intent* of these elements requires considerable creative problem solving. Ideally, potential research participants and the researcher should participate in a communication process constituted so that participants are able to question, discuss, comprehend and believe what they are told, and be given adequate opportunity to weigh relevant factors (such as whether the relationship is equitable and participation will be sufficiently convenient) in deciding whether to participate. In the first part of this paper, some approaches to achieving these conditions are discussed. In the second part of this paper, we consider some conditions under which consent is not obtained, and ways of reducing the potential harm or wrong of deception in research, including procedural and research design considerations and debriefing.

Both consent and debriefing are communication processes. They should be conducted using the best clinical skills available for creating rapport and empowering persons to think and decide for themselves. Courtesy, procedural fairness, relative informality, provision of information in an engaging, usable and readily comprehended form, and promotion of autonomous decision making are essential to fulfilling the intent of the informed consent requirement. Fortunately, skills of communication and human relations are among the tools of trade of many social scientists. Unfortunately, however, because social scientists have emulated the detached research style of physical scientists, the application of human relations skills to the consent process and to the research process in general remains underdeveloped and underemphasized. Here, let us consider some of the creative approaches that may be taken to fulfill the requirements of informed consent. We shall also consider fieldwork, an area of social research in which it often is not literally possible to fulfill the requirements of informed consent.

---

*The last three sections of this paper are adapted with permission from articles by the author which appear in *IRB: A Review of Human Subjects Research*.

Communicating what the research involves may be difficult for a variety of reasons. It is often a good idea to have groups of potential research subjects participate as a group in the consent process so that questions and expectations can be discussed among themselves. In some cases, equipment and procedures are complex and difficult to describe, especially if the research participants are unsophisticated. Among the approaches that have been used to solve these communication problems are: to show a videotape of someone participating in the study; to let a group of potential participants go through the procedure or try out any apparatus that is involved; to have a group of potential participants interview one or more persons who have already participated; to give potential participants a booklet that describes the pertinent details of the research.

The description of reasonably foreseeable risks typically is given from the researcher's point of view. This is too narrow an approach. If a participant is likely to worry about a risk or discomfort that he or she perceives as possible, this *is* a risk and a discomfort. The researcher needs to learn what concerns the participants will have, as well as what concerns seem to be legitimate or reasonable ones from the perspective of the researcher. An important part of the pilot testing of an experimental procedure is to query the pilot subjects about the kinds of concerns they would have. All subjects' concerns, real and imagined, need to be brought up in the consent process and discussed. Where steps have been taken to prevent or reduce certain risks, these steps should be discussed. Groups of subjects might be asked to brain storm to see what concerns they might have, after which the researcher would address those concerns. An open, nondefensive dialogue about possible risks is far better than a speech by a defensive researcher who feels compelled to create the impression that all bases are covered, and a group of potential subjects made defensive by the formality of the process. Researchers and IRBs are often motivated by concern to protect themselves from accusations, but defensive actions may cause more trouble than they prevent.

Benefits to the subject or others can be fostered in a number of ways. Most social and behavioral research can be done in ways that will provide personally meaningful information or experience to the participants. The investigator who sets out to provide such benefit and who discusses the nature of this benefit during the consent process enhances the likelihood that these benefits will occur. Unfortunately, investigators sometimes are tempted to make unrealistic promises about feedback from the research. Often, the length of time required to complete the data gathering and analysis makes it impossible to give participants information about the outcome of the research within a reasonable amount of time. It may be more useful to give participants a handout on the concepts and issues involved in the study, and some useful, well-established information pertinent to the topic studied. A post-study discussion on relevant issues of interest to participants might be conducted. This is also an excellent opportunity for debriefing, and for the researcher to learn more about the experiences, perceptions and backgrounds of those who participated in the research.

During the consent process subjects should be encouraged to ask about potential benefits that *they* may expect, but that the researcher may not plan to provide. For example, subjects often assume that social scientists are psychotherapists, and may expect clinical services or insights that will not be forthcoming. A benefit that can be given to such subjects is an explanation of pertinent limitations of current knowledge, limitations of the skill of the researcher, sources of good clinical services (e.g., the university counseling center), and sources of pertinent information.

"*A disclosure of alternative procedures*" is an element of consent that originated in medical research, and that refers to alternatives to an experimental medical procedure. In social research, this may be taken to mean "alternatives to participating in the study." When research is conducted on a natural setting such as a classroom, an office, a research laboratory, or a neighborhood, it is not often evident what non-involvement in the research means. In settings such as elementary school programs, children whose parents refuse to allow participation may be in the disappointing position of being barred from attractive activities. Some of the problems of creating an equitable control or non-involved condition are discussed by Conner (1982).

The contact person for participants who have problems or questions needs to be chosen with care. Much social research is done in academia where participants depend on the institution for a degree, or in the context of program evaluation where program participants dependon the program for services. In either setting, it may be desirable to give subjects the option of contacting more than one person in the hierarchy. One should have the option of contacting someone low in the hierarchy (e.g., the researcher), so that simple matters can be easily rectified without making a big issue out of a little problem. One should be able to contact a friendly liason person fairly low in the hierarchy (e.g., the research coordinator or the department chair) when the problem is a sensitive one about the research that cannot be taken up comfortably with the researcher. And one should be enabled to contact, easily, someone high in the hierarchy, such as the vice president for research of the university. Research participants might be given a list of their rights as subjects and the name, title, address and phone number of various persons they might contact in case of questions or problems.

The voluntariness of participation is rarely communicated effectively. Most participants are recruited in a way that conveys the researcher's desire that they participate. A more effective way to foster their autonomy is to stress that it is important that they decide whether it is in their best interests to participate. It might be stressed that persons often volunteer because they feel they "should," yet they really haven't decided to do so in an independent way. Persons who participate under these conditions may do so grudgingly, appear late for their session, and feel defensive about some of the things they are required to do. This is neither good for science nor for the participant. An approach that has been used effectively to promote autonomous decision making is to use some version of the decision balance sheet devised by Irving Janis and Leon Mann (1977). Students might be asked to engage in group discussion and individual thought about the following issues, to fill out their own balance sheet privately, and, on the basis of that information, to make their decision:

Decision-Making Balance Sheet

Criterion	**Reasons to participate**	**Reasons not to participate**
Utilitarian reasons of my own	E.g., I'll enjoy it.	I don't have time.
Utilitarian reasons of significant others in my life	E.g., I'll have some interesting things to tell them.	My family won't see me during the time I'm participating.
Value considerations of mine	E.g., I think science is good.	I doubt the value of this study.
How others will feel about my participation	E.g. My mother will be interested in this.	My friends will be mad that I'm taking time to do this.

Forthrightness and clear communication in the consent process are generally advantageous. For example, Singer (1978) found that when subjects are told ahead of time about the kind of difficult, embarrassing or personal matters that will arise in the research, they tend to be far more candid than when subjects are surprised with these matters. In unpublished research, I found that persons who were given extensive opportunity to discuss their forthcoming research experience and to fill out a decision balance sheet were far more likely than those given a more standard consent process to keep their appointments to participate in the research, and to answer questions candidly.

So far, we have treated consent as a one-time process. In many settings, consent should be considered an on-going process. When researchers conduct a long-term study in a place of employment, a community, or a private home, unexpected issues will continue to emerge that concern the relationship between participants and researchers. For example, organizational researchers who are studying the communication, productivity and attitudes of researchers, factory workers or some other group in a work setting cannot possibly anticipate the organizational crises that may arise during their stay, or the concerns that will arise about their research roles. If a particular manager behaves in ways that are very upsetting to employees who then discuss this event with the investigator, those employees will develop concerns about confidentiality that did not exist at the outset. And, the researchers should well be concerned about their ability to assure that confidentiality. Indeed, in such a setting, it is not unusual for management to impose, as a condition of the researchers being allowed to stay, that they provide to managers information that will assist them in their decision making. Likewise, other sectors of the organization, such as the union, may become suspicious of the role of the researchers and seek to stop the research in midstream. In such settings, the informed consent process is more like an "advise and consent" process. It requires that the investigator be highly skilled at developing communication channels to all sectors of the organization and at maintaining a dialogue with all sectors so that problems can be addressed and negotiated before they reach crisis proportions. The researcher typically has little direct power in the research setting and must use communication skills and good human relations to promote multilateral solutions to ethical dilemmas that may emerge. These processes of communication and group dynamics are discussed in detail in Mirvis and Seashore (1982) and in Mirvis (1982).

Fieldworkers have stressed that informed consent is not the correct name or model for their process of communicating with the persons they observe. Fieldwork is the method of cultural anthropology and is often chosen by social psychologists, sociologists, political scientists, educators, nurses, management scientists, criminologists and others who seek insight into a subculture such as that of the alcoholic, the school child, the dying, members of a feminist movement, or a white collar criminal. It is necessary for the fieldworker to participate in the host culture long enough to interpret the events that occur there. There is no experimental design, no interview schedule, no treatment and no measuring instruments. The fieldworker is the measuring instrument, and information is gathered by creating a natural human relationship with one or more members of the group to be studied, and learning from them by interacting with them, talking with them, and observing them.

While the method of fieldwork resembles friendship, fieldwork is not an ordinary human relationship. Fieldworkers are strangers who learn the ways of others, then leave and write about certain aspects of the host culture from the perspective of their discipline and their own culture. They may receive support from an agency that has more than an academic interest in the findings, and they may receive permission to enter that subculture from someone who has a vested interest in the research. Thus, many potential ethical issues are involved in fieldwork. These should be addressed at the outset and on a continuing basis as the fieldwork reveals pertinent new information.

Once they have entered the host culture, fieldworkers need to create a relationship with members of the host culture that is fair and respectful. They need to establish a viable way to survive and gain knowledge of the host culture and to allay fears and prevent stresses that might be caused by their presence. It may be difficult to communicate accurately about the scientific nature of the fieldwork to those being studied, yet fieldworkers must be careful not to wrong members of the host culture by lying or betraying their trust. Fieldworkers must learn how information might be used harmfully in the host culture, so that confidentiality can be protected in important ways. After developing close ties with members of the host culture, fieldworkers must be sensitive, yet detached enough, to complete the field work by writing a report that is of scholarly value yet compassionate enough to warrant the confidence of the informants. The findings should be disseminated in a responsible and nonharmful way, preserving privacy and confidentialty as appropriate.

The elements of informed consent are impossible to incorporate, literally, into some fieldwork. For example, in some tribal settings, obtaining the chief's consent, not individual consent, is the only permissible approach. And, in some organizational settings, obtaining management consent, not individual employee consent, is the acceptable procedure; being studied may be one of the conditions of employment. In field settings, the researcher has little control over how the study will evolve, thus a comprehensive discussion of risks and benefits is not possible. Moreover, there is no powerful research administrator within the setting who can set aright any wrongs. Indeed, the researchers, typically, are among the lowest powered persons in the setting. Thus, the problems of treating research participants and others equitably must be conceived more broadly. Many have written about the kinds of problems that arise in field settings. The reader is referred to Loo (1982) for a discussion of research in minority settings, Levine on research on the aged, Johnson (1982) on research in communities, Wax on the general issue of reciprocity in fieldwork, and Glazer (1982) on the meanings of reciprocity in modern field settings.

Fully informed consent is not always possible for a variety of reasons. In some cases, outright deception occurs. Social scientists and IRB members recognize that deception research has the potential for wronging and harming subjects, and should not be used without serious consideration of its risks and of alternative methods. However, the regulatory and methodological literature on social research does not adequately distinguish among deception paradigms in terms of their potential for wronging or harming. The researcher and IRB members have only their intuitions to guide them in evaluating the relative acceptability of deception research proposals. The kinds of wrongs and harms that might arise from deception research depend on the kinds and means of deception, the nature of the research, and the loci of the upsets it may cause.

KINDS OF DECEPTION AND THE WRONGS THEY MAY INVOLVE

First we consider a framework for assessing the potential of deception research procedures for wronging or harming persons, and for selecting valid procedures involving the weakest or least harmful procedures. In this section, we examine seven major *kinds* of deception research and the potential of each for wronging persons. The next section builds on this taxonomy and considers the *means* of deception, the *nature of the research*, and the locus of its potential *upsets* in relation to potential for harm. The last section considers *debriefing*—what it is, how it is done and when not to do it.

CASE 1: I WASN'T FOOLED, I WAS JUST DISGUSTED

As an undergraduate, I participated in a lot of deception research. It was all harmless; it was also disgusting. Is this the way it has to be? Is this what science is about? In one study, I entered the lab and followed a sign saying "FEMALES THIS WAY." There was another sign that said "MALES THIS WAY." The experimenter had me fill out an autobiographical form, took a Polaroid picture of me, and left. She returned with similar information on a guy. I was shown his picture and the autobiographical data. He was the most absolutely gorgeous guy I have ever seen. A junior; spends Saturdays helping underprivileged kids; GPA 3.99. Then, she explained to me that I was to answer questions based on the information about the guy and that he would do the same based on my information; later the guy and I would get to meet each other. She then asked me such questions as: Would you like to meet this guy? Would you go out with him? ... and more and more intimate questions. I started to think—ah yes, they are using the Guttman Scale. And a friend of mine told me yesterday about being in an experiment and being shown a picture of the ugliest guy in the world.

—Reflections of a student who prefers to remain anonymous.

The reasons why negative values are attached to deception research are many and complex. One major reason concerns the ways deception research may wrong people, that is, may violate ordinary moral obligations that decent people hold towards one another—moral obligations of the kind that, if generally met, enable human relationships to function constructively. For example, if most people tell the truth most of the time, constructive and meaningful communication is possible and trusting relationships may be built; otherwise, communication becomes a tangle of deception and counter-deception from which few good outcomes can be realized. Most people believe that our moral obligation to do such things as tell the truth, and respect the privacy and autonomy of others are not absolute, but rather may be violated if for a reason of overriding moral importance. The objection to deception research expressed in Case 1 appears to be based on the perception that the ordinary moral obligation to be honest and respectful of another's privacy was violated in order to do trivial and probably invalid research. The student felt wronged even though she was not harmed (or even fully deceived).

Other reasons why negative values are attached to deception research have to do with specific harmful consequences that might occur depending on the context and nature of the research. In the second section of this chapter, the context and nature of deceptive research and their possible causal connection with harmful outcomes are discussed, and some of the cases presented in this section are analyzed further.

What is Deception Research and Why is it Done?

According to *Webster's Third New International Dictionary*, the original sense of the word deception which survives today in special contexts is "to take unawares, especially by craft or trickery," and the modern meaning is "to cause to believe the false." Both of these meanings apply to deception as it occurs in social research. If a researcher informs subjects that their conformity to group pressure will be studied, all naturally occurring conformity will probably cease. The usual solution to this problem (illustrated in Case 2) is to deceive subjects about the purpose of the experiment—to make them believe that other people disagree with their answers (a false belief, since the others are confederates instructed to disagree) and then to observe their spontaneous conforming responses (taking them unawares).

CASE 2: DECEIVING TO STUDY CONFORMITY

Solomon Asch (1956) studied conformity by telling subjects that they were participating in a perception experiment in which each member of their group would select the line believed to be the same length as the standard line. Unknown to the subject, the other seven members of the group were confederates. On the first two trials, most of the seven confederates made the correct match. From the third trial on, the confederates all agreed on a wrong answer. Asch reported that the (real) subjects looked bewildered and anxious. Thirty-three percent of them gave the same wrong answer as the confederates, while the rest gave the correct answer despite obvious feelings of discomfort and confusion. The 33% error rate in the false majority condition was in sharp contrast to the 7% error rate in the normal condition. Most subjects had been made to doubt their own judgment, and a third of them caved in to the majority rather than believe their own eyes.

It is worthwhile to contrast Asch's findings with what persons report about their own tendencies to conform: Wolosin, Sherman and Mynat (1972) found that individuals perceive most other people as conforming sheep, but report that they themselves are independent of group influence. If these subjects' claims about themselves were valid, Asch would have obtained different results. Deception enabled Asch to obtain valid knowledge about human behavior that might have been unobtainable otherwise. There are other subordinate reasons for employing deception in research:

1. Deception may be necessary to obtain adequate stimulus control or random assignment of subjects (e.g., Cases 1, 2 and 3).
2. Deception may be the only economically viable way to study a given behavior. It may be impractical to wait in field settings for the natural occurrence of the event (e.g., Cases 1, 2 and 3).
3. Deception may be a means of obtaining valid data without serious risk to subjects. For example, in research on aggression, rather than allow or encourage real combat, it may be better to employ a confederate victim or aggressor and contrive the setting so that no one is hurt.
4. Deception may enable the researcher to obtain information that would otherwise be unobtainable because of the subject's defensiveness, embarrassment, shame or fear of reprisal (e.g., Cases 2 and 5).

To summarize, in deception research, the investigator deliberately causes or allows persons to believe that which is false for some or all of the reasons enumerated above. For purposes of this paper, then, we define deception research as follows: Deception research is research in which subjects are purposely allowed to or caused to have false beliefs or assumptions or to accept as false that which is true, and in which the researcher studies their reactions; the reactions and the study of those reactions are made possible by the incorrect beliefs or assumptions of the subject. Whether deception has occurred when the deception is seen through (as in Case 1) is an interesting question. Unconvincing deception inductions may involve most or all of the wrongs and harms that would have arisen had the induction been effective. (Later, the reader may evaluate this assertion by assuming the inductions of any of the cases presented herein to have been ineffective, and judging which of the wrongs described in Table 1 pertain to each case.) Moreover, given the willingness of many subjects to act as if they believe what the experimenter seems to want them to believe, some kind of mutual deception sometimes occurs when the deception induction is unconvincing. This raises even more serious ethical problems (e.g., problems of validity) than would occur if the deception had been totally convincing to subjects.

Kinds of Deception

While there are good reasons for social scientists to consider using research methods that involve deception, it is important to recognize that such methods may chip away at the privacy, self-determination and even the material well-being of subjects, and at the general quality of relationships between research participants and social scientists, and among people in general. As we shall see, all deception research, even the study of self-deception, poses some threat to subjects. It is important, therefore, to be clear about the conditions under which deception research seriously violates the moral obligations that ordinarily exist among decent people. We begin with an examination of various kinds of deception, then proceed to examine the ways in which each may violate ordinary moral obligations to others. In the next section, we build on this taxonomy to show how the content of research, coupled with the means and kind of deception, may potentially harm subjects.

Deception Not by the Researcher

Sometimes researchers observe existing deception and do not, themselves, deceive. The researcher may study self-deception, or deception perpetrated by a third party for purposes other than those of the research:

Self-deception. A weak form of deception occurs in research on persons who hold idiosyncratic views, in which the researcher studies and critically analyzes these views. Whether it is the subject or the investigator who is misinformed depends, of course, on one's point of view. For present purposes we consider subjects self-deceived when they independently choose to believe something that the researcher considers incorrect or notably lacking in perspective. For example, middle-class Americans who believe in ghosts or voodoo might be regarded as self-deceiving.

Sometimes researchers can be honest about their skepticism or criticism of the belief. When studying behavioral phenomena accompanying belief in ESP, one might openly solicit subjects who believe in ESP, making it clear that their beliefs and behaviors concerning ESP will be studied from a position of skepticism. This raises only a minor ethical problem, since presumably the subject is informed and consents; the problem has to do with being honest without being abusive and demeaning towards those having different beliefs than one's own.

Often, in the interest of creating rapport, researchers do not honestly express their criticism or skepticism. However sound this practice may be from a humanitarian and scientific point of view, it creates ethical problems. Subjects may reveal private information on the assumption that they were among like-minded people, placing the researcher under serious obligation to maintain strict confidentiality. The ethical implications of this practice depend on contextual factors. If the researcher is a cognitive psychologist writing a pure research paper on the thought processes of psychotics or preliterate peoples whose identity is cloaked, the potential magnitude of wrong or risk is far less than if the researcher is an applied anthropologist gathering data about the vulnerabilities of a tribe whom the sponsor of the research seeks to subjugate.

Deception by a third party. Another weak form of deception research involves study of a person who has been misinformed by someone else for purposes other than those of the research. For example, a social scientist might study the processes or effects of "therapeutic privilege"—physicians' lying to patients when they judge that the truth would harm or confuse their patients. As in the study of self-deception, confidentiality is crucial to maintaining the well-being of both parties studied, and debriefing may be out of the question unless the deceiver agrees to do the debriefing.

When studying relationships in intact groups (e.g., families, classrooms, romantic relationships, and so on) one may unexpectedly witness lying and deception. The unanticipated deception—particularly if it appears harmful—places the researcher in a most uncomfortable position. The researcher has an incomplete understanding of the relationship under observation and an obligation to cause no harm to subjects, and has probably promised them confidentiality. Yet, the researcher could be the only witness to serious fraud, and the presence of the researcher may be used to persuade the duped individual that what occurred is above board, since it was witnessed by a distinguished scientist. There are no simple solutions to such dilemmas. Social scientists should be aware that they might witness unanticipated and harmful deception in the course of research. They should take this into account when deciding whether to undertake research, and be prepared to seek the counsel of an attorney and others qualified to offer sound legal and moral perspective, if needed.

Deception by the Researcher

A stronger form of deception occurs when the researcher arranges for subjects to hold false beliefs. Deception by the researcher may be divided into five categories and placed on a continuum from weaker to stronger kinds of deception:

Informed consent to participate in one of several conditions. Subjects consent to participate in any one of various clearly described conditions, knowing that the researcher will conceal which condition actually occurs.

Consent to deception. Subjects consent to be deceived.

Waiver of right to be informed. Subjects waive the right to be informed but are not explicitly forewarned of the possibility of deception.

Consent and false informing. Subjects consent to participate in research and are falsely informed about the nature of the research.

No informing, no consent. Subjects are not informed, do not consent and do not know that research and deception are occurring.

Possible Interchangeability of Kinds of Deception. Much research requiring deception can be done about as well with weak forms of deception as with strong. Consider how the weakest and strongest forms of deception by the researcher might be used to study behavioral effects of LSD: The following is a hypothetical example of the weakest form of deception by the researcher. Subjects are asked to participate in a study of the effects of LSD on specified behaviors. They are told they will receive either a salt tablet (a placebo) or an LSD tablet, but that they cannot be told ahead of time which they will receive. The main form of deception that can occur here is self-deception; subjects experience affective states and may deceive themselves by falsely attributing the cause of their affective states—hence the need for a placebo group.

The following is a true example of the strongest form of deception by the researcher. This research was supported by the CIA. The investigators set up an elaborate laboratory in a brothel. As clients arrived, the madam gave them drinks containing LSD. The men's behavior was then filmed from behind a two-way mirror. The subjects were never debriefed. One of the subjects committed suicide while still under the influence of the LSD. The cause of his suicide and the details of the research remained secret until many years later when the victim's family finally found clues that led them to the truth (Goldman, Clark & Marro, 1975).

These examples are informative: Strong forms of deception generally occur in settings where random assignment of subjects, assurance of privacy and confidentiality, adequacy of standby medical aid, and other features of scientifically and ethically sound research are hardly possible. Outlandish staging often accompanies strong forms of deception. The subsequent news coverage of the CIA research illustrates the public outrage that such research may evoke. Weak forms of deception by the researcher are often much easier to perform. They permit the researcher to operate in a setting where accurate measurement and proper controls and safeguards are convenient to employ.

Weak forms of deception by the researcher. The weaker forms of deception by the researcher are ones in which subjects consent to procedures knowing that there will be some kind of concealment. These procedures are attractive because they overcome the main objection to most deception research—they are respectful of subjects' right of self-determination. In the weakest form of deception by the experimenter, the subject is specifically informed about the purpose, procedures and actual risks and benefits of the various experimental conditions that might occur, without being told which condition the subject is actually assigned to.

The two next stronger forms of deception—consent to be deceived and waiver of the right to be informed may be used in either of two ways. Members of a subject pool might give prior consent to be deceived from time to time or to waive the right to give informed consent, or persons may consent in a particular instance to participate in a study that may involve deception or to waive the right to be informed. When any risks are involved, subjects should be told of the magnitude and general nature of the risks. If it seems questionable whether subjects would consent to the specific risks, were they known, the investigator might seek surrogate consent—the consent of a similar group of persons—to determine whether the risks are considered generally acceptable ones to take for the purposes of that research. Or, one might seek informed consent from a proxy designated by the subject. These procedures respect subjects' right of self-determination; subjects may elect to live dangerously though they do not know the exact nature of the danger. However, the validity of these two procedures sometimes depends on how cleverly the researcher can catch subjects off guard. In the case of very risky or unpleasant treatments, these procedures may become highly objectionable.

Strong forms of deception by the researcher. The two strongest forms of deception, consent with false information and having no knowledge that research or deception are occurring, are the more typical forms of deception research used in the social sciences. Examples have already been cited (Cases 1 and 2). These deny self-determination and may increase the possibility of harm to subjects and society in various ways as we shall see in the next section. It is important to note, however, that even the very strongest form of deception, and the form that violates the largest number of ordinary moral obligations to persons, can be used in utterly harmless and delightful ways as well as in potentially dangerous and objectionable ways, depending on the means of deception and the nature of the research. That is, knowing only the *kind* of deception that is used tells us almost nothing about how harmful or objectionable a particular study may be. To illustrate this point, consider the following two examples of the use of no informing and no consent, the very strongest form of deception in research:

CASE 3: COOKIES AND KINDNESS

Isen and Levin (1972) investigated the effects of a person's positive affective state on subsequent willingness to help others. "Feeling good" was induced in half the subjects by handing out free cookies to them while they were studying in the library. The other half did not receive cookies. Half the students in each group were then approached by another person and asked if they would be willing to volunteer to serve as confederates in a psychology experiment designed to study creativity in students at examination time as opposed to other times of the year. It was added that the experimental procedure is something students find helpful. The other half of the students were asked if they would volunteer to serve as confederates in a study requiring that they drop books, make noises, and so on, while the experimenter unobtrusively recorded the subjects' reactions to distraction, at examination time as opposed to other times of the year. It was added that the distraction would be generally regarded by subjects as an unpleasant annoyance. The results indicate that students who received cookies were far more willing to engage in helpful behavior and less willing to engage in distracting behavior than those who did not receive cookies. A debriefing and discussion period followed each subject's reply. Subjects indicated that they had regarded the handing out of cookies as some person's kind gesture and not connected it in any way with the subsequent request to participate as a confederate in a study.

Contrast Case 3 with 4, in terms of potential for harming or wronging subjects:

CASE 4: TEAROOM TRADE

Laud Humphreys, a Ph.D. candidate in sociology at Washington University in St. Louis, recognized that the public and law-enforcement authorities hold highly simplistic stereotyped beliefs about men who commit impersonal sexual acts with one another in public restrooms. "Tearoom sex," as fellatio in public restrooms is called, then accounted for the majority of homosexual arrests in the United States. Humphreys believed that it would be of considerable social importance for society to gain more objective understanding of who these men are and what motivates them to seek quick, impersonal sexual gratification. Humphreys stationed himself in "tea rooms" and offered to serve as "watchqueen"—the individual who keeps watch and coughs when a police car stops nearby or a stranger approaches. He played that role faithfully while observing hundreds of acts of fellatio. He was able to gain the confidence of some of the men he observed, disclose his role as scientist, and persuade them to tell him about the rest of their lives and their motives. Those who were willing to talk openly with him tended to be among the better educated. To avoid bias, Humphreys secretly followed some of the other men he observed and recorded the license number of their cars. A year later, and carefully disguised, Humphreys appeared at their homes claiming to be a health service interviewer and interviewed them about their marital status, job, and so on.

Humphreys' findings destroy many stereotypes: 54% of his subjects were married and living with their wives, and superficial analysis would suggest that they were exemplary citizens who had exemplary marriages; 38% clearly were neither bisexual or homosexual. Most of the 38% were Catholic or their wives were, and since the birth of their last child conjugal relations had been rare. Their alternative source of sex had to be quick, inexpensive and impersonal. It could not entail any kind of involvement that would threaten their already fragile marriage and jeopardize their most important asset—their standing as father of their children (Humphreys, 1970). Humphreys' study was responsible for reducing the number of arrests for this victimless crime. He was praised for this work by the gay community and the Society for the Study of Social Problems chose Humphreys' book for its prestigious C. Wright Mills Award. However, the fact that he spied on subjects and risked the subpoena of his data and the arrest of his subjects caused considerable furor, including demands that his Ph.D. degree be rescinded, and scathing criticism by journalists and others.The angry words of columnist Nicholas von Hoffman (1970), which appeared in the *Washington Post* illustrate the extent to which some members of society felt wronged by Humphreys' research:

> We're so preoccupied with defending our privacy against insurance investigators, dope sleuths, counter-espionage men, divorce detectives and credit checkers that we overlook the social scientists behind the hunting blinds who're also peeping into what we thought were our most private and secret lives. But there they are, studying us, taking notes, getting to know us, as indifferent as everybody else to the feeling that to be a complete human involves having an aspect of ourselves that's unknown (1982).

Summary of kinds of deception research. Seven kinds of deception have been presented, two in which the researcher does not do the deceiving, three in which the researcher deceives but with some kind of consent, and two in which the researcher deceives without consent or forewarning of any kind. The two forms of deception not by the researcher are not necessarily the most harmless or morally acceptable.

They are weak forms of deception only in reference to the roles of the research and the researcher, since the only thing that the researcher may conceal is the fact that he or she knowingly observes deception. However, the deception that is observed may be highly insidious. The advantage of studying deception not by the researcher is precisely that the researcher merely observes rather than causes the deception. By analogy, it is more acceptable to observe the personality development of children who have been abused by their parents than to abuse children in order to do the research. Likewise, the strongest form of deception, deception with no informing and no consent, is not necessarily harmful or morally unacceptable as suggested by the contrast between Cases 4 and 5. How harmful and morally objectionable deception research is depends on many factors, and is considered in detail in the next section. Here, we consider only what wrongs may be involved in each of the seven kinds of deception considered, not on how serious or harmful the wronging might be. The following are seven wrongs that seem most pertinent to one or more of these kinds of deception research:

1. *Invasion of privacy.* The researcher arranges to extract kinds of information that the subjects probably would not agree to reveal if they understood the true purpose of the study.
2. *No informed consent.* The researcher does not honestly state what to expect regarding procedures and risks.
3. *Denial of self-determination.* The researcher does not give the subject a reasonable opportunity to decide whether to participate in the study.
4. *No debriefing.* The researcher does not (and it may be imprudent to) explain the deception after the study is completed.
5. *Researcher actively lies or misrepresents.* The researcher actively falsifies or misrepresents pertinent information.
6. *Researcher conceals.* The researcher conceals pertinent information.

Table 1 shows which of these moral objections are likely to accompany each of the seven kinds of deception. Note that the system for indicating the likelihood of each objection permits one to rate research according to the likelihood that it raises moral issues. Note that this numerical key represents a code, and not a weighting scale. For example, the number 3 does not necessarily indicate that a problem is present; it suggests that one should carefully scrutinize the research. Do not use the numbers as scores but as guides to further scrutiny.

As Table 1 indicates, the weak kinds of deception by the researcher deserve serious consideration for use in future research. Strong forms of deception by the researcher raise many problems—and these are the forms most frequently used in social research.

Table l. Potential Harms or Ethical Objections to Kinds of Deception in Research

Kind of Deception	**Potential Harm or Ethical Objection**					
	Invades Privacy	**No Consent**	**No Self-Determination**	**No Debriefing**	**Researcher Lies**	**Researcher Conceals**
Deception Not by the Researcher						
Self-deception[a,c]	4	3	3	3	2	3
Third person deception[a,b,c]	4	4	4	3	2	4
Deception by Researcher						
Informed consent	1	1	1	1	1	1
Consent to deception	3	1	1	1	4	4
Waives informing	3	4	1	2	4	4
False informing	4	4	4	2	4	4
No informing[a]	4	4	4	3	4	4

Key: 4=accompanies, 3=likely to accompany, 2=unlikely to accompany, 1=does not accompany.

[a]The category *No informing* may involve a combination of research on self-deception and deception by a third party as well as deception by the researcher.

[b]In some naturalistic observation, such as family research, the investigator should consider the possibility that deception may be observed and plan accordingly.

[c]Conceivably, a forewarning procedure could be used with one of the *Deception Not by the Researcher* procedures, but this possibility is ignored for purposes of this table.

Surprisingly, deception not by the experimenter has the potential for raising about as many problems as do strong kinds of deception by the experimenter. But the point is not that one should necessarily use weak kinds of deception; rather it is that one must consider not only the kinds of deception, but also the means and contexts employed. The power of the researcher to solve ethical problems raised by deception lies not just in the ability to use weak kinds of deception, but in the ability to take into account various dimensions of research design that affect the degree to which deception may be objectionable and harmful. In the next section, we complete this argument.

FACTORS INFLUENCING THE MAGNITUDE OF POTENTIAL FOR HARM OR WRONG OF DECEPTION

We have already noted that the magnitude of the wrong and potential for harm to subjects is determined largely by factors other than the kind of deception employed. As an example, if a researcher pretends to be a student handing out the bounties of a cooking class, and hands out cookies to study their effects on mood, the magnitude of wrong and risk involved in this deceptive procedure would vary greatly depending on whether the cookies contain raisins—a nonconcealed, positively regarded, nutritious substance, or LSD—a concealed, negatively regarded, illegal, and harmful substance.

In this section, we discuss those other factors and the way they may combine with one another and with the kinds of deception to affect the potential magnitude of the wrong or harm that could be caused by the research. The taxonomy of factors presented here is intended to serve as a guide in risk/benefit assessment of deception research proposals by increasing awareness of possible sources of risk, motivating a search for safeguards to reduce or remove those risks, and raising the issue of whether the likely benefits of the research can justify the level of risk that remains. It is also intended to build on the notion of *wrong* developed in the prior article: even if harm does not occur, certain combinations of factors in deception research are morally offensive and predispose members of society at large to feel wronged and concerned that such research is permitted. Concern of this sort is clearly expressed by journalist Nicholas von Hoffman, regarding Humphreys' research, described in Case 4, prior article.)

A Taxonomy of Deception Research Characteristics

I. Means of deceiving. Researchers deceive by using *devices*, with specific *kinds* of deception and involving *mental reservations* or *explicit lies*.

A. *Devices.* The devices that may be used to deceive are *implicit deception*, *technical deception* and *role deception*. All three of these devices are used in Milgram's (Case 5) study of obedience:

CASE 5: "SHOCKING OBEDIENCE"

Stanley Milgram, an experimental social psychologist at Yale University, ran newspaper ads inviting the public to participate in a learning experiment. Volunteers were told they would be divided by lot into learners and teachers. Actually, the aim was to study obedience, not learning, and all of the volunteers found themselves in the role of teacher, where they were instructed to teach lists of words to learners, and to give learners increasingly severe electric shocks at every mistake. Unbeknownst to the teachers, the "learners" were not really wired to shock apparatus, but to a box that looked like a shock generator; they were paid confederates who feigned both failure to learn and pain at being shocked. The results were surprising. Although a panel of psychiatrists had, before the experiments were performed, predicted that only about three persons in a thousand would obey instructions and deliver shock at a lethal level, in fact in one of Milgram's conditions about two thirds of his subjects did so.

At the end of each session, the actual purpose and procedure was explained to the subject, and those who had obediently delivered "severe shock" were assured that obedience under these conditions was not unusual. A one year follow-up was carried out to determine whether participation in the study had detrimental effects. The majority of the participants were grateful for the insight that their participation had provided, and only 1.3% of subjects indicated that they wished they had not participated (Milgram, 1974).

1. In *implicit deception*, the aims and methods of the research are so different from what subjects expect that subjects behave under incorrect assumptions, even though there may be no role or technical deception to reinforce the incorrect assumption. That is, subjects generate their own false assumptions and the investigator conceals the truth by not correcting those assumptions. For example, suppose a researcher says to a child "Draw me a good picture of a man," and later codes the picture according to a system considered indicative of the child's anxiety level. In all likelihood, the child drew the picture so that the researcher could admire it, not so that it could be coded for indicators of anxiety. In part, implicit deception depends on self-deception, but it also depends on the use of a procedure that induces the subject to act on naive beliefs. Because implicit deception depends on attributions made by the subject, debriefing may be difficult— subjects may find it difficult to understand that they were deceived because, in effect, they were deceiving themselves. Another example of implicit deception is research on "incidental learning" or learning that occurs without one's intending to learn: the experimenter gives subjects an obvious learning task such as learning pairs of nonsense syllables, and then tests subjects on other attributes of the stimulus material such as its colors. The experimenter does not explicitly lie about the nature of the learning task; having instructed subjects to try to learn pairs of syllables, subjects automatically assume that that is what they will be tested on. A third example can be found in Case 5, in which Milgram made the "teacher" rather than the "learner" the object of his study; Milgram explicitly lied to subjects about the role of the "learner," but the lie about the role of the "teacher" was implicit since subjects readily assumed that *only* the learner would be the subject of study.
2. In *technical deception*, objects, equipment or procedures are misrepresented. For example, Jones and Siegal (1971) hooked subjects to a formidable looking device and persuaded them that it was an electromyograph that functioned as a lie detector by measuring muscle movements that reveal one's true feelings. They then asked subjects questions to which people ordinarily give dishonest answers. Indeed, the subjects gave more candid answers than are ordinarily obtained. Milgram (Case 5) also used technical deception in the form of fake shock apparatus

and recordings of screams and pleading to stop the experiment.

3. In *role deception*, one or more persons are represented as other than who they are. For example, Humphreys (Case 4) pretended first to be a watchqueen and then to be a public health department interviewer; Milgram's (Case 5) confederate pretended to be a subject trying to learn paired associate words; Piliavin, Piliavin and Rodin's (Case 6) confederate pretended to be a sick man.

   It is proposed that none of these *devices* for deception is inherently wrongful or harmful, except when combined with certain other elements of deception research. Note that the popular TV show Candid Camera, which employed all of these devices, was not regarded by the public as wrongful or harmful. Note also that Candid Camera combined these devices with other elements of deception such that, by the system presented here, their deceptive stunts would receive a rating indicative of no harmfulness or wrongfulness. And, all of Candid Camera's "victims" were debriefed, thanked in a way that expressed sincere appreciation for the entertainment they had given to others, and given an opportunity to withdraw their videotaped data.

B. *Kinds of deception*. These include the seven kinds of deception described in the prior article: (1) informed consent (without revealing which of the fully described conditions will obtain), (2) consent to deception, (3) waiver of right to be informed, (4) consent and false informing, (5) no consent, no informing, (6) self deception, (7) deception by a third person.

C. *Mental reservations or explicit lies*. Either mental reservations or explicit lies accompany the creation of the device and context for deception.

1. *Mental reservations* are omissions of explanation which, coupled with a kind of deception and a device for deception, lead the subject to hold a false assumption about the situation (e.g., Isen & Levin, Case 3; and Piliavin, *et al.*, Case 6).

2. *Explicit lies* are conveyed by intentionally giving untrue verbal or written statements to the subject (e.g., Humphreys, Case 4, when in role of interviewer; Milgram, Case 5, when explaining to prospective subjects the nature of the equipment, the research, and the selection of the teacher and learner).

CASE 6: STIGMA AND BYSTANDER INTERVENTION

Piliavin, Piliavin and Rodin (1975) tested the notion that stigma makes bystanders feel uneasy and less willing to help. The "victim" whom bystanders might help was a student who rode a subway where he staged a false fainting spell. He moaned, fell, and lay on the floor of the subway. In the "stigma" condition, the "victim" used makeup to create a large, unattractive "birthmark." In the nonstigma condition, he had the same fainting spell, but no ugly disfigurement. If one of the bystanders did not come to the aid of the "victim" within a few minutes, a confederate "bystander" came forth and helped him up. The results indicated that helping was significantly lowered when the "victim" had a birthmark.

II. Nature of the research. This refers to aspects of the research other than its deceptiveness that influence its potential for harming or wronging persons. Four aspects are identified here: social perception of the behavior that is being studied, privacy of the behavior, confidentiality of the research procedure, and the extent to which the behavior is induced by the experimenter. Lack of confidentiality and induction of behavior, *per se*, do not make deception research harmful or objectionable; but when the induced behavior is private or is socially perceived as negative, the induction or lack of confidentiality may result in harmful or wrongful research.

A. *Social perception of the behavior.* The behavior studied may be located along a continuum from behavior that is perceived as neutral to behavior perceived as negative:

1. *Neutral* behavior refers to classes of behavior unlikely to evoke concern or distress in anyone. For example, a field study might be designed to study the effects of various kinds of prior experience on altruism. Subjects might experience having a door held for them as they leave a store, not having a door held, or having the door temporarily blocked; the dependent measure might be whether they donate a coin to the Salvation Army solicitor standing outside. Both the act of donating and of not donating are likely to be considered neutral by the subject and by observers.
2. *Mildly negative* behavior includes acts perceived as mildly harmful, offensive, unpleasant or undesirable. The subject may be induced to act in ways indicative of low ability, low self-respect, low respect for others, social immaturity, and so on, and may experience disappointment in self or the disapproval of others as a result. For example, the subject might do poorly on a test, litter a public area, or fail to help someone in distress. Note that the act need not be genuine; for example, "failure" on a test may consist of being told one has failed, irrespective of actual performance.

3. *Negative* refers to the perception that behavior is quite offensive, reprehensible, illegal, or damaging. The behavior need not be harmful or wrong by a universal standard, but only by some local standard. Milgram's obedient subjects engaged in negative behavior: although the shocks they delivered were not real, the subjects thought they were, and experienced strong negative emotions as a consequence. However, degree of harmfulness does depend partly on whether the act was real; had Milgram's subjects delivered real electric shocks in near lethal or lethal doses, their behavior would be classed as very negative.
4. *Very negative* refers to behavior that could have serious negative consequences for the subject or for others due to social perceptions of it. Although the distinction between categories 3 and 4 is blurred, some examples will illustrate the value of a fourth category. Category 3 might include smoking marijuana, petty theft, inflicting pain on others, or unmarried gay San Franciscans going to gay bars. Category 4 might include selling heroin, grand larceny, endangering the life of another, or married persons engaging in homosexual acts in public lavatories in the Midwest.

   The more negative (or apparently negative) the behavior that is studied, the more harmful or wrong the use of deception is likely to be, other conditions being equal. The kind and extent of harm that arises from studying behavior perceived as negative depends, to a considerable degree, on the extent of induction and on the lack of confidentiality and privacy, as discussed subsequently.

B. *Privacy of the behavior*. There is a continuum from private to public behavior. Private behavior is not intended for others to observe; public behavior may be freely observed. Deception research generally involves some invasion of privacy, since deception is employed to study behavior that most subjects would choose not to display to the investigator if they correctly understood the nature of the research. (Privacy may be further jeopardized by cross-validation procedures in which the researcher consults other sources of data—persons who know the subject, administrative records or archives—to corroborate direct research findings. These cross-validation procedures should also be evaluated in terms of the degree of privacy of the acts being studied and the degree of confidentiality of the method of data handling.)

1. *Public behavior* is performed for an audience to observe (not merely for members of one's primary group). Examples include a teacher's behavior before a class, and a speaker's behavior

before a convention audience. When a social scientist covertly observes public behavior, this is not an invasion of privacy but it does involve concealment; subjects do not know they are subjects or that data are being collected systematically.

2. *Private behavior in public places* is behavior that is observable by others but not done for others to observe. For example, when persons in public places talk to themselves, fight with friends, conform to group opinion, use lies and smiles to ingratiate, cry, and so on, they typically do not want outsiders to observe the details.
3. *Private behavior in restricted settings* is not intended for outsiders to observe. It occurs in settings where membership is strictly defined, and where nonmembers may enter only by invitation. Restricted settings include families, clubs, work organizations, crime organizations, jury chambers, offices where members of a profession meet their clients, and so on. Because members of restricted groups generally do not want to be studied, social research in these settings usually occurs through concealment and deception. The social scientist enters, often in the guise of membership, to observe typical behavior therein. Scientists have entered thus, as "patients" in the offices of physicians, as "penitents" in the confessional, as "workers" in factories, and as "new members" of encounter groups, Alcoholics Anonymous, religious cults, "tearooms," and so on. A setting is restricted to the extent that subjects assume it provides freedom from the prying eyes of outsiders such as social scientists. Thus, from Humphreys' (Case 4) role as watchqueen, we know that "tearooms" are highly restricted settings, though they are public lavatories.

CASE 7. TOILET BEHAVIORS

Middlemist, Knowles and Matter (1976) used hidden periscopes to study the effects of closeness of others on speed and rate of urination by men in a public lavatory. (Yes—you guessed it: closeness was manipulated by having confederates rush in and begin to urinate at the urinal next to the subjects who were designated for the "crowded" condition.) The investigators defended their research on grounds that anonymity was preserved and no harm was done to subjects, but their critics remained convinced that the induction and secret observation was immoral, since they judged the research to be trivial (Koocher, 1977).

4. *Private, nonsecret behavior* is not generally intended for the eyes of others, but others know it exists. For example, people

normally do not defecate in front of others, but it is no secret that people defecate. It is simply an act that prevailing culture defines as private. General cultural definitions are sometimes violated, however, so that acts normally considered private become public. For example, sexual intercourse in a couple's bedroom falls into category 4, but sex on a nude beach falls into category 3; at a regular beach, category 2; and as a scene in a movie, category 1.

5. *Secret, private behavior* is not meant for others to know about. There are many reasons for behavior to be secret and private: shame, guilt, modesty, self-consciousness, fear of reprisal, fear of negative evaluation, pride, and so on. Among private acts, whether an act is secret usually depends on special circumstance. Celibacy is no secret if the individual belongs to a celibate order, but it typically is a secret if the person purports to have a happy marriage. Praying is not usually secret behavior, except in countries that prohibit religious worship. The more private the behavior, the greater the potential for harm or wrong in the study of that behavior, other conditions being equal.

C. *Induction of the behavior studied.* Research varies from the observation of naturally occurring behavior to the observation of behavior that is powerfully induced.

1. *Naturally occurring behavior* is not induced by the experimenter. It is induced by some natural course of events and probably represents the kind of thing the subject often does. (Subjects in Humphreys' study, Case 4, were engaging in naturally occurring behavior.)
2. *Weakly induced behavior* as an experimental induction is not so powerful as to produce behavior that is highly unusual for the person. Weak induction was involved in Case 6, the crowded condition in Case 7, and the cookies condition in Case 3. Another example of weak induction is the presentation of unsolvable problems to college student subjects to solve; the level of anxiety induced is probably not very different from that experienced by the student when unable to answer a quiz question.
3. *Powerfully induced behavior* is induced by the experimenter, and the induction is so powerful that subjects are likely to do things that they would not normally do. For example, in order to study decision making under extreme stress, air crews were persuaded that their planes were about to crash (1976). Milgram (Case 5) induced his subjects to deliver "possibly lethal" levels of shock to persons.

D. *Confidentiality* refers to an agreement by the researcher that the information gained in the research will be used only for the bona fide purposes of the research. Confidentiality usually is not an important issue when studying public behavior that is generally perceived as neutral. Even when the researcher deceives the subject and induces the behavior, it may matter little who knows about it. However, if the researcher causes subjects to misunderstand a situation and then induces behavior that is private or generally perceived as negative, confidentiality becomes a critical means of reducing risk to the subject. We distinguish four levels of confidentiality:

1. *Anonymity*. Unique identifiers are not gathered (e.g., Case 3).
2. *High confidentiality*. Names or other unique identifiers are gathered, but data are stored by number and a key linking names and numbers is stored in a secure place elsewhere. The key and other identifiers are destroyed when they are no longer essential to the research (e.g., Case 4).
3. *Low confidentiality*. Names accompany data. Data are stored in a file out of sight. In any reports or publications the identity of individual subjects is cloaked. But the individual data, including unique identifiers, could be found, stolen, subpoenaed or misplaced.
4. *No confidentiality*. Individual data with unique identifiers (e.g., names, social security numbers) are available for others to see (e.g., research assistants, other researchers who wish to perform secondary analyses of the data, passersby).

Effects of These Factors on Possible Degree of Wrongfulness and Harmfulness

It is the *combination* of conditions that determines the possible degree of wrongfulness or risk of harm. In deception research on a *neutrally perceived* and *public* act, such as picking up litter in a park (or not doing so), even if the act is *highly induced* (e.g., by peer pressure) it matters little if the data are not kept confidential. In contrast, confidentiality matters greatly when studying a behavior *perceived as negative* such as drug abuse. The data should be *anonymous* or handled with *high confidentiality*, since they could be stolen for purposes of blackmail, subpoenaed, and so on. In the case of *private*, *secret* behavior that is negatively perceived (e.g., drug abuse by physicians who steal from hospital drug cabinets),the degree of risk and the importance of confidentiality are still greater.

Let us now consider deception research on behavior that is merely *private*, not harmful or offensive—behavior such as: family arguments, urination, sexual intercourse, disciplining one's children, and the expression of grief. Society holds that invasion of privacy is wrong because it reduces autonomy and is disrespectful of persons; the use of deception to study any private behavior is objectionable unless the research is of considerable social value.

In conclusion, deception research calls for scrutiny when it involves induction of behavior that is private or perceived as negative. Even when appropriate safeguards are employed (e.g., anonymity, protection of confidentiality, sensitive debriefing), the research may receive severe public criticism. Although scientific freedom should not be jeopardized by fickle public sensitivities, it is appropriate to weigh the importance of the research against one's willingness to deal with public and even professional outrage. Even in the case of research judged to be of great value, public outrage could lead to temporary curtailment of legitimate channels of scientific inquiry.

III. *Upset caused by deception.* Emotional upset may occur in four ways:

1. *The treatment* may cause upset. For example, many of Milgram's subjects were upset because they thought they had delivered high levels of shock to another person.
2. *The debriefing* may leave subjects feeling foolish and incapable of independent judgement or feeling that their environment is untrustworthy. For example, subjects who feel good about being praised for their "creative" responses may feel foolish and incapable of independently assessing their capabilities on learning that their reinforcment schedule was randomly assigned. When debriefed, Milgram's (Case 5) subjects experienced self-doubt about their own judgment and trustworthiness.
3. *Knowledge of the research* may cause upset. This upset may occur to persons who read or hear about the research, as well as to subjects. The upset may arise from concern that science would condone a dishonest or harmful treatment of subjects. If the research is important enough to warrant being conducted, it is important enough to mention in text books. If it is likely to evoke widespread anger, cynicism, fear of science, or generalized suspicion, the net value of the research is reduced. In Cases 4 and 5, the major upsets occurred not to subjects but to some members of society at large who learned about the research.
4. *Participation in the deception* by investigators, their assistants and their confederates may cause them upset. The principal investigator is less likely to experience upset than are those directly involved in each act of deception. The confederate role, in particular, which must be reenacted perhaps hundreds

> of times, can be extremely upsetting. Often, the confederates are graduate students being socialized for a research career. One may question the appropriateness of training that is either repellent or deadening to moral sensitivities.

Despite the obvious subjectivity of "upset" ratings, this category serves as a useful way for researchers and IRB members to increase their own awareness of ways their research might upset persons. Having identified possible upsets of subjects, appropriate desensitizing procedures can be developed (as discussed in the third section of this paper). Some possible kinds of upsets include: concern about lack of privacy; confidentiality; autonomy or freedom; embarrassment; self-doubt; concern about hurting or disrespecting others; anger; guilt about wrongdoing or having false pride; distrust or cynicism; and anxiety or dislike concerning the activity involved in the study. The researcher, peers of the subjects, and pilot subjects might participate in assessing the nature and degree of upset likely to result from the research or debriefing, and the effectiveness of the desensitizing procedures. For purposes of this taxonomy, degree of upset is divided into three categories: 1. No upset seems likely, 2. Mild upset seems likely, 3. Substantial upset can probably be expected.

Use of the Taxonomy to Evaluate Deception Research

Actual application of the taxonomy will provide the reader with clearer ideas about when deception research may be harmful and about ways to change research design to reduce risk. The three categories of *means* of deceiving are coded only by checking the *devices, kinds* and *lies* that seem to pertain to the given study. However, a *numerical code* is used for rating *nature of research* and *upsets*. Note that the numbers represent a code and not a weighting scale. A high score on an element of deception indicates that one should pay particular attention to that factor, not that it necessarily is harmful. This rating system should be used to guide the exploration of risk in research, not to "score" protocols on riskiness.

TABLE 1. Rating System for Applying Taxonomy

Case Studies to be Rated	**1**	**2**	**3**	**4**	**5**	**6**	**7**
Means of Deceiving (check relevant ones)							
Devices of deception							
Implicit deception							
Technical deception							
Role deception							
Kinds of deception							
Informed consent							
Consent to deception							
Consent to waive informing							
Consent and false informing							
No informing, no consent							
Self-deception							
Deception by third party							
Kinds of lies							
Implicit lies							
Explicit lies							
Nature of research							
Social perception of the behavior[a]							
Privacy of the behavior[b]							
Induction of the behavior[c]							
Confidentiality[d]							
Upset caused by Deception[e]							
Upset due to the research							
Upset due to the debriefing							
Upset due to knowledge of research							
Upset to research staff							

[a]Rate social perception as: 1=neutral, 2=mildly negative, 3=negative, 4=very negative
[b]Rate behavior as: 1=public, 2=private in public, 3=private in restricted setting, 4=private, nonsecret, 5=private, secret
[c]Rate as: 1=naturally occurring behavior, 2=weak induction, 3=powerful induction
[d]Rate confidentiality as: 1=anonymity, 2=high, 3=low, 4=none
[e]Rate upsets as: 1=no upset likely, 2=mild upset may occur, 3=substantial upset

What conclusions can be drawn from the rating of these cases? For purposes of this discussion, let us limit our attention to Cases 3, 4, 5, and 6, Isen & Levin, Humphreys, Milgram, and Piliavin, *et al.:*

The *means of deception* in all four of these studies involved role deception. All but Milgram's research clearly involved no informing and no consent. Yet, observe the effect of the other characteristics of these studies on the objectionableness of the role deception and the lack of informed consent. We see that the *role deception* of Piliavin *et al.*, and of Isen and Levin is rendered less objectionable by the use of *mental reservations*, by the *perceived harmlessness* of the behavior studied and by the fact that the behavior was not *private*, *powerfully induced* or the cause of much *upset*. In fact, Isen and Levin's role deception was so minimal that it is difficult to agree on whether it should be called role deception at all. Subjects observed that *someone* gave them cookies; there was role deception only in that subjects failed to realize that those people were research assistants. We must conclude that it is important to evaluate the means of deception in connection with the other aspects of the research procedure. When the *nature of research* or *upset* components earn high numerical values, deception research is likely to be risky or offensive. However, the use of deception—even strong forms of deception and of two or three devices of deception—coupled with other components rated no higher than 1, probably is no riskier than a Candid Camera stunt or a surprise party.

The *nature of the research* differed widely among these studies. Isen and Levin's study is about as harmless in nature as a deception study can possibly be. The Piliavin *et al.*, study was *harmless* to *mildly harmful*—some mild stress may have been experienced by passersby who were mildly induced to respond to a victim, but who chose to ignore him. Ignoring could have caused guilt, but this was minimized by having someone else help him. The behavior was public and the subjects remained anonymous. In contrast, the Milgram and Humphreys studies illustrate the potentially harmful effects of studying behavior perceived as very negative, and that is either highly induced (Milgram) or highly private (Humphreys). Milgram studied an incredibly "harmful" behavior by means of powerful induction. However, the behavior occurred in a laboratory—a nonprivate setting— and the harm was not real. The major objection to this study is that the researcher induced the subject to do something "horrible." The Humphreys study illustrates a different combination of these potentially harm-producing elements. Humphreys studied a behavior that most Midwesterners in the 1960s considered reprehensible. The behavior was real, and occurred in a highly restricted (private) field setting. The follow-up feature of the study precluded total anonymity but *any* disclosure whatsoever of the identify of the subjects would have posed dire threat to their long-term well-being and to the well-being of their families.

The upset scores show us a number of interesting things about possible harmfulness of deception research. Use of a powerful induction such as Milgram's surely calls for subsequent debriefing of the manipulated subject. Yet, the debriefing may be as upsetting as the induction. After a powerful induction of a "harmful" behavior, the researcher seems in a no-win situation in attempting to restore subjects' emotional well-being. However, Milgram's follow-up interview a year later indicated that 98.7%

of his subjects regarded the study and debriefing as worthwhile personal experiences.

The Humphreys study posed even greater possibilities for upset, but he went about things very differently: Since he used no induction, he felt free not to debrief his subjects. Most people would agree that this was the right decision, since debriefing would have horrified some of his subjects and their subsequent worries might have been life-long. Thus, Humphreys was able to avoid upset of both kinds. However, his research has a chilling effect on many who learn of it since its harmlessness and lack of upset to subjects hinged entirely on one assumption—100% confidentiality. Humphrey's good intentions and methods might not have been enough to ensure the meeting of that assumption, and the results could have been catastrophic. A foolproof procedure for assuring confidentiality is needed in research of this kind.

When is deception research risky? Only a few simple generalizations can be made here. Devices and kinds of deception, alone, seem not to be harmful. Consider an applied social scientist doing contract work for a nutrition foundation. Disguised as an ice cream vender, he surreptitiously studies children's reactions to sugar-free fruitcicles. We note that he is using the most powerful kind of deception and all three devices of deception. Moreover, he does not disclose the identity of the sponsor of his covert fieldwork. Yet, few would object. Risk appears to arise when the nature of research and upset scores are higher than one, and it is the combination of various high scores on these factors that forewarn of substantial risk.

The taxonomy and rating system, *per se*, do not provide a basis for deciding when deception is too risky, or when it is justified. This decision must be weighed in relation to the particular character of the specific investigation, its importance, the viability of alternatives to deception, and the adequacy of the reparation made to subjects. However, the taxonomy can be used as an aid in determining the potential risk of wrong or harm involved in a particular research design and can suggest design modifications that will reduce risk. The decision to employ one or another form of deception and to debrief should be based on an understanding of the nature and limitations of debriefing.

THE NATURE AND LIMITS OF DEBRIEFING

When research does not involve deception, two benefits that subjects should receive are: (1) the satisfaction of contributing to science or society, and (2) the educational or therapeutic value of gaining new insight into the topic under study. These benefits are derived primarily through the informed consent and debriefing procedures in which subjects learn about the nature and purpose of the research, the value of the information that it is expected to yield, and the importance of research participation.

In deception research, the subject is denied at least some powers of self-determination and is deliberately misinformed. To compensate for this, the debriefing should provide subjects with (1) satisfaction from having contributed to science or society, and (2) new knowledge that will be of educational or therapeutic value to them. In addition, subjects should receive six other benefits or reparations: (3) dehoaxing, (4) desensitizing, (5) restoration of confidence in science, (6) information on ways risk was anticipated and circumvented, (7) an opportunity to ask questions, and (8) an opportunity to withdraw one's own data.

Dehoaxing. The researcher should effectively dehoax the subject. This means that the subject should be given whatever explanation or evidence is needed to convey the truth about the research and to clear up any misunderstanding. This is not always easily accomplished. Having been deceived once, why should subjects believe the next thing they are told? Diligence and creativity are required to *demonstrate* the truth convincingly, and thus to restore the investigator's credibility in the eyes of subjects:

Whatever the *device* used to deceive, it should be *demonstrated* to be fraudulent. When *technical* deception is employed, convincing demonstration of the deception is usually easy to arrange. For example, when equipment such as a phony shock apparatus is used (as in Case 5), the bogus nature of the equipment can be demonstrated as part of the dehoaxing. Or, when a subject is given false feedback, supposedly based on a test performance, the dehoaxing might include returning to subjects their tests, still in sealed envelops as subjects turned them in (Holmes, 1976). When *role* deception is used, the dehoaxing should include an introduction of subjects to the *real* person, along with the presentation of whatever information is needed to establish the authenticity of the person's real identity. *Implicit* deception is the most difficult to dehoax, since essentially subjects have misinformed themselves. Here, it is tactful and beneficial to assure subjects that many or all misinterpret the situation and that the research was designed *so that* misinterpretation would occur.

After dehoaxing, the nature of the observation, data collection and analysis that occurred in the research, and a fairly detailed explanation of the *purpose* of the study should be explained. This fulfills the requirements discussed above, that the debriefing provide to subjects (1) satisfaction from having contributed to science, and (2) educational or therapeutic value derived from gaining new knowledge.

Since generalized mistrust is psychologically harmful and the social scientist is obligated to prevent its occurrence or to quickly remove any generalized mistrust engendered by the research, the practice of *double deception* is particularly harmful. The American Psychological Association has this to say about double deception:

> This practice involves a second deception presented as a part of what the participant thinks is the official postinvestigation clarification procedure. Then some further measurement is made, usually using covert means to assess the impact of the conditions upon the true dependent variable. In such cases there is a particular danger that the participant, when finally provided with a full and accurate clarification, will remain unconvinced and possibly resentful. Here confidence in the trustworthiness of psychologists has realistically been shaken (American Psychological Association, 1973, p. 80).

It is difficult to imagine a condition under which double deception could be ethically justified, particularly in view of the difficulty of effectively dehoaxing and desensitizing a doubly deceived subject.

Desensitizing. In addition to dehoaxing, the investigator should detect any undesirable emotional consequences of the research for participants and effectively desensitize them, that is, restore them to a frame of mind that is at least as positive and constructive as the frame of mind in which they entered the study. Deception research may induce subjects to reveal what they would prefer to have kept secret, or it may inflict on subjects new insights about their own personal weaknesses. Embarrassment, self-doubt, guilt, fear of damage to one's reputation, and other negative emotional consequences may occur. *Desensitizing should alter subjects' feelings concerning the way they behaved or were treated in the study so they are restored to a state of emotional well-being.* This aspect of debriefing should not be confused with dehoaxing. To dehoax subjects or convince subjects that they were misinformed does not necessarily return them to their prior emotional state. In fact, dehoaxing may contribute to subjects' emotional difficulties. For example, Milgram's obedient subjects felt stressed because they believed they had shocked and harmed another person (Case 5). Dehoaxing changed this belief, but, in turn, focused subjects' attention on the poor quality of their own judgment, and on their hitherto unrecognized potential for irresponsibility. The investigator should have adequate facilities (and in some cases, a budget) to handle any emotional reactions to stress that may arise from participation in the study or the debriefing. The specific steps needed to desensitize subjects depend on the nature of the research and are discussed subsequently.

Confidence in science. Subjects should receive an adequate enough explanation of the research that they will consider it reasonable and feel no loss of confidence in the investigator, in others who were involved, or in science.

Risk control. Subjects should be informed of the possible risks of the study that the researcher anticipated, and should be told what steps (e.g., use of confidentiality-assuring mechanisms) were taken to minimize those risks. In particular, any unwarranted concerns subjects have about harm that could result from their participation should be detected, fully discussed and allayed. The researcher should also be receptive to subjects' concerns about unanticipated forms of harm and should be prepared to do everything possible to prevent those forms of harm from occurring.

Questions. Subjects should be given an opportunity to ask questions they may have about the study, and to have their questions answered satisfactorily.

Withdrawal of data. Subjects should be given an opportunity to withdraw their data from the study if they so desire. This ethical requirement follows from the American Psychological Association's Principle 5 which states:

> *Ethical research practice requires the investigator to respect the individual's freedom to decline to participate in research or to discontinue participation at any time. The obligation to protect this freedom requires special vigilance when the investigator is in a position of power over the participant. The decision to limit this freedom increases the investigator's responsibility to protect the participant's dignity and welfare.*

The American Psychological Association's Ad Hoc Committee on Ethical Standards in Psychological Research notes that if the investigator has withheld or distorted information that would influence the participant's consent to participate, the right to withdraw data substitutes for the right to refuse to consent to participate (1973). This option gives subjects a choice in the matter: subjects may feel better, or less wronged, if allowed to withdraw their data.

Although APA does not explicitly relate the right to withdraw one's data after debriefing to the requirement that privacy and confidentiality be respected, it is useful to note the connection between the two requirements: The right to withdraw one's data is particularly important when data on private behavior are gathered and subjects experience discomfort about having revealed things about themselves that they would prefer not to have revealed, or concern about possible harmful uses of the data. Just as respondents to an in-depth interview may regret having been skillfully drawn into a discussion in which they revealed more personal data than they would have wished to reveal, so too participants in deception research may discover, upon being debriefed, that they revealed something about themselves that they would not have chosen to reveal. In either case, they should have the option of withdrawing their data.

Summary. Providing appropriate reparation for deception might be a routine matter if it were always easy to give subjects these eight benefits.

Unfortunately, it is not always easy to discover whether a subject has been successfully debriefed (dehoaxed and desensitized), and these eight benefits are not always mutually compatible. We turn now to these problems.

When are Dehoaxing and Desensitizing Successful?

Holmes (1976) has pointed to the importance of evaluating the effectiveness of debriefing; social scientists' license to do deception research depends partly on their ability to demonstrate that they can and do effectively debrief (dehoax and desensitize) subjects. Holmes shows that debriefing can be done effectively, but that the problems of discovering effective means of debriefing and evaluating the effectiveness on each subject are not trivial. These problems require more attention than they usually receive.

Dehoaxing—the effective removal of any misconceptions gained from participation in deception research—is particularly difficult under the following circumstances:

1. When the study has involved effective deception, the subject has every reason to wonder if the dehoaxing is not yet another clever deception. Consequently, the investigator needs to demonstrate *convincingly* the nature of the deception and the actual nature of the devices that were used to deceive.
2. Deception that alters a subject's beliefs about such matters as their self-worth or the trustworthiness of others may create undesirable and unanticipated side effects that are hard to remove. For example, if a deception induction successfully persuades a subject that he lacks intelligence, he may immediately reinterpret some of his past experience (e.g., poor performance in a course) to achieve consistency with his new self-perception. This reinterpretation may remain even after the initial misinformation is corrected.

Can the researcher correctly anticipate side effects and take effective steps to dehoax wrong beliefs? Does it take time for the dehoaxing to "sink in" and should the researcher therefore engage the subject in lengthy or intermittent dehoaxing sessions to be sure that the subject truly understands the implications of the true state of affairs? How can investigators maximize the chances that the subject will feel free to raise any questions or concerns that the dehoaxing has left unanswered? How might the researcher go about telling the subject that persons often maintain their first impressions even when they learn that those impressions were based on false information? From these considerations, a formidable desensitizing task emerges: the researcher should effectively motivate subjects to seek out wrong impressions that need to be corrected, yet should be careful not to arouse undue fear or worry.

Holmes (1972) presents extensive evidence indicating that dehoaxing can be effective, along with some evidence of instances when it has not been effective. Holmes concludes that effective dehoaxing may be difficult to achieve and reminds investigators that they have a responsibility to devote care, effort and vigilence to the creation of the most effective dehoaxing techniques. In particular, he urges researchers to test the effectiveness of their dehoaxing as thoroughly as possible before many subjects have participated in the study.

Desensitizing is done to enable subjects to deal comfortably and healthily with the fact that they behaved in a way they consider inappropriate. As Holmes indicates, desensitizing is difficult for two reasons:

1. It is an irrefutable fact that the behavior has occurred; the dehoaxing does not disprove the existence or inappropriateness of the act.
2. The subject's own evaluation of the behavior is probably rooted in his or her own well-ingrained value system and is not easily altered.

A third problem that Holmes does not discuss is whether the research should help the subject to rationalize away an immoral or undesirable act. Clearly, the researcher's first responsibility is to restore subjects' sense of well-being, not to improve their morals. However, one could point to instances where the two are inextricably related. For example, Milgram (Case 5) evoked "horrible" acts in which the subjects had never before engaged. It is perhaps not possible to restore subjects to a sense of well-being without also helping them to grow in sense of responsibility after they have confronted evidence that they are irresponsible and weak-willed.

Researchers have taken various approaches to desensitizing subjects, but the three difficulties enumerated above are not easy to resolve, as the following approaches (taken from Holmes) suggest:

1. The researcher can indicate that the behavior was due to situational factors rather than to the character or personality of the subject.
2. The researcher can point to the powerful induction used in the research and suggest that such powerful inductions do not normally exist outside of the laboratory.
3. The researcher can present behavioral norms for the research situation showing that the subject's behavior was not abnormal, unusual or extreme. This can be done by indicating that others in this and other experiments behaved in about the same way.

If subjects are concerned about their behavior, they probably will be highly receptive to such information. However, there is anecdotal evidence (1975) that some very conscientious individuals may be dissatisfied with the view that their poor behavior is normal and excusable under the circumstances. Clearly, then, the researcher has a serious obligation to remain open to further discussion, and to help subjects examine and clarify their feelings, if they so desire.

Holmes (1975) reviews the literature on desensitization and concludes that very little is known about it. Since it is difficult for researchers to know whether their desensitization has been effective, deception research requiring desensitization should not be entered into lightly.

Finally, we turn to the dilemma of deception research in which debriefing is more harmful than deception.

When Not to Debrief

When studying behavior that is socially perceived as negative and when the behavior is typical of the subject, desensitizing is usually unnecessary and dehoaxing may be harmful. The following examples illustrate this point:

As any parent or child psychologist knows, young children steal—often, innocently, and without a sense that stealing is wrong. Suppose a researcher studies stealing in young children by making toys or coins available for stealing. After observing subjects stealing, should the researcher then debrief them by telling them that they were observed stealing or by telling them that the study was about stealing? It is generally held that the researcher should not tell the children that they were observed stealing or that the study was about stealing. The researcher's business is not to punish, to shame, or try to produce accelerated moral development, but only to study how children normally function. Further, the ethical guidelines of the American Psychological Association hold that children should not be debriefed when debriefing would upset them.

This example raises an additional problem: In obtaining parental consent to perform the research, should the researcher agree to inform parents of their child's response in the experiment? In any case, the researcher would be obligated to give parents accurate information about typical behavior for children of that age, and about parental responses to stealing that are considered to be constructive for children of that age. With this background, most parents might be expected to handle feedback about their own children in a responsible way. However, the researcher would need to be highly sensitive to the needs of particular parents and children, and to seek consultation with a competent family therapist about the handling of difficult cases.

To take a second example, some adults have attitudes or habits that the researcher and most of society consider undesirable, but that the adults in question would view differently and would not readily change. After participating in a deception study of parental authoritarianism, should subjects be told that their authoritarian child rearing practices have been studied? What would this do to the subjects? What would the subjects do to the researcher? What would the resultant outrage do to science? These issues must be considered when deciding whether to undertake the research, and if so, whether or how to debrief. If subjects are unaware that they have been studied, debriefing may cause upset and harm. However, if subjects are aware that the research occurred but unaware of its true purpose, debriefing should be done without demeaning the subjects. The nature of the research can be described in general and neutral terms. For example, "This research was done to see what different ways parents have of coping with their children's crying"; rather than: "This research was done to study whether authoritarian parents tend to abuse their children for crying." Subjects can be educated by giving them feedback about the kinds of response choices persons actually have in such situations, without derrogating their particular response choice. It might be appropriate, in addition, to give subjects an opportunity to learn more about their response choices if they indicate a desire for such information or assistance.

To take a third example, there are behaviors with which some members of society are unsympathetic, but towards which the experimenter may be sympathetic or neutral, such as homosexual behavior. This raises subtle problems about rapport and trust between researcher and subject. Suppose, for example, that the sympathetic researcher dehoaxed subjects, but failed to convince them that the data would be kept confidential or that the researcher truly respected the subjects' lifestyle? In Humphreys' study of the Tearoom Trade (Case 4), this problem was resolved by debriefing only those subjects with whom Humphreys had been able to establish rapport and trust during the study.

Two other reasons sometimes are given for not debriefing subjects:

1. The research may be of long duration and the nature of the deception may need to be kept secret until all subjects have participated.
2. The deception may reflect so badly on the scientist or on the institution of science—at least from the perspective of some subjects—that it is deemed better not to debrief subjects.

These circumstances for deceiving and not debriefing are very difficult to justify on ethical grounds. It clearly is not the prerogative of any individual researcher to decide alone not to debrief on these or any other grounds. It is conceivable that these reasons for not debriefing might be ethically justified in the case of research of over-riding importance, but that decision would have to rest with a broadly constituted IRB that clearly represents community and scientific interests.

REFERENCES

American Psychological Association. *Ethical principles in the conduct of research with human participants.* Washington, D.C.: APA, 1973.

Asch, S. Studies of independence and conformity: A minority of one against a unanimous majority. *Psychological Monographs*, *70*, 9, (Whole No. 416), 1956.

Baumrind, D. Metaethical and normative considerations covering the treatment of human subjects in the behavioral sciences. In E.C. Kennedy (Ed.), *Human rights and psychological research*. New York: Crowell, 1975.

Berkun, M., Bialek, H.M., Kern, P.R. and Yagi, I. Experimental studies of psychological stress in man. *Psychological Monographs*, *76*, (15), 1-39, 1962.

Conner, R. Random assignment of clients in social experimentation. In J.E. Sieber (Ed.), *Ethics of social research: Surveys and experiments*. New York: Springer-Verlag, 1982.

Glazer, M. The threat of the stranger: Vulnerability, reciprocity and fieldwork. In Sieber, J. E. (Ed.), *The ethics of social research: Surveys and experiments*. New York: Springer-Verlag, 1982.

Goldman, P., Clark, E., and Marro, A. No one told them: Suicide of F.R. Olson linked to CIA drug experiment. *Time*, July 21, 1975, 15-19.

Holmes, D. Debriefing after psychological experiments. I. Effectiveness of post-deception dehoaxing. *American Psychologist*, *31*, 858-67, 1976.

Holmes, D. Debriefing after psychological experiments. II. Effectiveness of postexperimental desensitizing. *American Psychologist*, *31*, 868-75, 1976.

Humphreys, L. *Tearoom Trade*. Chicago: Aldine, 1970.

Isen, A.M., and Levin, P.F. Effect of feeling good on helping: Cookies and kindness. *Journal of Personality and Social Psychology, 21,* 384-388, 1972.

Janis, I., and Mann, L. *Decision making*. New York: Free Press, 1977.

Johnson, C.G. Risks in the publication of fieldwork. In J.E. Sieber (Ed.), *The ethics of social research: Surveys and experiments*. New York: Springer-Verlag, 1982.

Jones, E.E., and Sigal, H. The bogus pipeline: A new paradigm for measuring affect and attitude. *Psychological Bulletin*, *76*, 349-364, 1971.

Koocher, G.P. Bathroom behavior and human dignity. *Journal of Personality and Social Psychology*, *35*, 120-121, 1977.

Levine, E.K. Old people are not all alike: Social class, ethnicity/race, and sex are bases for important differences. In J.E. Sieber (Ed.), *The ethics of social research: Surveys and experiments*. New York: Springer-Verlag, 1982.

Loo, C.M. Vulnerable populations: Case studies in crowding research. In J.E. Sieber (Ed.), *The ethics of social research: Surveys and experiments*. New York: Springer-Verlag, 1982.

Middlemist, R.D., Knowles, E.S., and Matter, C.F. Personal space invasions in the lavatory: Suggestive evidence for arousal. *Journal of Personality and Social Psychology*, *33*, 541-546, 1976.

Milgram, S. *Obedience to authority*. New York: Harper & Row, 1974.

Mirvis, P. Know thyself and what thou art doing: Bringing values and sense into organizational research. *American Behavioral Scientist*, 1982, *26*, 177-198.

Mirvis, P., and Seashore, S. Creating ethical relationships in organizational research. In J.E. Sieber (Ed.), *The ethics of social research: Surveys and experiments*. New York: Springer-Verlag, 1982.

Piliavin, I.M., Piliavin, J.A., and Rodin, J. Costs, diffusion, and the stigmatized victim. *Journal of Personality and Social Psychology*, *32*, 429-438, 1975.

Singer, E. Informed consent: Consequences for response rate and response quality in social surveys. *American Sociological Review*, *43*, 144-62, 1978.

Warner, C., and Laslett, B. Privacy and secrecy: A conceptual comparison. *Journal of Social Issues*, *3*, 43-51, 1977.

Wax, M.L. Research reciprocities rather than informed consent in fieldwork. In J.E. Sieber (Ed.), *The ethics of social research: Surveys and experiments*. New York: Springer-Verlag, 1982.

Wolosin, R., Sherman, S., and Mynatt, C. Perceived social influence in a conformity situation. *Journal of Personality and Social Psychology, 23,* 184-191, 1972.

von Hoffman, N. Sociological snoopers. *The Washington Post*, January 30, 1970, pp. Bl; B9.

PART 3
RESEARCH DESIGN AND EQUITY

11. EQUITY AND RANDOMIZED EXPERIMENTS

Robert F. Boruch

Introduction

Our special interest here lies in randomized experiments, settings in which individuals or institutions are randomly assigned to one of two or more program variations in the interest of gauging the relative effectiveness of the variations. Such experiments are undertaken in education, welfare, law and criminal justice, health, and other fields. They are politically imporant in that they can inform decisions about initiating, operating, or terminating public programs. They are scientifically important insofar as they confirm, disconfirm, or sharpen theory and add to understanding.

They can engender ethical and legal problems in that random assignment may appear to put some individuals at risk, deprive them of rights, and so on.

Distinctions and Themes

First, there is need to distinguish between legal problems and difficulties of judging moral correctness of activities, since little can be gained by combining the two, and, at worst, we may confuse matters. Asking certain questions, for instance, may be legal, but the act may be unethical in the sense that there is grave discomfort for a respondent or in the sense that responses cannot be protected from uses that harm the respondent. That the two frames of reference often need not differ appreciably in their implications, despite the need to distinguish them, must also be kept in mind.

The second theme is that there are multiple approaches to resolving equity and risk problems in randomized experiments. Each has some costs and benefits.

The privately sponsored experiment is generally immaterial to the Fifth and Fourteenth Amendments, since they bear only on government action, though in a few cases a private institution's violation of other laws may bring research to the court's attention. For publicly supported experiments, the due process clause is pertinent in requiring that rights established under the law cannot be denied. In some cases, the clause may present a clear obstacle and an intractable legal problem in supporting the entitlement of individuals to benefits that program offers and supporting a prohibition against downward adjustment of those benefits. Entitlement laws ordinarily specify only a few conditions for denial of benefits, and experimental tests that require manipulation of benefits within those constraints constitute an intractable problem. The remarkable exceptions involve laws, such as the demonstration project provisions of the Social Security Act, that permit adjustment of benefits within limits in the interest of improving the laws themselves. Experiments falling into this category appear to present more tractable problems, the solutions being part of law itself.

Technical Design Approaches

There are a variety of strategies for tailoring experimental designs so as to avoid legal and ethical problems. One obvious tactic is to ensure that the number of people exposed to potentially burdensome treatments should be kept to a minimum, by choosing the appropriate sample size with statistical advice and by coordination of efforts to avoid unnecessary redundancy in risk-laden studies. The technology for minimizing the number of questions that must be asked and minimizing sample size under a variety of constraints is adaptable from sample design technology, developed to reduce costs without appreciably reducing precision in research.

Second, the experimental treatment should be that which will have a desired effect. Thus, one would evaluate the impact of smoking on health not by encouraging a nonsmoking experimental group to begin smoking but rather by having a smoking experimental group either stop or reduce smoking. At times, it may be necessary to restrict experiments to a limited socially acceptable range on some variables. So, for instance, when evaluating the effect of college scholarships, the benefit may not be randomly assigned for the whole applicant group but may be randomly assigned within a range of equally needy or deserving applicants if the resource, scholarship support, is scarce and it makes no sense to spread it thinly.

Testing components of programs rather than full programs, for example, is often warranted on management grounds, since full-blown tests are expensive and may not be worth the effort, as well as on ethical or legal grounds. Similarly, variations in program intensity may be compared to skirt the ethical problem of testing a program against a no-program control condition. For instance, several durations of a program designed to influence serious traffic offenders may be testable, under the assumption that the outcome of a no-program condition can be extrapolated or that the condition is meaningless since "no program" is not a realistic political option. One may alter the units of analysis, randomizing institutions where that process is legal and ethical, but where randomization of individuals is not, this being in the interest of indirectly estimating impact on institutions. Graduated introduction or withdrawal of benefits whose effect is not clear can be tailored to designs that capitalize on the stagewise character of the process.

Judgments as to whether designs other than randomized tests yield fair results are difficult partly because biases that can be generated in nonrandomized trials cannot always be anticipated or verified. At one extreme, the situation is clear. For some medical research, for instance, historical controls can be useful and are sensible when the time series implied by such controls is uncomplicated and stable, with deaths occurring soon after onset of a particular disease being a clear example. The other extreme usually involves fragmentary data, instability, and little coherent theory; this is much more typical in social, medical, health services field research. The possible sources of bias described in texts such as Campbell's and Stanley's (1963) are identifiable. But estimating them is difficult or impossible.

Empirical Approaches

If one looks at carefully designed studies of primary and secondary medical therapies, notably new surgical and anesthetic treatments, one finds the new treatment labeled as successful about half the time. In about 20% of the cases the innovation performs more poorly than standard treatment; in about 30%, far better. The implication is that the ethical dilemma of depriving people of benefit randomly is gratuitous to the extent that available information does not justify confidence in one or the other candidate treatments.

Evidence of this kind has also been generated for other fields. For instance, Smith's and Glass's quantitative integrations of results from different studies also provide numerical estimates about how often innovations work in mental health and other areas. Gordon and Morse review the published reports of high quality evaluations of social interventions and find that 35% of new programs succeed notably but that just over 20% are clearly failures relative to control conditions.

A separate stream of empirical work that is relevant suggests that nothing so improves the chances of apparently successful innovation as lack of experimental controls. Marked enthusiasm for an innovation is negligible in reports on controlled trials and typical in uncontrolled or poorly controlled trials; enthusiasm is considerably more evident in the latter. Declarations that a program is successful are about four times more likely in research based on poor or questionable evaluation designs as in that based on adequate ones.

The weight of the evidence then supports a more general point, made by Zeisel in considering criminal justice research and by Rutstein (1969) in considering medical research, that badly designed research can yield misleading results and is ethically unacceptable on that account.

Legal Approaches

Some conflicts between research and law require statutory or judicial resolution. The administrative authority for conducting social experiments, Congress's role in specifying statutes that avoid problems, and the courts' interpretation of each are especially important.

The administrative authority stems from the enabling statutes of the various federal agencies. The statutes may be specific, as in the case of law that directs the Department of Housing and Urban Development to undertake housing allowance experiments. Or the laws may be general, as in the case of statutory provisions that an agency head may waive compliance with other statutes for purposes of experimentation or demonstration projects, as for example, the waiver authority of the secretary of the Department of Health and Human Services permits social experimentation, within limits.

Federal authority for randomized field tests of social programs has been challenged in the courts on at least two occasions. The courts have interpreted the authority broadly, rejecting the challenges in *Aguoyo v. Richardson* and *California Welfare Rights Organization (CWRO) v. Richardson.* It is worth remembering in this respect that the legal history of experimentation—experimentation being defined broadly—is long and compatible with contemporary court decisions. In the *Truax v. Corrigan* decision of 1914, for example, Justice Holmes rendered a dissenting opinion that "there is nothing I more deprecate than the use of the Fourteenth Amendment beyond the absolute compulsion of its words to prevent the making of social experiments...in the insulated chambers of the several states, even though the experiments may seem futile or even noxious to me and to those whose judgment I most respect." A similar spirit was reflected by Justice Brandeis in *New York State Ice v. Liebmann.*

The use of a safety-valve category in randomized tests has been a device to ensure that unfairly harsh or severe burdens are not imposed as a consequence of blind randomization in traffic-offender experiments. It is one of an array of such devices that can reconcile institutional responsibility to take action on the basis of special needs or conditions of the individual in law, medicine, and elsewhere with the need for fair assessments of innovative practices.

Attitudes about Randomization

Do individuals involved in such trials find randomized assignment objectionable or demeaning, as some have claimed? What do we know about attitudes, preferences, and opinions, or about the accuracy of information on which the opinions are based? In fact, we know too little, but evidence is accumulating.

Laboratory studies on attitudes are just beginning. In Australia, for instance, J.M. Innes has executed small studies to understand how individuals view random assignment to new family therapy programs when various justifications for such assignments are stressed to the eligible families: scientific need for evidence on the program's effect, the equity of randomization when resources are scarce, and the possible negative effects of innovative treatment. The results suggest that the appeals to scientific or equity arguments do not appreciably affect a favorable attitude toward randomization but that the possibility of negative program effects on participants does.

Studies by Hillis and Wortman in the United States on medical research suggest that randomization is indeed viewed in a more favorable light when scientific merit of the design is emphasized and that it is viewed in a less favorable light than are alternatives when resources are scarce. Subsequent unpublished work by Wortman suggests that in the absence of self-interest randomization is, on the average, preferred as a method of allocation of scarce educational resources by individuals eligible to receive them.

REFERENCES

Boruch, R.F., and Cecil, J.S. *Solutions to ethical and legal problems in social research.* New York: Academic, 1983.

Breger, M. Randomized experiments and the law. In R.F. Boruch and J.S. Cecil (Eds.), *Solutions to ethical and legal problems in social research.* New York: Academic, 1983. pp. 97-143.

Campbell, D.T., and Stanley, J.C. *Experimental and quasi-experimental designs for research.* Chicago: Rand McNally, 1966.

12. SOME ISSUES IN IRB CONSIDERATIONS OF RANDOMIZATION

Charles R. MacKay

In the Belmont Report of the National Commission for the Protection of Human Subjects, the principle of justice was illustrated by the need to insure in research the equitable distribution of risks and benefits by selecting subjects so that no unfairness resulted by placing burdens on groups who would not benefit from the research. In the broader sphere of social and political considerations, however, it is much less obvious how to apply the principle of justice and even more difficult to see how we would reach agreement on any application. Plato was not always clear in how justice would be achieved. In our own day, Professor Rawls has formulated an elaborate model for a fair distribution of goods in society, and he certainly, for other reasons, seems to me even less clear than Plato. I am not advocating nihilism—no solutions—but proposing that practical solutions may be very pragmatic or political, and ethics may have to content itself with seeing to it that whatever comes about is accomplished by "fair and open" means—that it is at least procedurally equitable.

Let me illustrate. In medical research, randomization often serves a specific purpose. While the aim is to show that one treatment is superior to another, everyone is dealt with in a procedurally equal way; that is, they are all told up front the conditions of participating in the research and they all theoretically have an equal opportunity to be helped, assuming that no one is denied needed treatment to the extent of causing them harm. However, in social research, there is seldom so clear-cut a situation. The aim is, perhaps, to improve the efficiency or economy of a program. Thus, if a program involves possible benefit of like nature to the whole body politic, we would assess it very differently from the situation in which benefits to a portion of the population are being assessed against the costs to a larger portion that do not currently receive them and are not likely to receive them. In this latter case, justice and equity can and need to be assured by a societal debate which openly allows all parties to have a hearing on the merits of changing elements of a program through a rational process that builds on empirical data through "social experiments." It is, thus, my view that the IRB is not the forum in which wide-ranging philosophical, political and ideological views surrounding tax-supported social benefit programs are to be debated or resolved.

Thus, despite reservations about the technical drafting of the recent Exemption Six and a personal bias or two about the intrinsic merits of the ideology behind the new exemption of certain types of research on social benefit programs (promulgated in March of 1983), I am relieved that IRBs are not saddled with having to deliberate this set of issues. The rationale for the exemption is sensible: there is extensive review by public officials— elected and appointed—which offers a measure of procedural protections. More importantly from the view point of IRBs, they will not be faced with potentially acrimonious and destructive ideological debates or the practical difficulty of orchestrating agreement on the wording of consent forms among several IRBs in large scale multi-center research projects.

The recently promulgated exemption from the requirement of IRB review of research and demonstration programs of the Department of Health and Human Services (HHS) designed to evaluate public benefit programs shifts the arena of discussion of the equity in randomization for those research projects to a more appropriate level. The regulations had earlier sounded a similar cautionary note when they advised IRBs not to consider the long range effect of applying the knowledge gained in the research as among the risks IRBs are called on to assess. My point here is that IRBs ought not to get caught up in debate of issues that may impair their effectiveness.

But what about the cases which IRBs do not have to consider and come to a decision about? IRBs may face two types of problems here: One is administrative—how can agreement be reached among several IRBs on carrying out a randomized study involving multiple locations? Negotiating skills and trust may be the answer in this case, although the regulations provide for a cooperative or joint review mechanism that might mean development of a combined or representative IRB.

The other problem is ethical. In a reasonably well-designed study, most IRBs would accept randomization when the subjects were provided an opportunity to give informed consent. But there are situations in which obtaining informed consent may not be feasible or might thwart or undermine the research. One approach is to select a control population whose experience remains free of any manipulation of variables as proposed to be done in the corresponding population who will have some changes introduced. But when this may not be practical or possible, a single population may be divided into several cohorts and each cohort dealt with differentially. The regulations provide for a waiver of the informed consent by the IRB when certain criteria are verified:

1. The research involves minimal risk.
2. The rights and welfare of subjects are protected in other ways.
3. Carrying out the research would be impractical without the waiver.
4. Where appropriate, subjects are informed afterward.

When the IRB waives the informed consent requirement under the above conditions, the "forced" randomization could be accomplished in accordance with the regulations. What the IRB needs to assess in making its determination that the risk is minimal and that the waiver doesn't adversely affect subjects is, of course, the matter of equity: are the risks and benefits evenly distributed? For example, let us suppose that the introduction of some innovative health screening and disease prevention program is planned in a city. It would not appear to be equitable to offer that plan only to affluent sections of the city while withholding it from poor sections in an effort to demonstrate how effective the program is. The randomization itself must be equitable. Similarly, if an experimental program of crime prevention is instituted to benefit some citizens while not helping, or actually being detrimental to, others then clearly the IRB ought not to waive informed consent and might reasonably question whether such research be permitted at all.

In conclusion, it is perhaps an overall advantage to IRBs that they do not find themselves grappling with politicians' attempts to tinker with Federal benefit programs, or caught in the middle of the wrangling about the changes. Still, IRBs do have to address the matter of equity in randomization in many types of social and behavioral research when they determine whether informed consent may be waived in accordance with the regulations as may happen in some research designs. That may be an arduous task. Consequently, I am uncertain whether to be uneasy, as a citizen, when I think of many social experiments that do not get anything like an ethical review, let alone an IRB review, or whether to be relieved, as an IRB member and advocate, when I realize that so much is initiated that does not intersect with these customary circuits that feed into IRBs.

PART 4
PRIVACY AND CONFIDENTIALITY

13. METHODS FOR ASSURING INDIVIDUAL PRIVACY AND CONFIDENTIALITY OF INFORMATION IN SOCIAL AND BEHAVIORAL RESEARCH

Robert F. Boruch

Some Distinctions and Themes

Privacy is a characteristic of the individual, *confidentiality* a characteristic of information, and *security* is a property of the information system. The approaches described below assure that information, once collected, will remain confidential. Some methods also protect privacy in the sense that not even the researcher knows the true status of the individual although thoughtful analysis of data is possible.

The functional distinction between *research information* and *administrative information* is critical to law, regulations, and development of privacy protection methods. Administrative information is defined as that used in making judgments about specific identifiable individuals. Research information uses individuals' identification only as a tracking device; it is not material to conclusions that one wishes to draw.

The first major theme of this paper is that there are *multiple solutions* to protecting privacy or confidentiality of individual responses in applied social research. They can be costly and have clear benefits, but there are no perfect solutions. The second theme is that the *risk* of forced or accidental disclosure of sensitive information is very low. Fewer than a dozen subpoenas have ever been issued; few cases of accidental disclosure have ever been discovered. This implies that one must make a sensible balance between the cost of privacy protection and (weak) threats.

Procedural Approaches

These are nontechnical approaches to assuring confidentiality or privacy. In mail surveys, for example, anonymous responses and alias responses (where study is longitudinal) are not uncommon approaches. Inquiry that is indirect may be made through brokerage agencies, an archive or the census bureau, for example, to obtain data without necessarily obtaining identification, for both cross-sectional and longitudinal studies. Insulated data bank approaches may be used to link records from different archives without breaching privacy rules governing each archive.

The strategies are imperfect to the extent that deductive disclosure is possible and the procedures are burdensome and time consuming. At times, the more important cost is degraded quality of research since it may be difficult or impossible to assay validity of sampling and quality of response.

Statistical Approaches

Over the past ten years, a variety of clever statistical devices have been developed to obtain information from identifiable responses in direct surveys without degrading either privacy or quality of research.

The simplest such device involves presenting two questions to a respondent, one sensitive (e.g., Did you strike your child last week?) and an innocuous one (e.g., Did you use the telephone today?) that is independent of the first. The respondent is asked to choose one based on the roll of a die, and to answer it *without* disclosing which question is being answered. The interviewer receives only yes or no responses. Given a large sample and the odds on answering either question, the statistician can legitimately estimate the fraction who struck their child, yet privacy is protected. Such devices amount to having the respondent inject his or her response with random error, or answering one of several questions randomly so that the interviewer cannot link a response with a specific question or state of the individual. Tested in the U.S. and abroad, the methods have considerable promise and appear to work well.

The direct costs of their use, however, are increased complexity of analysis and increases in sample size. They are useless with small samples and with clinical inquiries.

Statutory Approaches

Statutory approaches refer to laws which state that identifiable information collected for research purposes cannot be used for judicial, legislative, or other purposes against the individual. The level of protection available varies. In some cases, identification and information are protected; in others only identifiers are protected.

Formal statutes have been created to protect respondents in federally supported research on criminal justice, mental health, drug and alcohol abuse, and a few court cases have helped to clarify limits of protection. They apply to data on individuals, not on institutions.

The statutes most pertinent to social, educational, and behavioral research include:

Public Health Services Act, P.L. 93-282, section 303

Crime Control Act of 1973, P.L. 93-83, section 524(a)
Drug Abuse Office and Treatment Act, P.L. 92-255, section 408

and there are others. New bills are being introduced to improve protection, but professional association support for these is often feeble.

Red Herrings and Errors

Privacy/confidentiality problems are often tangled with other ethical or political issues in research. They need to be separated out for any solution to work.

The other problems include cases in which individual privacy is used as a shield against inquiry about institutions (e.g., schools and discrimination, prisons and mistreatment). They include cases in which individual privacy is confused with group privacy (e.g., IQ and race). They include instances in which administrative programs are (a) set up without proper regard for privacy and (b) basically ought to be regarded as research; so regarded, privacy problems are more tractable. They include the fact that threats of legal appropriation or accidental disclosure of research files are a remote risk, and most researcher inquiries are innocuous.

REFERENCES

Boruch, R.F., and Cecil, J.S. *Assuring confidentiality of social research data.* Philadelphia: University of Pennsylvania Press, 1979.

14. THE USE OF VIDEOTAPES AND ISSUES OF PRIVACY AND CONFIDENTIALITY

Deborah Lowe Vandell

A major technological innovation in behavioral and psychological research has occurred in recent years in the form of the greatly increased use of videotapes and audiotapes. It is the purpose of the current discussion to outline how the use of videotapes and audiotapes of behavior introduces issues for those concerned with the protection of human subjects. The particular focus of the current discussion will be on the balance between privacy or confidentiality and the increased knowledge to be gained from using videotapes and audiotapes.

Several research advantages are associated with the use of videotapes and audiotapes. These advantages should be stated at the outset: using tapes, samples of behavior can be analyzed in more detail than is possible from live observation. Second-by-second microanalyses of social interaction, for example, have revealed information about the structure and timing of communication which was not available without the type of play and replay made possible with videotape systems. Similarly, audiotapes have enabled language researchers to collect more accurate and detailed language samples than were previously available with "live" observations. In addition, videotapes and audiotapes have enabled researchers to examine a much broader range of observational variables or categories within a single study. In "real" time, observers can only note and record a limited number of variables, but videotapes can be repeatedly replayed allowing researchers to include all variables they believe to be important. A third use of videotaped samples of behavior has been to train other researchers in particular coding procedures. As coding schemes have grown more complex, it has become necessary to provide extensive training for observers within researchers' own laboratories as well as training for outside researchers who wish to learn particular observational schemes. Videotaped samples which can be played, discussed, and replayed are an ideal training device and have facilitated training observers in a way that was impossible with "live" behavior. The advantages of combining instances of behaviors which are rare in natural time onto a sample videotape are obvious. Finally, videotapes and audiotapes have another significant, long-term benefit. If the tapes are properly and securely stored, they can ultimately represent important archival information. A major problem in long-term longitudinal research is that ideas about critical variables change over time. If videotapes or audiotapes are used, however, as our knowledge about social, cognitive, and language processes advances, these video and audio samples will be available for reanalysis.

At the same time, there are potential pitfalls and dangers introduced by the use of videotapes and audiotapes which should be enumerated. In this paper, I would like to discuss the need to balance privacy of research participants with the benefits of videotape and audiotape procedures. Let me provide four examples of studies that were conducted at the University of Texas at Dallas and elsewhere which illustrate somewhat different issues relating to this balance.

A colleague of mine recently completed a study (Lederberg, 1983) in which she examined bilingual Spanish/English speaking individuals. A number of psycholinguists had noted that bilinguals sometimes combine words from their two languages within a single sentence. Lederberg was interested in the apparent rules bilinguals use in these combined sentences and in the question of whether speakers use the grammatical rules of one language, both languages, or whether the combinations represent a third, somewhat independent grammar. To address this question, bilingual adults and children were presented with 80 different sentences and asked to rate the utterances as correct or incorrect. They were then asked to rephrase sentences which they judged to be incorrect. The sessions were audiotaped and the utterances were transcribed. Prior to the session, subjects completed a consent form in which the purpose of the study and the procedure were outlined.

I use this study of code switching as my first example because I believe it illustrates a case of minimal risk with regard to videotapes/audiotapes and issues of privacy. The information contained on the audiotapes was not of a personal or sensitive nature. The particular task was nonevaluative in that there were no "right" or "wrong" answers. Privacy and confidentiality were assured because the transcripts were labeled using a subject number rather than the individuals' names. Furthermore, when the audiotapes were played it was difficult to recognize an individual's identity from his/her voice. Lederberg has also adopted a final precaution. The audiotapes have not played outside of the laboratory where the transcripts were completed.

The second example of an observational study I take from my own laboratory where we have been studying social development in twins and singletons. In this project, we are addressing issues such as (a) whether there are differences in social skills associated with twinship, (b) whether there are differences in sociability associated with zygosity, i.e., whether monozygotic twins are more similar socially than dizygotic twins, and (c) whether there are inter-relationships between mother-child, sibling, and peer interactions over time, i.e., how do interactions with one partner affect interactions with another partner over time.

In addressing these questions, infants were videotaped in a laboratory playroom as they played with one another, with unfamiliar peers, and with their mothers. The peer sessions were basically unstructured play situations in which the babies were placed together with some toys. The mothers were present but asked not to initiate interactions with the infants during this period. During the mother-child sessions, only a single family was present and the mother was asked to pretend that she and her baby (or babies) were in their own home with a few free minutes. Sessions were analyzed using a variety of coding schemes including a microanalysis of interaction sequences which specified who initiated interactions and the complexity of sequences and a time-sample code which specified amount of time spent in both social and nonsocial activities.

This study differs from the Lederberg project in several ways which introduce additional issues relating to privacy and confidentiality. First, these sessions were videotaped rather than audiotaped so that the identity of the participants was easier for observers to ascertain. Second, because the sessions were essentially free play, it was also possible to examine a much wider range of behaviors on these tapes. The question then becomes how individuals' privacy and confidentiality were maintained.

Contact was initially made on the telephone and the purpose and methods of the study were outlined. When the mothers brought their infants in for the first session they were given a consent form to read and sign. The consent form stated that we were interested in social development in infants and that we wanted to videotape the children as they played with their twin, with an unfamiliar peer, and with their mother. The consent form also stated that the videotapes would not be shown publicly without prior approval from the mother. Once the videotaped sessions were completed, mothers were asked if they would give their permission for the videotapes to be shown for teaching and research purposes. To date, all mothers who have been contacted have given permission for videotapes to be shown in undergraduate and graduate classes. The mothers have apparently felt comfortable in having these videotapes (1) collected, (2) saved, and then (3) publicly shown. I believe it is important to note that the mothers, in fact, gave permission on all three counts.

Now let me describe another study conducted at a different university which relies on videotaped observations and differed from my twin/singleton study in some interesting ways. In this study, mother-child and father-child interactions were videotaped in a laboratory playroom.

During separate counter-balanced 20 minute sessions, mother and father were asked to have their toddler sons play with each of four different toys. These sessions were then analyzed in terms of the styles of play adopted by mother and father and by the types of behavior the toddlers used with mother and father.

In terms of the current discussion, an interesting aspect of this study was that permission to show the videotapes was requested prior to the sessions; several parents who participated in this study did not grant permission for the videotapes to be viewed outside of the immediate research staff responsible for coding the tapes. They did grant permission for the videotapes to be collected and saved. One wonders if the differences in the parents' responses were related to when permission was sought (before as opposed to after the videotape was collected) or to the particular parents involved. Each individual who did not want the videotapes to be shown publicly was either an academic or clinical psychologist who lived and practiced in the community. At the least, I think that the differences in parental responses to the two studies illustrate the importance of stating at the onset what will become of the videotapes and to whom the videotapes will be shown. Not all parents may be willing for videotapes of themselves or their children to be shown publicly.

The fourth set of studies I would like to outline are concerned with attachment patterns in infants. Attachment is believed by many developmental psychologists to be a critical emotional bond tying infants to significant others, particularly their mothers. Mary Ainsworth and her colleagues have argued that there are critical differences in the quality of infants' attachment to mother, with some infants being securely attached while other infants are insecurely attached. Ainsworth has argued that these attachment distinctions are apparent in both the home and laboratory. Of critical importance, researchers have also found these early patterns of attachment to be related to subsequent development. Securely attached infants have been found to be more competent explorers at 2 years, more competent with peers at 4 years, and more competent problem solvers at 5 years than are insecurely attached infants. Ainsworth and others also contend that quality of infant attachment is related to quality of mothering. Mothers who are warm and responsive with their infants are expected to have securely attached children, while mothers who are cold and unresponsive with their infants are expected to have insecurely attached children.

Although Ainsworth and her colleagues initially observed attachment in the home, attachment quality is now primarily assessed in a 30 minute laboratory procedure in which the mother and an adult stranger are observed with the baby. Infant attachment is determined by looking at the pattern or configuration of infant behavior over seven episodes in which the mother and an adult stranger go through a series of departures from and returns to a laboratory playroom. In order to discriminate attachment patterns, videotapes are used so that the sessions can be examined as a whole and then repeatedly replayed to determine particular response patterns.

With this brief background of attachment research, I would now like to talk about some issues relating to privacy and confidentiality. Unlike the other videotaped and audiotaped studies reviewed earlier, the attachment work has a very evaluative component. Some infants (the "B" infants) are seen as securely attached and their mothers are believed to be responsive, warm, and cooperative, while other infants (the "A" and "C" babies) are seen as insecurely attached and their mothers are believed to be either inconsistent or cold. Given the relatively sensitive nature of these data, what effort should be taken to preserve the confidentiality and privacy of the participating families?

There are several areas that should be considered. On the one hand, the best way of teaching observers to identify particular attachment patterns is to observe multiple examples of these patterns. Unfortunately, because it would be impossible to "stage" these behavior patterns using infant actors, examples of "A," "B," and "C" babies are typically taken from real research protocols. Also, a current practice around the country has been for various laboratories to exchange videotapes to insure that similar assessments are being made by the different laboratories. These exchanges have been viewed as crucial to establishing cross-laboratory reliability of assessment.

An important issue, then, becomes whether the rights to privacy and confidentiality of the participating families are violated by using these videotapes as training devices. In this regard, several questions have not yet been satisfactorily resolved. Namely, when permission to show a videotape is solicited, should researchers tell the parents the comments that will be made about the session and the participants? Would parents be willing to have their infants identified (even to other researchers) as insecurely attached, with all the potential implications of such a statement? At the same time, is it a disservice to tell parents that their child is "insecurely" attached, given that our knowledge of this area is still fairly limited? Another question concerns obtaining the parents' approval concerning to whom the videotapes can be shown. Should separate approval be solicited from parents for videotapes to be sent to other laboratories, for videotapes to be shown to graduate students, or for videotapes to be shown to undergraduate students?

I would contend that the conditions in which these videotapes are shown should be carefully considered. At the least, parents should grant permission for the videotapes to be shown in teaching or research settings and researchers should use discretion in not showing the videotapes if there is a reasonable possibility that the viewers will know the identity of the participants.

From this outline of four different studies using either videotapes or audiotapes, another question emerges for consideration by researchers and by IRBs; namely, whether videotapes or audiotapes should be destroyed after their initial analysis. I would affirm that the reply to this question is dependent on the type of behaviors videotaped or audiotaped, the research purposes specified in the project proposal and the consent form, and the extent of the effort to insure that the videotapes are only viewed by individuals or groups specified in the consent form. If the behaviors are nonsensitive, if the purposes of the study are clearly outlined, if individuals are informed about what is being said about them relative to their taped performance, if the participants grant permission for the tapes to be saved, and if the participants specify the conditions under which the tapes may be viewed, then I believe that the potential for abuses of privacy or confidentiality are minimized. Researchers are then free to take advantage of the multiple benefits associated with the use of videotapes/audiotapes outlined at the beginning of this paper. However, researchers have a real responsibility to insure that these tapes are used ethically and that the research subjects' privacy and confidentiality are protected.

15. SOME SPECIAL CONFIDENTIALITY PROTECTIONS FOR RESEARCH ON DEVIANT BEHAVIOR

Lorraine B. Torres

Research on socially deviant behavior brings into unusually sharp focus the issues and dilemmas regarding individual privacy with which the research community must deal. These issues arise from the tension (a) between the individual's right to privacy and some other social good, (b) between competing or conflicting social goods, and (c) between the individual and collectivities which may be seeking to know more about his or her behavior, to "correct" or treat that behavior, or to protect against that behavior.

In *Personal Privacy in an Information Society*, its 1977 report, The Privacy Protection Study Commission examined the relation between the citizen and the government and observed that:

> First, research and statistical activities generally do not lead to an immediate or direct benefit for the individual subject as such. The researcher asks for the individual's participation or for information about him, but society as a whole, rather than the individual, is the ultimate beneficiary.
>
> Second, research and statistical activities depend heavily upon the voluntary cooperation of the individual in providing accurate and reliable information. On the theory that responses will be more candid and complete if individuals are convinced that the information they provide will not come back to haunt them, researchers who directly question subjects usually assure them confidentiality, and when the study design calls mainly for observation, the observer usually promises anonymity.
>
> Third, assuring that information will not be disclosed to third parties in individually identifiable form is especially important in research on deviant behavior such as drug and alcohol abuse, gambling and prostitution, in studies of topics such as abortion and institutionalized discrimination, and in probes of public attitudes on controversial social issues...

While individual researchers, research institutions, and some states have provided protection of subjects' privacy, all of those protections are vulnerable to proceedings from other levels of government.

In several instances, Congress has moved to balance the individual's right to privacy with the public need for knowledge about behaviors that are individually and socially unacceptable and destructive. Such Congressional interventions have been of two kinds: one has placed restrictions on the amount and kind of information collected and on the conditions of its storage and use; the other has provided a discretionary immunity, or shield, for the researcher protecting the identity of research subjects.

The first kind of intervention, automatic or blanket immunity against forced release of information, was provided in Section 524 (a) of the Omnibus Crime Control and Safe Streets Act of 1968 (42 U.S.C. 3771) and incorporated in the 1973 amendments to that Act and in the Juvenile Justice and Delinquency Prevention Act of 1974. That section states:

> Except as provided by Federal law other than this title, no officer or employee of the Federal Government, nor any recipient of assistance under the provisions of this, shall use or reveal any information furnished under this title by any person and identifiable to any specific private person for any purpose other than the purpose for which it was obtained in accordance with the title. Copies of such information shall be immune from legal process, and shall not, without the consent of the person furnishing such information, be admitted as evidence or used for any purpose in any action, suit, or other judicial or administrative proceedings.

Implementing regulations require applicants to certify that the above privacy protections will be provided.

A discretionary authority to extend immunity was provided in Section 303(a) of the Public Health Service Act (42 U.S.C. 242a) which states that:

> The Secretary of Health and Human Services may authorize persons engaged in research on mental health, including research on the use and effect of alcohol or other psychoactive drugs, to protect the privacy of individuals who are the subject of such research by withholding from all persons not connected with the conduct of such research the names or other identifying characteristics of such individuals. Persons authorized to protect the privacy of such individuals may not be compelled in any Federal, State, or local civil, criminal, administrative, legislative, or other proceedings to identify such individuals.

The Secretary has implemented this authority by delegating to the Directors of the three Institutes of the Alcohol, Drug Abuse, and Mental Health Administration authority to issue on application, confidentiality certificates for specific research projects which extend the above protections. While certificates are issued for a specific term or to the termination of a project, the protection they afford is permanent with respect to subjects who participate in the protected research while the certificate is in effect.

Under the Supremacy Clause of the Constitution, this statute is considered to supersede state laws requiring reporting. By its own provisions, it is considered to stand against any federal reporting laws in effect at the time of its enactment.

Implementing regulations do not require federal funding of research to be protected, nor do they determine the soundness of the research, if risk is involved in it, nor if there is a need for a certificate. They require only that the activity be bona fide research and that it be within the scope of the statute.

An applicant for a certificate must provide assurance that it will be invoked against any attempt to compel disclosure, although voluntary disclosure is not prohibited, and must agree to provide subjects detailed information on the existence, effects, and limits of such a certificate.

Even broader protection has been extended by two identical Federal statutes which govern the confidentiality of alcohol abuse patient records and drug abuse patient records. The broad scope of implementing regulations reflects the Congressional intention of encouraging treatment through comprehensive and strict confidentiality protection. The regulations are applicable to "records" of the identity, diagnosis, prognosis or treatment of any "patient" maintained in connection with performance of any "alcohol abuse or drug abuse prevention function" conducted, licensed or assisted (through grants, contracts, or revenue sharing) by any agency or department of the United States, or assisted by the Internal Revenue Service through the allowance of tax-exempt status for, or income tax deductions for, contributions to the program carrying out the prevention function. The term "record" is broadly defined to include any information relating to a patient, whether recorded or not. A criminal penalty is provided for violation of the regulations.

Because these regulations are applicable to all records of the identity, diagnosis, prognosis, or treatment of any patient which are maintained by a covered program, they apply to any federally assisted project testing the effectiveness of treatment or evaluating the performance of a treatment program. There may be disclosure to qualified personnel for scientific research.

It should be noted that Congress has repeatedly refused to extend blanket immunity to researchers protecting the identity of subjects. Instead, specific areas of high public concern and special sensitivity have been identified and, within them, increase in knowledge through protecting the privacy of research subjects has been given priority over other social and individual concerns.

PART 5
MANAGEMENT OF IRB DATA

16. THE NEED FOR A COMMON DATA BASE FOR HUMAN SUBJECTS IN BIOMEDICAL RESEARCH STUDIES

Robert E. Krebs

Following World War II there has been increasing concern for the welfare of humans who participate as experimental subjects in biomedical and behavioral research. This concern has led to the establishment of task forces, committees, commissions, etc., to study specific issues and make recommendations. These recommendations have led to new regulations and revisions of existing regulations.

One of the consistent concerns of these study groups was the lack of comparable and quantifiable data regarding research that utilizes human subjects. Even today there is only a handful of institutions that know for sure just how many persons are involved as research subjects in those institutions—much less the number per type of research or the number who may have reacted adversely to the experimental procedures.

The landmark regulation that recognized that human subject research placed participants at risk and legally required that effective informed consent must be obtained was published by HEW in the *Federal Register* on May 30, 1974.

Shortly after this date, an HEW Task Force was formed to explore means of compensating persons who may have been injured as a result of their participation in research. Their recommendations were sent to the National Commission for the Protection of Human Subjects of Biomedical and Behavioral Research in January 1977 (hereafter referred to as the "Commission"). The Commission generally agreed with the Task Force's recommendations and in turn recommended that subjects should be informed as to "whether treatment or compensation is available if harm occurs." The Commission also recommended that some mechanism be developed to provide for compensation. There has been limited study of the degree of risk involved for unanticipated harms because there is no common experience data. This lack of experience data also causes problems for establishing insurance rates.

This recommendation led to the infamous January 2, 1979 administrative edict by the Secretary of HEW. In essence it required that institutions must include a statement in the informed consent, for both biomedical and behavioral research, as to whether or not medical treatment or compensation will be available in the event of physical injury occurring as a result of the subject's participation in the research.

Universities and other research institutions began looking at their insurance plans and other options. It soon became apparent that any external or self-insurance plan for compensation would require much more and better data than were available within most institutions.

The Commission's report included two institutions that had collected some information. The University of Washington analyzed data over a nine year period that involved 530 protocols and an estimated 356,000 subjects who were covered by their self-insured compensation plan. Of some interest is that in the year before the insurance plan only 10 out of 14,942 subjects had been reported as adversely affected (0.07%). None were seriously injured or disabled and there were no deaths.

The Quincy Research Center in Kansas City, Missouri is a drug testing facility whose subjects have been covered by workers' compensation since 1975. Because of the nature of their research, the record keeping was far more extensive and reliable than for most universities.

The Public Health Services and FDA have not gathered significant types and amounts of institutional based data related to human subjects, IRBs, procedures, etc., but The Survey Research Center of the University of Michigan did a study of IRBs for the Commission in 1975. To my knowledge this is the first systematic collection and analysis of information on the characteristics of subjects (age, sex, racial and income distributions). In 1977 the Survey Research Center published other data dealing with therapeutic versus nontherapeutic research for different population groups and different types of institutions. Additional data were reported on exposure to invasive procedures most frequently used in research.

In June, 1982 the Commission recommended that the Secretary of HHS conduct a small-scale experiment in which several institutions would receive Federal support over three to five years for the administrative and insurance costs of providing compensation on a nonfault basis to injured research subjects, to determine if a full-scale program is needed and what type of program is best suited to obtain the desired results. HHS has recently formed a committee at NIH to study the feasibility of implementing the Commission's recommendation to conduct an experiment on compensation plans at several universities.

The NIH Office for Protection from Research Risks collects data from Study Sections who review applications for research involving human subjects. This information is more general and national in nature than are the data collected by individual institutions. It is mostly used for PHS internal records and reporting. NIH is in the process of coding, developing automated retrieval programs, and analyzing information by types of subjects, potential harms for certain types of subjects, IRB and research procedural problems that are identified by the Study Sections, and comparing multiple IRBs within an institution. They also analyze the data to identify patterns of reviews by IRBs.

This background leads to my concern for the need of an adequate data base, at the institutional level, for information on the results and effects of human subject research. Some months ago at the Health Sciences Center of the University of Illinois at Chicago, Dr. Gordon Humphrey, Senior Research Biologist and our in-house microcomputer expert, Ms. Joe Ann Ferguson, the IRB Secretary, and I developed HESIS (Human Experimental Subject Information System). The system uses an Alpha Micro 100/1 multiuser microcomputer with Control Data Phoenix 90 megabyte hard disc (a 20 megabyte Winchester system hard disc could be used). It is programmed in Alpha/BASIC using the ISAM indexing systems. HESIS has an ACTIVE and COMPLETE file each with a 3,000 record file capacity plus 10 indices that require 500-600 blocks of 512 bytes each. The hardware, including a CRT input terminal, phone modems, and letter quality printer cost about $15,000, but a much less expensive PC system could be used. Our equipment expenses are shared by several other internal data bases.

The first thing we did was to make a list of all the questions we are asked, for which we have no data, or for which the data is difficult and time consuming to generate. Then we talked with other IRB administrators, our risk manager, and OPRR representatives about what minimal data would be useful. To prevent the input of everything including the kitchen sink we tried to design for simplicity and utility. I'm sure, after more use, we will find that some of the information is of little value and that we excluded some data that is desired by others.

The attached input format may give you an idea of what HESIS is all about. To us it is obvious that the small-scale experiments recommended by the Commission will need something like HESIS; and it goes without saying that if HESIS could be developed further and tried out at several universities it may improve the human subject information available for decision makers.

HESIS
(HUMAN EXPERIMENTAL SUBJECTS
INFORMATION SYSTEM)

A COMPUTER DATA BASE FOR INFORMATION
ON THE PROTECTION OF HUMAN SUBJECTS

DEVELOPED FOR
THE GRADUATE COLLEGE
THE HEALTH SCIENCES CENTER
THE UNIVERSITY OF ILLINOIS AT CHICAGO

BY

DR. ROBERT E. KREBS, ASSOCIATE DEAN
GRADUATE COLLEGE

DR. GORDON L. HUMPHREY,
SENIOR RESEARCH BIOLOGIST
RESEARCH RESOURCES CENTER

MS. JOE ANN FERGUSON,
EXECUTIVE SECRETARY
UIMC INSTITUTIONAL REVIEW BOARD

USING THE ALPHA-MICRO 100 COMPUTER
AND CONTROL DATA HARD DISCS

DIAL: X____ ____ ____ ____

PLEASE SIGN ON: HESIS

PASSWORD: HUMAN

HESIS LOGGED IN AT: ____/____/____/

HIT THE RETURN KEY TO CONTINUE

THIS IS AN HESIS ACCOUNT

YOUR OPTIONS ARE:
ACTIVE: TO ADD OR EDIT ACTIVE RECORDS
COMPLT: TO ADD OR EDIT COMPLETED RECORDS
DONE: TO MARK INDIVIDUAL RECORDS AS COMPLETED TO TRANSFER THEM TO THE COMPLT FILE, AND TO DELETE THEM FROM THE HESIS FILE
COUNT: TO OBTAIN A RECORD COUNT
LIST: TO GET A LIST OF IRB NUMBERS
LOGOFF: TO DETACH TERMINAL FROM COMPUTER COMPUTER
CHOOSE:

IF YOU CHOOSE "ACTIVE" THE FOLLOWING APPEARS:

THE COMMANDS ARE:
(N) NEW
(E) EDIT
(P) PAGE
(Q) QUIT
(H) HELP
CHOOSE BELOW
COMMAND

PAGE 1 ACTIVE FORM

IRB SUBMITTED NUMBER ____/____/____/____
mo yr no R

IRB NUMBER IS MANDATORY

(IF R# IS GREATER THAN 0)

IRB RENEWAL DATE ____/____/
mo yr

PAGE 2 ACTIVE FORM

TYPE OF REVIEW REQUESTED ________

1. EXEMPT
2. EXPEDITED
3. FULL

TITLE:

NAME OF PI:

SSN OF PI:

SSN OF PI: ___ ___ ___/___ ___/ ___ ___ ___ ___

COLLEGE/SCHOOL OF PI ___ ___

DEPARTMENT/UNIT OF PI ___ ___

(USE OF CODES)

PAGE 3 ACTIVE FORM

APPROVAL FOR USE OF FACILITIES/PERSONNEL FROM OTHER UNITS? ________________

1. YES
2. NO

IND NUMBER, IF GIVEN ___ ___ ___ ___ ___

NAME OF SUPPLIER OF IND ________________

IS SPONSOR EXTERNAL?

1. YES ____________________
2. NO ____________________

STATUS OF THIS REQUEST FOR ETHICAL REVIEW

1. APPROVAL
2. RENEWAL/CONTIN
3. PENDING
4. COMPLETED
5. OTHER

PAGE 4 ACTIVE FORM

	EXP'D	ACTUAL *Number*
TYPES OF SUBJECTS INVOLVED (description)	___ ___ ___	___ ___ ___
ADULTS (Normal/Controls)	___ ___ ___	___ ___ ___
ADULTS (Experimental)	___ ___ ___	___ ___ ___
ADULTS (Pregnant Women)	___ ___ ___	___ ___ ___
ADULTS (Incompetent)	___ ___ ___	___ ___ ___
ADULTS (Prisoners)	___ ___ ___	___ ___ ___
ADULTS (Employees of U of I)	___ ___ ___	___ ___ ___
MINORS (Normal/Controls)	___ ___ ___	___ ___ ___
MINORS (Experimental)	___ ___ ___	___ ___ ___
MINORS (of U of I employees)	___ ___ ___	___ ___ ___
MINORS (Other)	___ ___ ___	___ ___ ___
FETUSES	___ ___ ___	___ ___ ___
ABORTUSES	___ ___ ___	___ ___ ___
OTHER		

PAGE 5 ACTIVE FORM

HAS PROTOCOL BEEN MODIFIED SINCE LAST APPROVAL? ________

1. Yes
2. No

WHO WILL PROVIDE COSTS OF RESEARCH? ________

1. PROJECT SPONSOR/GRANT FUNDS
2. SUBJECT (S)
3. THIRD PARTY/INSURANCE
4. U OF I
5. INVESTIGATOR (PERSONAL-NOT GRANT FUNDS)
6. OTHER

WILL SUBJECTS RECEIVE PAY FOR PARTICIPATION? ________

1. YES
2. NO

WHICH COMPENSATION STATEMENT CHECKED? ________

1. HSC Disclaimer Statement
2. For-Profit Sponsor's Statement

PAGE 6 ACTIVE FORM

WERE THERE ANY UNANTICIPATED ADVERSE EFFECTS? ________

1. Yes
2. No

WAS THERE LOSS OF EARNINGS OR ABILITY TO EARN? ________

1. Yes
2. No

WAS MEDICAL TREATMENT/HOSPITALIZATION REQUIRED? ________
1. Yes
2. No

DID ADVERSE EFFECTS RESULT IN DEATH? ________
1. Yes
2. No

GIVE DESCRIPTION OF INJURY BELOW:

....

DATE ADVERSE EFFECTS DISCOVERED __ __/__ __/__ __
mo dy yr

DATE ADVERSE EFFECTS REPORTED TO IRB __ __/__ __/__ __
mo dy yr

SAVE LAST ENTRY YES (Y) NO (N) ________

REPORTS FOR HESIS

DIAL: X__ __ __ __ (USE DIABLO PRINTER)

SIGNON: HESOUT

PASSWORD: BEINGS

TO PRINT DESIRED REPORTS TYPE AS: REPORT Al

REPORT Al: COLLEGE/DEPARTMENT REPORT (OF PI)
REPORT A2: TYPE OF REVIEW REPORT
REPORT A3: STATUS REPORT

REPORT B1: IND REPORT
REPORT B2: FACILITIES REPORT
REPORT B3: U OF I EMPLOYEE/SUBJECT REPORT

REPORT C1: SPONSOR REPORT
REPORT C2: TYPE/NUMBER OF SUBJECTS REPORT
REPORT C3: PRINCIPAL INVESTIGATOR REPORT

REPORT D1: REPORT OF ADVERSE EFFECTS REPORT
REPORT D2: SINGLE RECORD REPORT
REPORT D3: SINGLE INVESTIGATOR REPORT

17. RECENT MODIFICATIONS IN THE COMPUTERIZED DATA SYSTEM TO TRACK GRANT APPLICATIONS INVOLVING HUMAN RIGHTS

Joan P. Porter

Some Background

The National Institutes of Health (NIH) revised its internal instructions, Chapter 4107 of the NIH Manual System, that sets forth NIH policy and procedures for the protection of human subjects involved in NIH-supported extramural assistance awards, i.e., those funded by grants and cooperative agreements. This chapter implements Part 46, Title 45 of the *Code of Federal Regulations*. The Alcohol, Drug Abuse and Mental Health Administration has similar recent instructions.

One of the major features of the revised chapter is discussion of a new *computer coding system* to be used to characterize the grant (and cooperative agreement applications).* NIH has for some time had a data capture system that indicated whether or not human subjects were involved in the proposed research and whether or not there were any human subjects "problems" identified in the course of administrative and initial scientific/technical merit review (i.e., "initial review").

For several reasons, refinements in the coding system have been made after lengthy internal discussions. Several sources have made inquiries about the system of human subjects protections NIH uses and have made specific requests for the number and nature of human subjects protection problems identified in grant applications at applicant institutions. Within the last few years, for example, the President's Commission for the Study of Ethical Problems in Medicine and Biomedical and Behavioral Research, the FDA-NCI** Investigational New Drug Task Force, and the General Accounting Office have focused on the ability of the Office for Protection from Research Risks (OPRR) and NIH to account for human subjects considerations, and to develop mechanisms to assure that "nothing will slip through the cracks."

---

*The term "grant" will refer to both grants and cooperative agreements hereinafter in this discussion.

**Food and Drug Administration-National Cancer Institute.

Uses of the Coding System

The new coding system will now enable OPRR to identify, for individual applications and in the aggregate, for example, the following:

1. Involvement of human subjects
2. The type(s) of exemptions claimed
3. Whether the applicant institution has Multiple Project Assurance (MPA) or if a Single Project Assurance (SPA) needs to be negotiated before an award
4. If the initial review group or national advisory board or council has a "concern" or a "comment."*
5. Any "concern" identified in the course of review at NIH has been resolved.

Before the refinements were made in the coding system, all degrees and types of problems identified by NIH were classified under one category and so identified on the summary statement for the application as "protections inadequate." Problems might range from the absence of a signature on a Form HHS-596 to a serious ethical concern about a research procedure. OPRR will now be able to determine, when the data are aggregated, which institutional review boards (IRBs) continually seem to have problems in identifying research in which NIH review prompts concerns. OPRR will also be able to see which initial review groups and awarding units have identified the most problems. This will enable OPRR to target its scarce time and staff resources to addressing areas that are most in need of attention.

Finally—and this is new and quite important—OPRR has the ability to bar an award if the concerns indicated by the review groups are not resolved between the awarding NIH component and the institution or if an SPA is not in place. OPRR is the only office that can lift the bar to permit awards to proceed. Once the appropriate documentation has been forwarded to OPRR indicating that resolution of concerns has been made by the awarding component staff and the potential awardee, OPRR can lift the bar within a 48 hour period.

The human subjects coding system is linked to the NIH Division of Research Grants management information system, IMPAC (Information for Management, Planning, Analysis and Control), and hence can be added on to the data items added to the central record as the application flows through the review and processing system at NIH, and can also be linked to the award document generation stage.

---

*A "comment" is an IRG observation regarding the adequacy of human subjects protections to be communicated to the Principal Investigator (PI), but which does not require the recommendation of a bar to award or restriction on the project or activity. A "concern" is a statement by the IRG that clearly indicates that human subjects protections are inadequate. A concern constitutes a recommendation of a bar to award. The PI and institution are notified.

Specifics About the Codes

The codes used are two-digit and range through 10, 20, those in the 30s, 40s, and 50s. A much abbreviated explanation of the stages of assignment follows.

The grant application, Form PHS-398, comes from the institution with a coding on the face page in block 4, human subjects involved-yes or no, and the number of the exemption, if any, identified. A Form HHS-596 should accompany the application when human subjects are involved unless all of the human subjects research is exempt. By regulation, the Form HHS-596 must be in place, and at those institutions holding MPAs, IRB approval must have been given within one year of submission of the application before NIH initial review may occur.

In the Division of Research Grants, the computerized data record is begun and the information on the face page of the application is translated to a *10* for no human subjects and a *20* for human subjects involvement. The number of the exemption, if applicable, is entered into the system.

Following initial (scientific or technical merit review) the code 20 is translated to one of the following codes and ultimately printed on the summary statement (in a somewhat abbreviated fashion).

30 - H.(uman) S.(ubjects) involved - certified *
- No H.S. concerns or comments

32 - H.S. involved - certified - No H.S. concerns - comments regarding H.S. protections added by the IRG **

44 - H.S. involved - certified - IRG concerns expressed requiring further action for H.S. protection ***

45 - H.S. involved - No assurance - No H.S. concerns or comments ***

47 - H.S. involved - No assurance - No H.S. concerns - comments regarding H.S. protections added by the IRG ***

49 - H.S. involved - No assurance - IRG concerns expressed requiring further action for H.S. protections ***

Codes 32, 44, 45, 47, and 49 require a notation in the human subjects paragraph in the summary statement.

If exemptions are involved, the following will be printed on the summary statement:

*Means that a multiple project assurance is in place and the appropriate IRB has recommended approval.

**Initial review group.

***Once assigned, this code can only be changed by OPRR.

0072E1 - E6 H.S. involved - Exemption #1 (- #6) designated
or
E7 H.S. involved - Multiple exemption categories designated
E8 H.S. involved - Applicability of H.S. regulations waived

If no human subjects are involved, then the code is 10 - no H.S. involved.

Only OPRR can authorize change of codes in the 40s series. OPRR codes one of four codes in the 50s series when it makes a change. Codes may be changed in the system as a result of national advisory council or board review also.

Timing of New Procedures

The new codes are required on competing applications for the February and March 1983 receipt dates. Beginning October 1, 1983, no new award may be made if there is a code that results in the bar that OPRR lifts after being advised of adequate resolution of concerns by the awarding component.

The codes will also apply to noncompeting applications awarded after October 1, 1983, but through different procedures, of course, because there is not initial review.

Triggers for Communications with the Institutions about Human Subjects Protections

The assignment of codes 32, 44, 45, 47, and 49 require preparation of a human subjects paragraph in the summary statement. Principal Investigators receive the comments and concerns via summary statements before national advisory council or board review if they so request, and always automatically after that review.

All applications coded as 44-"H.S. involved, certified-IRG concerns" or 49-"H.S. involved, no assurance-IRG concerns," require special consideration by national advisory council or board, and the institution must be advised in writing of the nature of concerns by the awarding unit *whether or not an award is made.* Even if HHS does not choose to support the project, the institution and IRB should be apprised of concerns because other sources of funding may have been identified for the project by the institution. OPRR receives copies of these communications between the staff of the NIH institute to which the applications have been assigned and the applicant institution.

Conclusion

These are only highlights of the system. There are other procedural nuances. We feel this is a tight system, perhaps not fail-safe, but the new coding process will help to guide a process of internal NIH deliberations that will further the protection of human subjects and institutional and NIH accountability.

For additional information about the system, contact OPRR staff at NIH, Office for Protection from Research Risks, 9000 Rockville Pike, Building 31, Room 4B09, Bethesda, Maryland 20205. (301-496-7005).

PART 6
IRBS AS MONITORS OF RESEARCH

18. THE PERCEIVED AND ACTUAL ROLE OF THE IRB IN MONITORING RESEARCH

Joel Cooper

Our purpose is the discussion of the monitoring and legal functions of IRBs. I am not an expert in legal matters although I find them interesting. I have concerns about the question of legal liability that I will defer for a moment. Let us first talk about the monitoring function of the IRB.

My experience with IRBs suggests that we spend an overwhelming proportion of our time on the initial review of research projects. At my institution, Princeton University, we review all research projects regardless of whether they are funded by governmental agencies. We apply the same rules of the full and expedited review processes to all proposals, whether they are from faculty members applying for a grant, graduate students proposing their dissertation or undergraduates asking for permission to start their independent projects. The investigator responds to a lengthy questionnaire that helps us answer the very important questions concerning risk, informed consent, confidentiality and the costs and benefits of the research.

It may be a popular perception that the IRB then sits in judgment of the proposals, deciding which ones can be done and which ones cannot. Anticipation about having one's research proposal rejected may well be a fear on the part of researchers who respond to our questionnaire. In reality, that fear would be misplaced—a misperception of the role of the IRB. At Princeton, our IRB has not turned down a proposal during my six years on the panel. That does not mean that we have not had questions—indeed very serious questions. But, our next step is to work with the investigator to show him or her our concern and to see if we can arrive at a commonly agreed on response to our concerns about the adequacy of the safeguards and protections for the participants. About 30% of all the cases we consider reach the stage of negotiation. In a small minority of these cases, it is useful to have the investigator come to the full panel to discuss the situation. If there has been a disgruntled investigator during these six years who felt that he or she did not have the opportunity to conduct research in the most productive way, I have not heard about it.

The point of these comments is not to extol the virtues of our IRB. I am certain that most IRBs have their own procedures that are similarly effective. My comments are really intended to contrast the great concern and attention paid to research at the initial stages with the lack of attention paid to the ongoing monitoring of research. If we are to be confident that we are adequately protecting the welfare of our subjects, can we hide our heads in the sand during the several months to years that a project may take to its completion?

We monitor projects in three ways. First, we have a complaint procedure available if a participant in a research project feels that he or she was not treated fairly or was placed at more risk than was agreed on at the beginning of the research. This allows us to deal directly wth participants and allows them to deal directly with us. Second, we have a questionnaire available for investigators to report unforeseen problems or accidents directly to our committee. Third, we conduct an annual review of all projects to ascertain that the procedures that were agreed on at the beginning of the research are still the ones being employed. Although investigators are told that they should inform us of any substantial changes in the methodology of their research whenever they occur, it is more likely that we actually learn of such changes during the annual review.

The problem arises because of the lack of attention that is actually paid to any of these monitoring functions. Participants are usually only dimly aware of their rights as research subjects. Researchers rarely believe that they have changed their procedures to any substantial degree and annual reviews are usually conducted in a cursory manner. Isn't there a contradiction between our function as a monitor of a participant's rights and our lack of knowledge about what is going on during the evolution of a project?

On paper, the IRB would seem to be exercising its monitoring function. In reality, this is rarely the case. We are all aware of the danger of giving the impression that we are the Secret Police, spying on research projects to learn about what is actually happening. The actual conduct of a review process is likely to proceed along the following lines. An investigator, having held a research grant for a year, replies to an inquiry from the IRB by saying, "No changes have taken place since the last review." An enterprising member of the IRB then phones the principal investigator and inquires about the real changes that have occurred. "No," says the investigator honestly, "things are just as I outlined them last year in my grant proposal." When the IRB member checks back with the original proposal, he may find a series of studies outlined such that one was well defined, one was sketched out briefly, and several were alluded to only in the vaguest of ways. Yet, this investigator is likely to slide easily through the monitoring process.

Nothing in the foregoing example is meant to imply that the investigator tries to deceive the IRB or anyone else. Nor is it meant to imply that the IRB was being cowardly or lazy in its actions. Yet, the dynamics of research in a university or similar institution makes further monitoring very difficult indeed. In our example, the investigator lived up to his obligation to report to the IRB in a regular fashion, and the IRB lived up to its obligation to monitor the research. I think we can agree, however, that in reality little was done to protect the rights of human subjects in an ongoing fashion.

Do we not have a legal obligation to protect human subjects and to monitor the risks involved in research? Do we not have a moral obligation to protect subjects at the beginning of a research endeavor and also throughout the many years that the project may last? I believe that there is a very real dilemma whose answer I do not have. I hope the discussion that follows can help to shed some light on this issue.

As a final word, I want to point out a concern that I have with the liability that IRB members may have for the conduct of research. Individual members of review boards certify that, to the best of their knowledge, a research activity meets adequate standards of safeguards and protections. Yet, a research participant may turn out to suffer great pain, embarrassment or injury. Imagine a study in which an apparatus is constructed for measuring sensitivity to heat in a study of meditation. Suppose this electrical gadgetry is not built well and the subject suffers electric shock. Are the IRB members legally responsible for the damage since they certified their belief that the subjects were not at risk? Clearly, they never anticipated that the apparatus would be faulty. Imagine a different case in which, as part of a psychological investigation, subjects take a standard personality inventory. Suppose that one particular subject is exposed to items on the test that reinforce unique feelings of inferiority and worthlessness. The subject suffers psychological injury in a study whose investigator, with the concurrence of the IRB, felt would be free of risk. Are IRB members legally responsible? Can they be targets of litigation? Although I am not aware of legal precedent in these matters, I am aware that several respected members of universities have refused to serve on IRBs for that very reason. Can unforeseen situations cause even the most conscientious IRB member to be at even more risk than the research subjects? Can the problems that I have already alluded to concerning the reality of the ongoing monitoring of research lead to litigation and IRB liability? I will be intrigued to hear the experience of the workshop participants in this regard.

19. THE IRB'S ROLE IN MONITORING RESEARCH

Charles R. MacKay

There are some preliminary points to be made regarding the matter of IRB monitoring of research as prescribed by the code of federal regulations. First of all, the regulations do not use the word "monitoring" in connection with IRB activities and functions. Not that "monitoring" is not of interest to an IRB or that the results of "monitoring" aren't relevant to IRB determinations. The only place in the regulations in which the word "monitoring" occurs is in the section (46.lll) on "Criteria for IRB Approval of Research" in which the IRB is required to determine that, "where appropriate, the research plan makes adequate provision for monitoring the data collected to insure the safety of subjects." The regulations, however, do authorize the IRB to conduct continuing review of the research, which involves reports from the investigators and other sources, in accordance with institutional policies and procedures, which may involve monitoring on the part of the other sources or structures.

This leads us to the second preliminary point, that it is important to view the regulations as not merely a list of IRB responsibilities, but rather as a list of authorities which the IRB needs to ensure that subjects are adequately protected, not only by a well-designed research plan, but also in the course of research. These authorities are not sweeping, but they are broad. For example, the IRB or its designee is authorized: to observe the conduct of the research and the informed consent procedures; to obtain independent verification that no unapproved changes have been made without IRB approval; to require reporting on a more frequent basis; or to impose some special conditions on the conduct of the research.

I make these points to help clarify what the IRB's role is: The IRB has *authority* to monitor research or to set up or rely on measures which provide information obtained through monitoring procedures. But the IRB is not required to perform a monitoring function and many of us believe that, if the IRB were to attempt to monitor research on a large scale, it would be seriously hampered in trying to meet its primary responsibilities. Some argue that it is not staffed to do this; others, like

Dr. Herman Wigodsky, also point out that in principle, there is to be a separation of the "judiciary from the constabulary." The IRB ought not to "police" the activities of the researchers.

However, one may ask what is the IRB's *responsibility* in this regard. It is my view that the regulations specify a number of procedures which the IRB is required to follow in exercising its authority. By procedures, I mean not only the requirements for composition of the board, quorum, record keeping, etc., but also those involving substantive matters of judgment, such as the criteria that are to be followed in approving research and those involving continuing oversight that were described above in connection with IRB authorities. These are certainly important responsibilities, but they have to do with guiding IRB deliberations and determinations so that the IRB review and approval process reaches adequate conclusions. Inasmuch as these substantive matters of exercising judgment and discretion leave room for valid differences of view on complex decisions, the regulations envision some areas of ambiguity on the issues. The regulations, in this respect, are not unlike the sort of "instructions" a jury might expect from a judge prior to its deliberations; the jury must weigh the evidence, but the parameters of its considerations are defined to some extent. Thus, the criteria for approval or the extent of continuing review follow-up do not mechanically dictate the IRB's findings or actions. The criteria stand as guides for the IRB in reaching its conclusions; the authority to monitor provides the IRB with capability of seeing to it that its determinations are adhered to. But the criteria and authority allow for ample discretion by the IRB and it would only be in the case of willful disregard of the procedural standards and guides that one might consider that IRBs were acting negligently or irresponsibly.

In point of fact, legal liability of IRBs is a somewhat remote theoretical issue. In the case of monitoring, for example, an IRB would not appear to be legally liable unless it chose to disregard or subvert its own procedures, for example, by failing to respond to reports of noncompliance or harm to subjects. Even then, the primary liability would rest with the agent, the investigator, and the institution sponsoring the research rather than with the IRB. In most cases, it is the institution which, in fact, has taken remedial measures, even without consulting the IRB on occasion, when circumstances indicated.

IRB legal liability seems limited in other respects as well. For example, it is a well-established precedent in case law that individuals who serve in a volunteer capacity in furthering the public good do not incur liability for those decisons that may adversely affect some, provided they have acted in reasonably good faith in accordance with prescribed procedures. Thus, IRBs following federal regulations and institutional policies governing their deliberations could not be held liable because some harm ensued as a result. Moreover, in the event that someone would attempt to hold the IRB liable, virtually every institution has extended legal liability coverage to IRB members.

The fact remains that there are few, if any, legal cases involving research and only one or two involving IRBs. In one case in California, an IRB member, an attorney, sued the IRB because he disagreed with a decision they reached in his absence. The case was eventually resolved before the suit progressed to court. More recently, a case in Iowa involved the IRB in a decision which would have required the IRB to reveal the identity of a prospective bone marrow donor. Strictly speaking, this did not involve an issue of research and its resolution at appeal upheld the IRB's right to maintain confidentiality of the information it had access to.

In conclusion, the IRB has authority to monitor, but wide discretion in the exercise of that authority. In some ways, direct monitoring by the IRB, unless in specific and limited applications, may even prove counterproductive. However, IRBs do not and cannot operate in a vacuum: they need relevant information and can act on their own to obtain needed information when routine sources at an institution do not provide what is needed. All the same, the IRB's liability in the event of some noncompliance with the IRB determinations or harm to subjects seems entirely secondary, if it can be said to exist at all, to that of the researcher and the institution. In short, these and other factors do not reinforce the supposition of liability on the part of the IRBs. But to speak of liability is to imply a serious breakdown of the system. In fact, IRBs have a responsibility that they must execute to remain alert to the manner in which research they approve is actually carried out. So far, the evidence is that they meet their responsibility well.

20. POTENTIAL LEGAL LIABILITY OF IRBS—A LEGAL PERSPECTIVE

Roger W. Reinsch

The Department of Health and Human Services promulgated new regulations for the protection of human subjects, which became effective on July 27, 1981.[1] The purpose of this article is to examine some of these regulations and relevant case law, in order to explore the problems created by the regulations in regard to potential legal liability of an Institutional Review Board,[2] or its members. There will be no discussion of the legal liability that could arise if a research project that has been approved by the Board is somehow negligently conducted. The focus will be on the potential legal liability that could exist as a result of an error in judgment that is made during the Board's review of a proposed behavioral science research project. Because of the complexity of the regulations, such an error in judgment could be made even when the Board members believe that they are following the regulations to the letter.

If the regulations are somehow misapplied, even innocently, the most likely basis for a lawsuit by a research subject against an IRB or its members will be based on a claim that the research subject's consent was either defective or not acquired at all. In addition, the research subject could claim that the defect in consent or the lack of consent amounted to deprivation of a constitutional right without due process of law. For that reason, the best protection of an IRB from legal liability is to require full informed consent from every subject in every experiment. That, obviously, is not practical due to the expense and time involved. Since most of those involved in the review process would like to do "something less than that," and still retain a high degree of protection from a lawsuit, this article will explore those decisions which represent the highest risk of error in judgment. There will be no attempt to answer how the decisions should be made; rather, the purpose is to point out potential problems when making a decision. Each IRB will have to balance the risks of legal liability versus the desirability of doing the research in the manner proposed by the researcher.

The first portion will be an analysis of the decisions an IRB must make in deciding whether to exempt the research from the regulations or whether to have it conform to the regulations. The next portion will discuss the informed consent requirement, the law of informed consent, and why a defect could create legal liability. Finally, there will be a discussion of some possible defenses to such a claim.

Is the Research Within the Regulations?

The first decision to be made by an IRB is whether the proposed research project is within the new regulations or exempt from them. "The regulations are intended to guide an IRB in evaluating research involving human subjects conducted by the Department of Health and Human Services or funded in whole or in part by a Department grant, contract, cooperative agreement or fellowship."[3] That is the general rule, but the Department intended to exempt much behavioral science research from the new regulations as indicated by the statement that, "These amendments substantially reduce the scope of the existing HHS regulatory coverage by exempting broad categories of research which normally present little or no risk of harm to subjects."[4] Did HHS accomplish that goal? Probably not. Instead, their attempt to exempt "broad categories of research" most likely created a pitfall for an IRB and its members.

Making a correct decision based on Section 46.101 is crucial, because if an IRB decides that the research is exempt, based on this section, the IRB is also likely to decide to forego requiring informed consent. As will be pointed out later, that is a dangerous position for an IRB to be in. Therefore, an analysis of Section 46.101 (b) (1)-(5) is needed to show "most behavioral science research" cannot be *safely* excluded.

The first type of research intended to be excluded is found in Section 46.101 (b) (1). All a researcher may do under this section is to compare the effectiveness of several different teaching methods or practices, as long as nothing is done to "manipulate" the students.

If individual testing of the students is involved, then Section 46.101 (b) (2)[6] applies, and only research in which the individual information is recorded in such a manner that subjects cannot be identified, in any manner, is exempt. This section excludes only a very narrow category of research, and an IRB is only on safe ground exempting research when it is certain that the information cannot, *in any way*, be linked to the subjects. This is a very difficult standard to meet. The members of an IRB, on the date of reviewing the proposal, must be able to predict that the information will never be linked to the research subjects.

The intent of Section 46.101 (b) (3)[7] is to exempt interview or survey type research, for all but public officials, when the information could not be directly or indirectly linked to the subject and it could not reasonably place the subject at risk of criminal or civil liability or damage her or his financial standing or employability and the information does not deal with sensitive aspects of the subject's behavior. The section enumerates what kind of behavior is "sensitive," but it says "such as," making this an illustrative and not an exclusive list of sensitive behaviors.[8] This section leaves an IRB with the problem of defining concepts such as "damage to financial standing or employability" and "sensitive aspects of behavior." An IRB could easily decide to exempt research that arguably should not be exempt and if the kind of "harm" envisioned by this section results, the IRB could be liable. Under this section, the burden that an IRB has at the time when the IRB is reviewing the research proposal is whether a breach of confidentiality could ever occur, and if such a breach occurs, whether it could reasonably place the subjects at risk of being injured in one of the enumerated ways. Since there is no case law to clarify the "could reasonably" standard, an IRB is in a precarious position. In tort law, there is the concept of something being "reasonably foreseeable,"[9] and that might be applicable here, but that standard offers little comfort, since courts have found some results to be reasonably foreseeable that for many people would only have been a remote possibility.[10]

The fact that the "injury" does not occur for 20 years after the experiment was conducted is also no protection because in most states the statute of limitations does not begin to run on the cause of action until the injury is discovered.[11] This means that the potential for a lawsuit arising out of any experiment exists for as long as any subject remains alive, and, in some cases, it might even survive the subject.

Section 46.101 (b) (3) concludes with the statement that all survey or interview research is exempt, "without exception, when the respondents are elected or appointed public officials or candidates for public office."[12] What does that statement mean? Who is a "public official"? For instance, are the elected chairperson of a political ward, the elected president of the student body of a state university, the appointed president of a state university, and an appointed IRB member, all "public officials?" If someone is a public official, can a survey or interview involve only questions that ask about behavior during their "public official" status, or may the questions ask for information about behavior prior to such status and still leave the research within the exempt category? The same questions can be asked if the research involves only candidates for public office.

The regulations provide no answers to any of these questions. An IRB, to be safe, should define "public officials" and "candidates for public office" very narrowly and limit themselves to those respondents who are clearly within the definition as promulgated by an IRB. Perhaps the only time an IRB can safely exempt research based on "public official" status is when the respondent is so well known that he takes on the role of being a "public figure."[13]

The following example will illustrate the problem with subparagraph (b) (3) exemption: Assume that in a research proposal a researcher intends to ask students about their political beliefs and behavior during their four years on a university campus. The subjects will all be volunteers from several classes. There will be a list of volunteers so that each one can be contacted for the interview. There will be no identification on the interview sheet. For the purposes of publication, the researcher will break down the information by age, sex, and background. Therefore, each interview will contain that information. Even if the list of volunteers is destroyed after the interview it is still possible that the information and the interviewee could be linked if the interview sheets became public due to some breach of confidentiality. Political behavior could certainly be classed as "sensitive personal behavior"; therefore it meets the criteria. If the breach occurred five years after the interview, and a subject is now working for someone with totally opposite political beliefs and the subject loses his job or does not get a promotion (financial harm), could the IRB members be liable? The answer could be "yes," if the IRB had decided to exempt the research from the regulations. Had they decided *not* to exempt the research, and thereby conform to the regulations, then they would have the informed consent as a protective device. By exempting the research and foregoing the informed consent, they have no protection.

The preceding illustrates that, despite the comment by HHS that most social research is exempt, Section 46.101 is merely a trap for the unwary, because it contains many vague terms that have not been defined by any court of law. It is impossible to predict how the terms in Section 46.101 will be applied. Often when an "innocent victim" (the research subject) and a large institution come into conflict, the sentiment of a jury will be with the individual, especially if, as here, the individual was contributing to the public fund of knowledge and suffered an injury as a result. The suggestion is that if there is a question as to whether the research is exempt due to subparagraph (b) (3), an IRB should lean toward not exempting the research proposal. Most social researchers probably want less interference from an IRB, not more. However, there are no other logical choices for an IRB because of the legal uncertainties created by Section 46.101. The alternative to bringing all research within the regulations would be to exempt research that is borderline based on subparagraph (b) (3), but then to require informed consent for protection. HHS supports this alternative and seems to recognize the importance of informed consent as a prophylactic in their response to the public comments to Section 46.101.

"The Department disagrees with public comments suggesting that informed consent may not be necessary in observation research. The question whether informed consent is to be sought is to be judged *independently* (emphasis added) from the requirement for IRB review and approval. Exemptions from coverage under the regulations in no way changes any requirements of other federal, state, and local laws or regulations on informed consent."[14]

This statement by HHS acknowledges that even though the research may be exempt from the regulations, an IRB should decide independently whether or not to require informed consent. Therefore, if an IRB decides to both exempt the research *and* forego informed consent, there is very little protection in the event of a lawsuit. Making the correct decision based on Section 46.101 is, therefore, very important, even though, as HHS stated, there has been no "successful" litigation. The other type of research proposals an IRB will obviously review is research covered by the regulations. It is relatively easy to determine what type of research is within the regulations. The rule states that all research not exempted by subparagraph (b) is within the regulations.[15] If the research falls within the regulations, an IRB must then decide whether to approve the research proposal, based on the criteria for IRB approval of research.[16] This section will not be covered in any detail because it is fairly clear and does not create any pitfalls for an unwary IRB.

However, if an IRB decides that the research proposal meets the criteria of Section 46.101, and approves the project, that does not end the decision making process. The IRB must next decide whether the research involves "minimal risk" or "more than minimal risk." This decision is important because, depending upon the amount of risk involved, an IRB may alter what is required for adequate consent from the research subjects.

" 'Minimal risk' means that the risks of harm anticipated in the proposed research are not greater, considering probability and magnitude, than those ordinarily encountered in daily life or during the performance of routine physical or psychological examinations or tests."[17] Based on this definition, an IRB must not only be able to anticipate what harm could result "considering all the probabilities and magnitude" of the potential harm, but also whether that harm is greater than harm "ordinarily encountered in daily life." That certainly does not provide a clear guideline, and there is little to clear it up. In fact, in response to a public comment in regard to the "minimal risk" definition, HHS merely added to the confusion with this statement: "HHS has reworded the final regulations to reflect its *intention* that the risk of harm ordinarily encountered in daily life means those risks encountered in the daily lives of the subjects of the research."[18] (emphasis added) This adds to the confusion, because it sounds as if the Department intended to set a variable standard for placing a subject into the minimal risk category. The statement implies that instead of simply deciding whether or not a research project involves more than minimal risk for a subject, an IRB may have to decide whether it involves minimal risk to some subjects and more than minimal risk to other subjects, depending upon what kind of risks each subject encounters in her or his daily life. This is probably not what the Department intended to do. Most likely what HHS intended to say was that any risk is more than minimal if the "average" subject is likely to suffer some harm. But that certainly is not clear, and based on the regulation and the quoted statement, there is a good possibility that if a research subject's potential for harm is more likely than the "average" subject, that subject should have been placed in the "more than minimal risk" category, with the full informed consent procedure, in order for an IRB to be fully protected. For example, a research project that attempts to find out about alcohol use by college students would be a minimal risk project for most students, because even if the information became known, it is unlikely to "harm" most students. Nor are the questions themselves likely to cause emotional harm to most subjects. But what if a subject belongs to a religion that does not condone the use of alcohol? If that subject uses alcohol and the information became known, the type of harm defined in Section 46.101 (b) (3) could result. Or, the questions themselves could cause emotional harm to a subject who does not encounter such questions in "daily life," and therefore would be more than a minimal risk. Under either circumstance, an IRB is exposed to potential liability. What Section 46.102 (g) appears to have done is bring the "thin skull"[19] concept from tort law to these regulations, but they probably did not intend to do that.

An IRB may decide that only minimal risk is involved (Section 46.110) and permit either altered or no informed consent, or employ an expedited review procedure.[20] When the expedited review procedure is used, one person may do the review and exercise all the power of the entire IRB. Only if that person does not approve the proposal must the entire IRB review it. Therefore, the entire IRB never sees expedited proposals that are approved, yet the entire IRB is subject to legal liability arising from the approved expedited proposals. The IRB could be liable whether the person handling the expedited procedure is careless in the review, makes an error in judgment, or purposely misleads the Board members. Their liability is a question of fact and depends upon the law of agency because the Board has delegated its power to that member. The duty to keep the entire Board informed of all such research proposals is buttressed by subparagraph (c) which places the duty upon the Board to develop a procedure for keeping informed. Therefore, an IRB cannot claim as a defense that it did not know of the research proposal, because it has the affirmative duty to create a system that keeps it informed.

A section that creates similar liability problems is the cooperative research section.[21] This section, in effect, creates joint and several liability for each IRB involved in a cooperative research project. It allows each IRB to share the review burden or to leave the burden to the prime contractor.[22] If the review burden is shared, each IRB obviously carries the risk of potential liability. But even if the review is not shared, and the prime contractor retains the entire burden of reviewing the proposal, all the other IRBs involved risk liability. The reason each could be liable is because the section says, "each cooperating institution shall comply with these regulations as though it received funds—directly from the department."[23] This means that when the other institutions do not participate in the review process they have delegated their duty to the prime contractor creating an agency relationship.

In addition to the above problems, there are three other problems created by the regulations that should be briefly mentioned. The first problem is created by Section 46a.109 (e), which requires a yearly review of all research covered by the regulations, or more frequently, depending on the degree of risk.[24] The problem is that if an IRB properly decided that the research was exempt, based upon the criteria in Section 46.101(b)(1)-(5), does that mean the research does not have to be reviewed yearly? Because the regulation says all research "originally covered by these regulations," it appears that all research must be reviewed yearly or "more frequently, depending upon the degree of risk." Without a yearly or more frequent review procedure for originally exempt research, there would be no protection if the research moved into the category of research covered by the regulations, because there would be no consent, as that is usually not obtained for the exempt research.

A second problem is found in Section 46.113, which gives an IRB the power to terminate or suspend research that is not being conducted in accordance with the IRB's requirements or that has been associated with unexpected serious harm to subjects.[25] This Section places an affirmative duty on an IRB to terminate such research or they could be liable for any harm resulting from the research. The way to reduce the risk is to set up a procedure for identifying research which could potentially fall into this category and review it more frequently than yearly.

A third problem is the research that falls within the provisions of Section 46.116(c) (1) and (2) and (d) (1)-(4), which allows an IRB to alter or waive the full consent procedure in certain situations.[26] Research covered by this Section should also be identified for yearly or "more frequent" review because the research might move out of one of the categories covered by this Section and therefore require full informed consent.

The above analysis only deals with some of the more serious problems created by the regulations themselves. It does not attempt to cover all the potential problems that could exist based on an infinite variety of factual situations.

Informed Consent and the Regulations

The general rule in regard to informed consent is found in Section 46.116, which states, that unless provided elsewhere, informed consent is required for all research that falls within the regulations.[27] Therefore, once it is decided that the research is covered by the regulations, and there are no exceptions such as "minimal risk" research, it is extremely important for an IRB to know what constitutes legally effective informed consent, based on the regulations and case law. Proper informed consent will shield the researcher, the IRB and the institution from liability, unless, of course, the experiment itself is carried out negligently and causes injury to a research subject.

In regard to informed consent, the regulations clearly require that, "No informed consent, whether oral or written, may include *any* exculpatory language through which the subject or the representative is made to waive or *appear* to waive any of the subject's legal rights or releases or *appears* to release from liability for negligence."[29] (emphasis added) The important aspect of this statement is that the consent form cannot even *appear* to waive or release any right of the subject in regard to negligence. It only needs to *appear* to waive or release rights, for the form to be defective under the regulations. If the form is defective, there is the possibility that the consent will *not* be effective and that will have the same legal effect as if informed consent had not been acquired at all. This will leave an IRB vulnerable to legal liability. Therefore, the first step for an IRB is to be certain that the consent form itself meets both the letter and the spirit of Section 46.116.

Even though a research subject may not be forced to waive certain rights, under the regulations an IRB may waive or alter the informed consent procedure in certain situations. The criteria for waiving or altering this procedure is found in the general requirements for informed consent. If an IRB intends to waive or alter the informed consent requirement on Section 46.116(c) (l) and (2), it may do so only if the research involves the evaluation of a government research program or service without making any changes in the program, *and* the research could not practicably be carried out without the waiver or alteration."[30] That appears to be fairly clear and should present no problem in actual practice.

The procedure under Section 46.116 subparagraph (d) (l)-(4) however, would present some practical problems. Under the provision, all four elements must be met in order to waive or alter the consent requirement. That means an IRB must first determine whether the research involves only minimal risk.

The problems with that concept have already been discussed.[31] Next, the IRB must determine that the change "will not adversely affect the rights and welfare of the subjects."[32] This is not an easy task. There is no guideline as to what "rights" or what kind of "welfare" must be "adversely affected." Also there must be no alternative to carrying out the research without the waiver or alteration, and finally, "whenever appropriate, the subjects will be provided with additional pertinent information *after* participation (emphasis added)."[33] The decision to waive or alter the consent requirement is made by an IRB *prior* to the research being carried out, yet they must provide for a system of review to inform research subjects of pertinent information after their participation. It is up to the IRB to decide when it is "appropriate" and what information is pertinent. What is probably meant is the same information that would have been given had informed consent been initially required. That leaves open the question: How long after the research must an IRB give pertinent information? If pertinent information is acquired 20 years after the experiment, must all the subjects be found and informed? The answer appears to be "yes." That places on an IRB the burden of developing a system for keeping track of experiments and of subjects.

It is a basic principle of law that *volenti no fit injuris*; he who consents can receive no injury.[34] Therefore, when an IRB decides to require informed consent, either because the proposal falls under the regulations or it is not within the regulations but as a safeguard an IRB decides consent is necessary, it will need to know what is legally effective consent. There are three elements to informed consent:[35]

1. It must be voluntary.
2. It must be knowledgeable (information).
3. It must be competent[36] (cognitive).

If any one of those three elements fails, then there is defective informed consent. One writer states that, "unless consent of the subject is not a prerequisite, no human research should be conducted if the consent is defective in failing to comply with these minimum standards of information, cognition or voluntariness."[37]

There has been at least one suit naming IRB members as defendants, *Nielson v. The Regents of the University of California*,[38] and defective informed consent was the basis for the lawsuit. This case was instituted by James Nielson, an attorney, and a member of the IRB he sued. The defendents in the case were the University of California Regents and all the other members of the University's Committee on Human Experimentation (prior name for IRB). The challenged project had been approved by the committee and was funded by a grant from HEW (now HHS) and therefore, subject to its guidelines.

Nielson contended that the consent was not voluntary, because it was acquired through undue influence. The claim of undue influence was first based on the fact that a $300 stipend was offered to the families of the children who were to be subjects. The stipend was meant to compensate for the inconvenience and to absorb the cost of babysitting expenses. This aspect alone may not have been enough to make the consent involuntary, but, secondly, the children for the control groups were to be chosen from students and junior staff members of the University medical facility. Nielson claimed that this created undue influence over junior staff and students by the senior staff and any consent would, therefore, be defective because it was involuntary.

The *Nielson* case was apparently never resolved on its merits, because research attempting to discover what happened to the case was unsuccessful. One can only guess that the University, after the suit was filed, decided to drop the research project or modify it, and Nielson dismissed the suit. Therefore, the suit provides no answer to whether the consent was defective based on those allegations, but it does illustrate that an IRB can be named as a defendent in a suit based on defective consent.

Another case that was based on defective consent, albeit a more obvious defect, was *Clay v. Martin*.[39] The case involved a prisoner who had consented to an experimental procedure, but claimed coercion and lack of full disclosure. This case was dismissed at the trial level on procedural grounds unrelated to the merits of the case. This dismissal was reversed on appeal and the court said, "The legislative history of the Act (National Research Act) indicates that it was passed in reaction to reports of abuses similar to those alleged here. Of particular concern to the drafters was that a subject's consent be based on *full* disclosure, free from any type of coercion. In view of these expressions of public policy, a court should not be quick to dismiss, on pleading technicalities, an action involving experimentation on humans."[40] This decision sent the case back to court for trial on the merits. Unfortunately, research revealed no further action on the case. One can only speculate why it was never tried on the merits. Even though it was never tried, the case is important because the court's comments illustrate how strongly a court might react to a suit arising out of research involving human subjects. The court emphasizes the fact that any consent must be knowledgeable and voluntary. In addition, the court indicates that public policy in this area is strongly on the side of the research subject, and that outweighs any "mere" technicalities. That point of view could certainly be used to support an argument for an injured research subject.

Both of these suits involved basically biomedical research, rather than behavioral, but they are important nonetheless, because they contain statements that show how a court is likely to react to these types of lawsuits.

Nielson and *Clay* both illustrate the voluntary aspect of consent, which is probably the easiest element to challenge. Therefore, it is absolutely essential that all consent be voluntary. That raises the question: How "voluntary" does voluntary consent have to be? *Nielson* illustrates that, at least to allege coercion, the amount of duress does not have to be great. The *Nielson* situation is found daily at universities when a researcher is using students or staff members as subjects. "Duress occurs when there is physical coercion or when psychological and situational pressures are applied."[47] As seen in *Nielson*, the psychological and situational pressure can be implied from the circumstances and it does not have to be overt. Frequently these kinds of pressures are overt, such as when a researcher uses students and awards "extra points" for those who "volunteer." That psychological and situational pressure is very real and it makes any consent defective because it was not voluntary. The pressure could exist even if no extra points are given, because most students know that some of the grading process is subjective and the better a student is known to the instructor, the better the chance for a good grade. Any consent in such a situation would also be involuntary. "The restraint, intimidation or compulsion is sufficient if it induces the particular person claiming duress to perform some act which he is not legally bound to do, contrary to his will."[42] Relevant variables of the voluntariness issue are "relationship of subject to researcher, environment, and inducement. Even within a controlled environment, which is not inherently coercive, the power of the controllers may be applied in such a way as to constitute duress."[43] Ideally, each subject should be in a position to make his choice totally free of any real or imagined duress. However, that ideal setting rarely exists, especially on a campus where professors are the researchers and students the subjects. So, voluntariness must be looked at in relative terms. The question for an IRB then becomes whether the consent is "voluntary enough under the particular research conditions...the setting, the subject's relationship to the investigator, the benefits and risks which the subject perceives other than those implicit in the experiment itself."[44] One commentator, discussing *Nielson*, suggests that "a possible solution to the dilemma (of voluntariness) is that the peer group review committee be replaced by a committee composed of or including representatives from the lay community. Lay community representation would aid the committee in ridding itself of its inevitable self-serving attitude."[45]

The new regulations do, in fact, require just such diversity in IRB membership. Section 46.107(a) states, "research that involves a vulnerable category of subparts, including but not limited to subjects, covered by other subparts of this part, the IRB shall include one or more individuals who are primarily concerned with the welfare of these subjects."[46] All Boards, for their own protection, should have such individuals on their board and they should be used for the purpose of looking out for the subjects, as recommended by HHS. In addition, under Section 46.lll(a)(2), as one of the criteria for approving a project, an IRB has the duty to decide whether the risks to the subjects have been minimized as much as possible and that the risk is reasonable to anticipated benefits, if any, to the subjects.[47] In response to the confusion over the requirement in Section 46.lll(a)(2), HHS has clarified it by saying "that in evaluating risks and benefits to subjects, an IRB should consider only those risks and benefits that may result from the conduct of the experiment and not the possible long range effects of research on public policy."[48] This means an IRB may look only at the immediate risks versus benefits to subjects and not only balance the risk to subjects but the long range benefit to society from a successful research project.

Based on the above discussion, it would appear that any kind of "inducement" will make the consent involuntary, which is probably not true. Some of the literature suggests that some inducement *might* be acceptable. "Inducements are acceptable if sufficient benefits are offered so that a reasonable person in the subject's situation, upon balancing the risks and benefits, including the inducements, could rationally choose to undertake the risk. This is why outside review of the reasonableness of the inducement is required and why the reviewing body must include persons situated similarily to the potential subjects."[49] This means that giving a student a few extra points for answering a 15-minute survey questionnaire might be reasonable inducement and not destroy the voluntariness of the consent. On the other hand, giving a student any extra credit for a 24-hour isolation experiment is not reasonable inducement, making the consent involuntary. Since there is no standard for defining the *quid pro quo* of risk taking on behalf of society, each IRB member must decide when the inducement is unreasonable in relation to the risk taken. For some risks, no inducement whatsoever would be reasonable.

The next element of informed consent is that the consent be knowledgeable. This means the subject must be given adequate information in order to make a knowledgeable decision. The kind of information to be given a subject is detailed in the regulations.[50] Basically, it should be all the information available at the time, including the benefits and the risks. The most serious risks that have been documented should be described in detail. If new information becomes available during the course of the experiment, that information should also be given to each research subject, along with the option of dropping out of the research project at the time. Therefore, new information carries with it the idea that new consent probably may be informal, but to be certain that a claim of involuntariness does not arise, the subjects should at least be informed that they have the option of discontinuing their participation.

The case law on how much information is enough information is not very clear. The cases that have developed this area of the law have been cases involving biomedical research, instead of behavioral science research. Some courts have said that the standard is to tell a subject what a reasonable person would want to know in order to make a decision.[51] Other courts, according to one commentator, have required that almost all risks be detailed for the person, regardless of what impact that disclosure may have on the person.[52] This substantially conforms with what the new regulations require in order to meet the information component of consent. If an IRB follows it to the letter, it should be a legally adequate standard.

The final element of consent is competence or, as some writers say, cognition or "knowing." This means that once the information has been transmitted to the subject, there must be some standard to determine that the subject understands it. To make a competent decision, the subject must have the "cognitive capacity to comprehend the disclosed information and, if necessary, to engage in additional data seeking to make his own decision."[53] Determining whether the subject "understands" the information being presented will usually be left up to the person presenting the information. However, in some instances, it probably should be part of the IRB review process when there is a serious or irreversible risk to the subject. The review, in those situations, should go beyond a signature on a standard consent form, even if a signature technically meets the HHS guidelines. The IRB should determine that, when the risk is great enough, the subject has the level of understanding that is necessary to meet the element of competent consent. This cognitive component should *always* be reviewed by the IRB when the subjects are mentally incompetent or minors.

Because of that burden when minors are involved, an IRB must know the rights minors have in regard to informed consent. Do minor subjects have the right to be informed and then make a "knowing" decision on their own with the subsequent approval of their parents or guardians; or may the parents or guardians act entirely on the minor's "behalf"? In *Nielson*, it was assumed by the committee that parents act in the best interest of their children and, if parents had the information and cognitive ability, their interest in their children would outweigh any undue influence. The case challenged that assumption, but it was not resolved since it was never tried on its merits. A recent Supreme Court decision, *Parham v. J. L. and J. R. Minors, Etc.*, would support the claim that parents act in the child's best interest.[54] In this case, the parents committed a child to a mental institution and the court upheld their right to do that by saying, "More importantly, historically it has been recognized that natural bonds of affection lead parents to act in the best interest of their children."[55] However, the court did point out that, soon after commitment, there would be some independent determination of whether the child should remain at the institution. One may not be able to compare seeking mental health care for a child with subjecting a child to behavioral experimentation, but most would agree that seeking mental health care may be more benign than some behavioral experiments. Therefore, in an experimental setting, the parents' informed consent might be adequate, if the IRB later reviewed that consent to determine whether the parents considered all the information and acted as a reasonable parent would have acted. On the other hand, a recent Missouri case decided by the U.S. Supreme Court, supported the rights of minors to make decisions about their own bodies by holding that a minor does not need parental consent to obtain an abortion.[56]

There are, of course, ways to distinguish these cases, but they nevertheless illustrate that there is no consensus on what rights a minor does have. Since this area of the law is somewhat unsettled, the safest method for an IRB would be a two-step process, at least with minors who have reached the age of some cognitive capacity—normally age four or five. The first step should be to inform the child, just like an adult, and then ask if she or he consents. If the child's response is "no," then that decision would be final. If the child's response is "yes," then the second step is to supply the parents with all the information about the experiment and ask for their consent. A similar procedure should be used with incompetent subjects, the second step being the consent of the guardian. In either case, a "no" answer by the subject should be final. Anything else could be classified as coercion and the consent would be defective.

Constitutional Claims

In addition to a claim that the consent was defective and the IRB should be liable for any resulting injury, defective consent could be basis for a claim that the research subject's constitutional rights were violated. This claim could be made despite the fact that the entire experiment was carefully conducted and nothing else in the experiment was negligently done. In other words, the only "injury" was the deprivation of a constitutional right. The failure of the government—IRB members are "officials" of the government when they administer public funds or are part of a public institution—to meet the informed consent standard means that the "...(g)overnment 'compels' a person to participate in an experiment against his will (and that)...is a clear deprivation of liberty without due process of law."[57] The courts have said that most constitutional rights can be waived, if the person is capable of giving informed, competent and voluntary consent; then that consent will ordinarily be accepted as a waiver of the constitutional right in question.[58] This illustrates why it is crucial to acquire informed consent from research subjects, and why, without that, an IRB member leaves himself extremely vulnerable to a lawsuit and possible liability. The most likely basis for such a lawsuit will be under the Civil Rights Act 42 U.S.C. Section 1983.59.

The constitutional rights most likely to be violated by behavioral research would be First Amendment rights, such as the right of privacy or freedom of "mentation." The courts have recognized a right to privacy, a right "to be let alone," as one of the most comprehensive and important constitutional freedoms.[60] The Constitution, under the First Amendment, through protection of communication and privacy, protects freedom of "mentation" as a fundamental right.[61] When a fundamental right is involved, it requires compelling state interest to abridge that right.[62] Very little research would fall into the "compelling state interest" category, therefore, without adequate consent when a constitutional right is involved, an IRB is vulnerable.

As already indicated, there are no cases dealing directly with the liability of an IRB in regard to the deprivation of a constitutional right based on 42 U.S.C. Section 1983. However, there are cases that deal with this area of the law, and, by analogy, they can be used to predict what the result would be if a case such as *Nielson* or *Clay* were tried on its merits and one of the allegations was a deprivation of a constitutional right.

In *Mackey v. Procunier*,[63] the plaintiff, a prisoner, had consented to shock treatment, but not to receiving the drug, succinylcholine, prior to shock treatment. As a result of the drug, he alleged that he regularly suffers nightmares in which he relives the frightening experience and awakens unable to breathe. The complaint was dismissed at the trial level, but the appeals court reversed saying, "(t)he District Court treated the allegations of the complaint as claims of malpractice. . . . It is clear, however, that the claims were intended to go far beyond this. . . . Proof of such matters could, in our judgment, raise serious constitutional questions respecting. . . impermissible tinkering with the mental processes."[64]

This case illustrates that if the consent is defective, then a constitutional basis for a claim could exist, and that a mental, not just a physical, injury is compensable. In addition, it states that negligence (malpractice) is not the only basis for a lawsuit against a government official (Procunier was the warden), but that a constitutional basis exists when the official interferes with "mentation."

The First Amendment argument was again articulated and applied in *Kaimowitz v. Department of Mental Health.* When the court referred to protection of a person's mental processes, the communication of ideas, and the generation of ideas and expressions of thoughts, it equally emphasized: "*must protect the freedom to generate ideas.*"[65] (emphasis added). The Supreme Court in *Stanley v. Georgia* said, "Our whole constitutional heritage rebels at the thought of giving government the power to control men's minds. . . ."[66] These and other cases are precedent for, and clearly establish that, a suit against an institution or an IRB can be based on a violation of a First Amendment right. These cases also show that the courts feel very strongly about protecting such rights.

Defenses for an IRB?

Are there any defenses for an IRB or its members if they are sued by a research subject claiming a deprivation of a constitutional right, or making any other claim as a basis for a lawsuit? One defense might be sovereign immunity, but that, obviously, is not available for a claim of a deprivation of a constitutional right, since only government officials can violate one's constitutional rights.[67] If, instead of deprivation of a constitutional right, the basis for a lawsuit is negligence, then sovereign immunity is severly restricted, to the point of being practically non-existent. Today, sovereign immunity is basically limited to a qualified immunity for certain government officials, such as judges, when acting in their judicial capacity, and government officials, when they are merely setting policy or legislation, in the strictest sense of the word. An IRB would surely not fall into that classification. For example, in *Robinson v. City of Raytown*,[68] the court said that the aldermen and mayor were acting only in their official legislative capacity by passing an ordinance, which was never enforced and later declared invalid. This means that as long as an IRB only makes rules and regulations, *but* never implements them, it is safe from a lawsuit. This does not leave much safe ground since most IRBs do more than that. One might think that even if a regulation is implemented, as long as it was done in "good faith," there would be protection, but that is not correct. In *Owen v. City of Independence* the Supreme Court held that a municipality has no immunity from liability under 42 U.S.C. Section 1983 flowing from its constitutional violation, even though its officers assert good faith as a defense. The fact is that "good faith" simply does not matter when someone has been deprived of a constitutional right by some government "entity."

These cases offer little comfort to an IRB that wants to claim sovereign immunity. The cases show that sovereign immunity is no defense—unless an IRB has merely approved a research project and nothing has yet been done to carry out the research.

Another defense that has been attempted under 42 U.S.C. Section 1983 has been that governmental bodies are not "persons" within the meaning of the statute. The answer to this was resolved by the Supreme Court in *Monell v. New York City Department of Social Services*,[70] where the court held that government bodies are "persons" within the meaning of Section 1983. However, an IRB is not a government agency, but merely a board administering government funds at a state institution, and therefore, might claim that *Monell* does not apply. That argument is most likely precluded by a Missouri case, *O'Hearn v. School District of Springfield R-12.*[71] In that case, the court held that the city board *and* individual school board members were "persons" subject to suit under Section 1983.

Another attempted defense has been a claim that the person or persons being sued were too far removed from the one who actually caused the injury, or that they were not even aware the harm was caused. There must be "some" connection, as stated in *Mackey v. Camp*:[73] "With regard to defendant Camp, the plaintiff has failed to show a direct and personal participation on his part in the acts complained of. Such a showing is necessary where money damages are sought under 42 U.S.C. Section 1983, for the doctrine of respondent superior."[74] Therefore negligence on only the part of the researcher without any causal link to an IRB will not expose the IRB to liability. There will only be liability imposed on the IRB if some causal link between the action of the IRB and the injury complained of can be established. The point was made again in *Doores v. McNamara*,[75] where the only involvement of the Board of Police Commissioners in the challenged employment practices was the Board's approval of the affirmative action plan. The court held that approval by *itself* was not enough causal connection to hold the Board liable. These cases don't answer the question "How much involvement is needed before liability attaches?" That question was answered in *Rizzo v. Goode*[76] and more specifically in *Monell*,[77] where the court said that liability will attach if, "(t)he action alleged to be unconstitutional implements or executes a policy statement, by that body's officers."[78] The actions of an IRB certainly fall within this definition of the requisite involvement. A case that illustrates the required degree of causal connection even more is *University of Missouri, Etc. v. Dalton.*[79] The issue in the case was whether the named defendants—Dr. Schooling, the chancellor and Dr. Ratchford, the president of M.U.—had the requisite involvement in the matters which formed the basis of the lawsuit in order to subject them to liability under Section 1983. The court said, "It is...true that supervisory personnel cannot be held liable under 42 U.S.C. Section 1983 merely because an underling violates a person's federal rights...the action that is alleged to be unconstitutional (i.e., Chancellor Schooling's and Dr. Ratchford's denials of plaintiff's request for use of campus facilities) implements or executes a policy statement ...adopted and promulgated by the defendants in their capacity as members of the Board of Curator....Consequently, defendants may be held answerable, under 42 U.S.C. Section 1983 for the actions taken by various University officials...."[80] An IRB's actions clearly fall within those guidelines. A Pennsylvania court echoed similar sentiments when it said, supervisors cannot be held liable, "unless it is shown that they were personally involved in the alleged wrongful acts.... It is sufficient to show that they directed their subordinates to commit improper acts, or had actual knowledge that such acts were being committed and acquiesced in them."[81]

What Kind of Injury?

The cases and the regulations use the term, "injury," in regard to damages. That raises the question of what kind of "injury" is compensable in a lawsuit against an IRB? As seen in the cases, mental injury is sufficient, even without any physical injury. The new HHS regulations have adopted the same definition of "injury." The Department, in response to the public comments suggesting that the word, "injury," in Section 46.116, be replaced by the words "physical injury," explicitly rejects that with, "(t)he Department sees no reason to limit such disclosures to only one kind of injury."[82] HHS obviously intended to allow recovery for all types of injury, not just physical injury, since disclosure of all types of potential injury must be made. That simply adds to the potential risk of lawsuit.

Conclusion

The prior regulations applied to most research using human subjects. That aspect made them much easier to apply and reduced the risk of legal liability arising out of a misapplication of the regulations. The new regulations, with their attempt to reduce the scope of coverage, created ambiguities and uncertainties in regard to the application of the regulations. Therefore, the risk of legal liability has been greatly increased for an IRB that misapplies the regulations, even if done in good faith, or for an IRB that is not very careful in its review procedure and negligently excludes research from the regulations or from requiring informed consent. It is therefore interesting to see how HHS addressed the question of an IRB's legal liability.

In response to the question, "Should there be direct compensation and protection against liability for IRB members?" the National Commission for the Protection of Human Subjects of Biomedical and Behavioral Research recommended that there be direct compensation and protection against liability for IRB members by saying, "(T)his protection can be provided in several ways including sovereign immunity, insurance, indemnification by the institution, or specific provision of state law."[83] The National Commission at least recognized the problem, but the suggested solutions are not very sound. As seen, sovereign immunity is generally no defense.[84]

Indemnification by the institution, beyond providing legal counsel, is unlikely. Where would those funds come from? State legislation aimed at specifically providing immunity for IRB members is very unlikely.

The public policy is to protect those who take risks in order to advance the fund of knowledge of our society as a whole. A state is unlikely to pass legislation preventing research subjects from recovering for an injury that resulted from their participation in a research project. In fact, California has recently enacted legislation similar to the HHS regulations *without* granting any immunity of indemnification to IRB members.[85] That leaves insurance as the only alternative and that may not always provide adequate protection, especially in regard to punitive damages. It will be up to each IRB member to acquire the best protection possible.

The HHS decision in regard to the recommendation by the National Commission was that, "HHS has decided not to address in these regulations the issues of compensation for IRB members or liability protection for IRB members."[86] This certainly is not an answer, it merely avoids the issue. It is correct, as HHS itself said that, "(t)he Department is unaware of any successful negligence action which has named an IRB member as a defendant."[87] That should not offer much comfort to an IRB member. It merely leaves the question of the potential liability unanswered. There would be more comfort if there had been some successful litigation so that some parameters for liability would exist. Since the limits of liability have not been defined in this area of the law, the best advice, at this point, is that an IRB should be certain that the informed consent from every subject is adequate and that any proposal exempted from the regulations is clearly the type of research intended to be exempt.

What HHS should do to give more protection to the IRBs from legal liability is to reduce the ambiguities and define clearly what some of the terms mean. For example, Section 46.101 (b) (3) (iii)-(4) (iii) should contain an exclusive list of what type of behavior is sensitive by removing the words, "such as." That section should also define who is a public official or a candidate for public office, and how long that status is retained. Other examples are a clarification of the yearly review requirements found in Section 46.109(e), the expedited review procedure in Section 46.110, and the cooperative research of Section 46.114. These sections all need clarification in regard to what is required. In addition, a much clearer definition of "minimal risk" is needed.

It would also be of great benefit if HHS would come out and say that if the research is exempt from the regulations, then consent is not required. Right now they say that the requirement for consent is to be judged independently[88] and that leaves open the argument that even though the research was exempt, informed consent should have been acquired. Since one of the main reasons for attempting to exempt "most social science" research was to reduce the burden on researchers, it seems strange that informed consent would still be needed in order to protect the IRB. This puts the IRB in the position of saying to a researcher that the proposal is exempt from the regulations, *but* consent will have to be acquired anyway. This does not appear to reduce the burden on the researcher very much.

The suggestion is that instead of waiting for a court to clear up these problem areas, HHS should review the regulations and propose definitions or rewording to clear them up.

NOTES

[1]Protection of Human Subjects, 45 C.F.R. Section 46.101 et. seq. (1981).

[2]Institutional Review Boards are boards that are created by an institution receiving federal research funds. Their purpose is to review and approve or reject research proposals.

[3]45 C.F.R., *supra* Section 46.101(a).

[4]46 *Federal Register* 8366, (1981).

[5]Research conducted in established or commonly accepted educational settings, involving normal educational practices, such as (i) research on regular and special education instructional strategies, or (ii) research on the effectiveness of or the comparison among instructional techniques, curricula, or classroom management methods.

[6]Research involving the use of educational tests (cognitive, diagnostic, aptitude, achievement), if information taken from these sources is recorded in such a manner that subjects cannot be identified, directly or through identifiers linked to the subject.

[7]Research involving survey or interview procedures, except where all of the following conditions exist: (i) responses are recorded in such a manner that the human subjects can be identified, directly or through identifiers linked to the subjects, (ii) the subject's responses, if they become known outside the research, could reasonably place the subject at risk of criminal or civil liability or be damaging to the subject's financial standing or employability and (iii) the research deals with sensitive aspects of the subject's own behavior, such as illegal conduct, drug use, sexual behavior, or use of alcohol. All research involving survey or interview procedures is exempt, without exception, when the respondents are elected or appointed public officials or candidates for public office.

[8]"Such as illegal conduct, drug use, sexual behavior or use of alcohol."

[9]The question of foreseeability is actually part of the issue of what was the proximate cause of the injury. In order to determine if something was the proximate cause, the analysis often involves the question of whether the result was reasonably foreseeable. For example, see *Palsgraf Long Island R.R. Co.*, 162 N.E. 99 (N.Y. 1928). Prosser, speaking about foreseeability said, "There is perhaps no other one issue in the law of torts over which so much controversy has raged." Prosser, *Law of Torts* Section 43, 250(4th ed. 1971).

[10]For example, see *Walmsley v. Telephone Association,* 102 Kan. 139 (1917) where the plaintiff was riding on a wagon and hayrack with a large steel grain bin. He carried a loaded rifle and was standing at the front end of the hayrack. His employee was riding the team of horses at a walking pace. A low hanging telephone wire caught the grain bin and caused the wagon to upset and plaintiff was thrown to the ground. The bin struck the rifle, it discharged and shot the plaintiff in the chest.

He sued the telephone company and they were held liable, because all of that was reasonably foreseeable.

[11]For example, see K.S.A. 60-150, "Civil Actions. . .can only be commenced within the period prescribed . . . after the cause of action shall have accrued." This was interpreted in *Ruthrauff, Administratrix v. Kensinger*, 214 Kan. 185 (1974) with the statement "that tort actions accrue, not when the alleged tortious act is committed but on the date substantial injuries result therefrom," at 189.

[12]45 C.F.R., *supra* Section 46.101 (b) (3).

[13]*Gertz v. Robert Welch, Inc.*, 418 U.S. 323 (1974), the Court gave this definition of "public figure": "For the most part, those who attain this status (of public figure) have assumed roles of especial prominence in the affairs of society. Some occupy positions of such persuasive power and influence, that they are deemed public figures for all purposes. More commonly, those classed as public figures have thrust themselves to the forefront of particular public controversies in order to influence the resolution of issues involved. In either event, they invite attention and comment," at 345.

[14]46 *Federal Register, supra*, 8371.

[15]45 C.F.R., *supra*, Section 46.101.

[16]*Id.* Section 46.111. The section states: "(a) In order to approve research covered by these regulations, the IRB shall determine that all of the following requirements are satisfied: (1) Risks to subjects are minimized: (i) By using procedures which are consistent with sound research design and which do not unnecessarily expose subjects to risk, and (ii) whenever appropriate, by using procedures already being performed on the subjects for diagnostic or treatment purposes. (2) Risks to subjects are reasonable in relation to anticipated benefits, if any, to subjects, and the importance of the knowledge that may reasonably be expected to result. In evaluating risks and benefits, the IRB should consider only those risks and benefits that may result from the research (as distinguished from risks and benefits of therapies subjects would receive even if not participating in the research). The IRB should not consider possible long-range effects of applying knowledge gained in the research (for example, the possible effects of the research on public policy) as among those research risks that fall within the purview of its responsibility. (3) Selection of subjects is equitable. In making this assessment, the IRB should take into account the purposes of the research and the setting in which the research will be conducted. (4) Informed consent will be sought from each prospective subject or the subject's legally authorized representative, in accordance with, and to the extent required by Section 46.116. (5) Informed consent will be appropriately documented, in accordance with, and to the extent required by Section 46.117. (6) Where appropriate, the research plan makes adequate provision for monitoring the data collected to insure the safety of subjects. (7) Where appropriate, there are adequate provisions to protect the privacy of subjects and to maintain the confidentiality of data.

[17]*Id.* Section 46.102(g).

[18]46 *Federal Register, supra*, 8373.

[19]"Thin skull" means that a person takes the other person as they are and if that other person has a thinner skull than average, the risk is upon the IRB.

[20]45 C.F.R., *supra* Section 46.110 states: "(a) The Secretary has established, and published in the *Federal Register*, a list of categories of research that may be reviewed by the IRB through an expedited review procedure. The list will be amended, as appropriate, through periodic republication in the *Federal Register*. (b) An IRB may review some or all of the research appearing on the list through an expedited review procedure, if the research involves no more than minimal risk. The IRB may also use the expedited review procedure to review minor changes in previously approved research during the period for which approval is authorized. Under an expedited review procedure, the review may be carried out by the IRB chairperson or by one or more experienced reviewers designated by the chairperson from among members of the IRB. In reviewing the research, the reviewers may not disapprove the research. A research activity may be disapproved only after review in accordance with the non-expedited review procedure shall adopt a method for keeping all members advised of research proposals which have been approved under the procedure. (d) The Secretary may restrict, suspend, or terminate an institution's or IRB's use of the expedited review procedure when necessary to protect the rights or welfare of subjects."

[21]*Id.* Section 46.114 states: "Cooperative research projects are those projects, normally supported through grants, contracts, or similar arrangements, which involve institutions in addition to the grantee or prime contractor (such as contractor with the grantee, or a subcontractor with the prime contractor). In such instances, the grantee or prime contractor remains responsible to the Department for safeguarding the rights and welfare of human subjects. Also, when cooperating institutions conduct some or all of the research involving some or all of these subjects, each cooperating institution shall comply with these regulations as though it received funds for its participation in the project directly from the Department, except that in complying with these regulations, institutions may use joint review, reliance upon the review of another qualified IRB, or similar arrangements aimed at avoidance of duplication of effort."

[22]The "prime contractor" is the institution that received the grant for the research project and it is "subletting" part of the project to other institutions or is engaged in a cooperative project with other institutions.

[23]45 C.F.R., *supra* Section 46.114.

[24]*Id.* Section 46.109 (e) provides that: "An IRB shall conduct continuing review of research covered by these regulations at intervals appropriate to the degree of risk, but no less than once per year, and shall have authority to observe or have a third party observe the consent process and the research."

[25]*Id.* Section 46.113.

[26]*Id.* Section 46.116(c)(1),(2) and (d)(1) thru (4) provides: "(c) An IRB may approve a consent procedure which does not include, or which alters, some or all of the elements of informed consent set forth above, or waive the requirement to obtain informed consent, provided the IRB finds and documents that: (1) The research is to be conducted for the purpose of demonstrating or evaluating: (i) Federal, state, or local benefit or service programs which are not themselves research programs, (ii) procedures for obtaining benefits or services under these programs, or (iii) possible changes in alterations to these programs or procedures; and (2) The research could not practicably be carried out without the

waiver or alteration. (d) An IRB may approve a consent procedure which does not include, or which alters, some or all of the elements of informed consent set forth above, or waive the requirements to obtain informed consent provided the IRB finds and documents that: (l) The research involves no more than minimal risk to the subjects; (2) The waiver or alteration will not adversely affect the rights and welfare of the subjects; (3) The research could not practicably be carried out without the waiver or alteration; and (4) Whenever appropriate, the subjects will be provided with additional pertinent information after participation."

[27]*Id.* Section 46.116.

[28]*Id.* Section 46.116.

[29]*Id.* Section 46.116.

[30]*Id.* Section 46.116(c)(2).

[31]*Supra.* see discussion on pages 5 thru 6.

[32]45 C.F.R. *supra*, Section 46.116(d)(2).

[33]*Id.* Section 46.116 (d)(3)(4).

[34]*Black's Law Dictionary* 1746 (4th ed. rev. 1972).

[35]*Kaimowitz v. Michigan Department of Mental Health,* 42 L.W. 2063 (1973).

[36]The difference between "knowledgeable" and "competent" is that "knowledgeable" means that the person consenting must know the nature and consequences of the conduct, and "competent" means that the person must have the capacity to consent to the conduct.

[37]*Human experimentation*, 70 (R.L. Bogomolny, ed. 1976).

[38]Civil No. 655-049 (S.F. Super, Ct., filed Sept. 1l, 1973).

[39]509 F. 2d. 109 (2nd Cir. 1975).

[40]*Id.* at 113.

[41]Medical treatment and human experimentation: Introducing illegality, fraud, duress, and incapacity to the doctrine of informed consent, 6 *Rutgers-Camden Law Journal* 538, 552 (Winter 1975).

[42]*Smith v. United States*, 153 F. 2d 655, 661 (5th Cir. 1946).

[43]*Human experimentation*, *supra*, at 73.

[44]*Id.* at 78.

[45]Konkle, *Nielson v. The Regents:* Children as pawns or persons? *Hastings Constitutional Law Quarterly* 1151, 1172.

[46]45 C.F.R., *supra*, Section 46.107(a).

[47]*Id.* Section 46.lll(a)(2).

[48]46 *Federal Register, supra*, at 8378.

[49]*Human Experimentation, supra*, at 79.

[50]"(a) Basic elements of informed consent. Except as provided in paragraph (c) or (d) of this section, in seeking informed consent the following information shall be provided to each subject: (l) A statement that the study involves research, an explanation of the purposes of the research and the expected duration of the subject's participation, a description of the procedures to be followed, and identification of any procedures which are experimental; (2) A description of any reasonably foreseeable risks or discomforts to the subject; (3) A description of any benefits to the subject or to others which may reasonably be expected from the research; (4) A disclosure of appropriate alternative procedures or courses of treatment, if any, that might be advantageous to the subject; (5) A statement describing the extent, if any, to which confidentiality of records identifying the subject will be maintained; (6) For research

involving more than minimal risk, an explanation as to whether any compensation and an explanation as to whether any medical treatments are available if injury occurs and, if so, what they consist of, or where further information may be obtained; (7) An explanation of whom to contact for answers to pertinent questions about the research and research subjects' rights, and whom to contact in the event of a research-related injury to the subject; and (8) A statement that participation is voluntary, refusal to participate will involve no penalty or loss of benefits to which the subject is otherwise entitled, and the subject may discontinue participation at any time without penalty or loss of benefits to which the subject is otherwise entitled. (b) Additional elements of informed consent. When appropriate, one or more of the following elements of information shall also be provided to each subject; (l) A statement that the particular treatment or procedure may involve risks to the subject (or to the embryo or fetus, if the subject is or may become pregnant) which are currently unforeseeable; (2) Anticipated circumstances under which the subject's participation may be terminated by the investigator without regard to the subject's consent; (3) Any additional costs to the subject that may result from participation in the research; (4) The consequences of a subject's decision to withdraw from the research and procedures for orderly termination of participation by the subject; (5) A statement that significant new findings developed during the course of the research which may relate to the subject's willingness to continue participation will be provided to the subject; and (6) The approximate number of subjects involved in the study."

[51]See generally, *Cooper v. Roberts* 286 A. 2d 647 (Sup. Ct. Penn. 1971); *Scarcia v. St. Paul Fire and Marine Ins. Co.*, 227 N.W. 2d 647 (Wisc. 1974).

[52]Freud, Is the law ready for human experimentation, 2 *Trial* 46, 48 (Oct./Nov. 1966) states: "(the subject) should have sufficient knowledge and comprehension of the subject matter involved as to enable him to make an understanding and enlightened decision. This latter element requires that before the acceptance of an affirmative decision by the experimental subject there should be made known to him the nature, duration and purpose of the experiment; the method and means by which it is to be conducted; all inconveniences and hazards reasonably to be expected; and the effects upon his health or person which may possibly come from his participation in the experiment."

[53]*Human experimentation, supra*, at 75.

[54]442 U.S. 584 (1979).

[55]*Parham* 442 U.S. at 602.

[56]*Planned Parenthood of Central Mo. v. Danforth*, 428 U.S. 52 (1976).

[57]*Human experimentation, supra*, at 73.

[58]See generally, *Brady v. United States*, 397 U.S. 742 (1970); *Johnson v. Zerbst*, 304 U.S. 458 (1938).

[59]"Every person who, under cover of any statute, ordinance, regulation, custom, or usage, of any State or Territory, subjects, or causes to be subject, any citizen of the United States or other persons with the jurisdiction thereof to the deprivation of any rights, privileges or immunities secured by the Constitution and laws, shall be liable to the person injured in an action of law, suit in equity, or other proper proceeding for redress."

[60]"The right of privacy is broad enough to include the right to protect

one's mental processes from governmental interference." *Kaimowitz, supra*, at 2064. Also see *Mackey v. Procunier*, 477 F 2d. 542 (1969); *Griswold v. Connecticut*, 381 U. S. 479 85 S.Ct. 1978, 14 L. Ed. 2d. 510 (1965). "The roots of the right of personal privacy have been found in various Amendments, most notably the First, Fourth, and Fifth, in the 'penumbras of the Bill of Rights,' and in the concept of liberty guaranteed by the first section of the Fourteenth Amendment." *Roe v. Wade,* 410 U.S. 113, 152, 93 S. Ct. 705, 726, 35 L. Ed 2d. 147 (1973).

[61]See generally, *Cohen v. California*, 403 U.S. 15 (1970); *Tinker v. Des Moines School Dist.*, 393 U.S. 503 (1969); *Eisenstadt v. Baird,* 405 U.S. 438 (1972).

[62]"We must next consider whether some compelling state interest...justifies the substantial infringement of appellant's First Amendment right. It is basic that no showing merely of a rational relationship to some colorable state interest would suffice; in this highly sensitive constitutional area, '(o)nly the gravest abuses, endangering paramount interest, give occasion for permissible limitation." *Thomas v. Collins*, 323 U.S. 516, 530 (1944); *Sherbert v. Verner*, 374 U.S. 398, 406 (1963).
"(i)nfringement by the state of her constitutional rights...may be justified by a compelling state interest in the regulation of a subject within the state's constitutional power to regulate..." *NAACP v. Button*, 371 U.S. 415, 438; (1963); *Sherbert v. Verner, Supra* at 403.

[63]477 F. 2d. 877 (9th Cir. 1973).

[64]*Id.* 878.

[65]*Kaimowitz, supra*, at 2064. The emphasized portion of this quote explains what is meant by the term "mentation."

[66]See Note #61, *supra*, at 565.

[67]This rule is known as "state action." The classic case states that, "(c)ivil rights, such as are guaranteed by the constitution against state aggression, cannot be impaired by the wrongful acts of individuals, unsupported by state authority in the shape of laws, customs, or judicial or executive proceedings..." *Civil Rights Cases*, 109 U.S. 3, 17 (1883). See also *Burton v. Wilmington Parking Authority*, 365 U.S. 715, 81 S. Ct. 856, 6 L. Ed. 2d 45 (1961).

[68]606 S.W. 2d 460 (W.D. Mo. 1980).

[69]445 U.S. 622 (1980).

[70]436 U.S. 658 (1978).

[71]578 F. 2d 220 (8th Cir. 1978).

[72]415 F. Supp. 323 (D.C. Mo. 1976).

[73]*Id.* at 324.

[74]The "respondent superior" doctrine stands for the proposition that the employer, the master, is acting through the facility of an employee or agent...and tort liability is incurred during the course of this agency due to some fault of the agent, then the employer or master must accept the responsibility. *Black's Law Dictionary* 1475 (4th ed. rev. 1972).

[75]476 F. Supp. 897 (W.D. Mo. 1979).

[76]423 U.S. 362 (1976).

[77]*Supra*, at Note 70.

[78]*Id.* at 690.

[79]456 F. Supp. 985 (W.D. Mo. 1978).

[80]*Id.* at 995.

[81] *Sonder v. McGuire*, 423 F. Supp. 803, 832 (Penn, 1976).
[82] 46 *Federal Register, supra*, at 8382.
[83] *Id.* at 8385.
[84] *Infra*, beginning on page number 16.
[85] Protection of Human Subjects in Medical Experimentation Act, West's Ann. Health & Safety Code, Section 24170 *et. seq.* (1978).
[86] *Federal Register, supra*, art 8385.
[87] *Id.* at 8385.
[88] *Infra*, at page number 4.

PART 7
ETHICAL CONSIDERATIONS IN SOCIAL AND BEHAVIORAL RESEARCH

21. THE MODERN EVOLUTION OF HUMAN EXPERIMENTATION

Stanley J. Reiser

At the start of the nineteenth century, a scientific revolution began in medicine, which enhanced the capacity of investigators to learn about the secrets of disease within the interstices of the body. It was based upon the development of an extraordinary set of techniques to study the body. In 1829, an improved lens system enabled the microscope to become a dependable agent of investigation and an object of intense use. At this time, the techniques of chemical analysis gave scientists new abilities to understand the basic composition of many body fluids. And techniques of converting the movement of body organs and muscles into graphic patterns that could be analyzed and compared led to greater knowledge of physiologic function.

These techniques were often invasive and harsh. For example, to produce graphic patterns of blood flow required the insertion of a large needle into an artery; or to chemically analyze blood required large amounts with which to work. These problems created barriers to the use of these techniques on humans, and led the nineteenth century investigator to conduct basic experiments on animals.

By the early twentieth century, techniques such as those described and others had become refined in a way that made their use on people acceptable and desirable. This not only improved the diagnoses of diseases in patients, but encouraged investigators to recruit people into experiments. Now clinical investigation began to rival laboratory investigation for the attention of scientists.

The conclusion of World War II marked a watershed for human studies. Revelations of cruel behavior towards human subjects, inducted against their will into experiments by physicians and scientists stunned the research community. Those who prosecuted the war criminals at Nuremberg asked probing questions about these events, including whether human studies should be conducted at all.

They decided such investigations were morally permissible, but only if a wall of protections were drawn about people who were subjects in this work. Investigators were bound to tell subjects about benefits and risks, and to seek their consent before proceeding with the work. Before humans were even approached, investigators were to have conducted prior studies on animals and to use other experimental models to assure subjecting humans to any risk was justified. These protections became known as the Nuremberg Code.

Events that occurred for the two decades following the war and the development of the Code demonstrated the need for more formal bodies and rules to assure the protection of subjects in medical investigations.

In the late 1960s, human studies committees were impaneled across the country as the result of a promulgation of the United States Public Health Service requiring them in all institutions which accepted federal research funds in medicine. These committees were to review all experiments which involved humans, to insure that subjects had adequate knowledge of risks and benefits.

These actions raised the basic issue of the moral significance of beneficial knowledge in medicine. What place should search for this knowledge have, in relation to other meaningful values that are part of the ethical traditions of medicine and society, such as the autonomy of patients over what is done to them? The past fifteen years, since the IRB has become so ubiquitous in medicine, have been remarkable for the searching moral inquiry into the place of research activity in medicine, and for the reasonable administrative innovations designed to facilitate this process. The continuance of these discussions will strengthen and define the purposes and goals of research, to the benefit of us all.

22. EMERGING ETHICAL ISSUES IN SOCIAL AND BEHAVIORAL RESEARCH

Joan E. Sieber

Five years ago, I began to taxonomize and review the literature on ethical issues in social and behavioral research. I shall summarize the issues that seem to be emerging, but first I shall mention the historical context from which these issues arise, and outline the broader array of ethical issues within which these are located.

Ten years ago, the social sciences were concerned with the ethics of studying human subjects. Or rather, the social sciences were responding defensively to society's concern that human subjects were routinely being deceived and their privacy invaded. The spectre of federal regulation of social research took on unreal proportions in the minds of social scientists, who anticipated the demise of scientific freedom and of valid and rigorous research. It seemed incomprehensible to many social scientists that society could question the value of research or could have a say in how it was done. It seemed a misunderstanding on the part of society, that scientists trained in deception research techniques be required to obtain voluntary informed consent prior to research. It seemed obvious that the scientist was entitled to invade privacy in order to study sensitive personal matters that individuals would not knowingly disclose. It seemed that the scientific merit of random assignment of subjects obviously superceded any considerations of equity or benefit to subjects.

Now, out of the creativity of many social scientists who understood and were concerned with these ethical issues, and out of the insistence by the Federal Government that more ethical practices be employed, there is emerging a more ethical set of research practices. The issues of informed consent, privacy and confidentiality, research risk and institutional review of research are no longer new or very controversial. The question of whether scientific freedom is absolute—whether freedom can exist unbalanced by social responsibility—has been answered, and most recognize that the answer is "No."

In my reading of the literature, new ethical issues now seem to be emerging into the awareness of social scientists. Or rather, like the issues of a decade ago, they are being forced into our defensive awareness. This time, it is not the government or social advocates that force issues into our awareness. Rather, funding pressures focus our attention on problems of applied research. In this context, we perceive our failure to follow our own highest principles of open-mindedness and objectivity, to focus on important issues, and to serve society responsibly. The issues I am about to describe are not new. They are as old as humanity's efforts to understand humanity and to intervene in society so as to improve it. What is new is only the growing awareness of these issues as important ones within social and behavioral science.

These new issues lie just outside of what most in the social science disciplines consider their methodology, philosophy of science or ethics. These new issues are best understood in the systems theory terms of C. West Churchman (1979). Churchman has pointed out that the philosophy, methodology and ethics of science have traditionally meant the philosophy, methodology and ethics *within a well-defined science*. It has meant the working out of the detailed rules of doing that science. In contrast, these new issues raise radical questions about methodology, push beyond the confines of that methodology, and acknowledge the value or legitimacy of alternative methods, tastes or styles in doing science. Sciences, and especially social sciences, have remained embedded in their rather singular rational models, despite the pioneering efforts of a few who have moved past the traditional structure of science.

As one example of pioneering scholarship, the historian of science, Kuhn (1962), has shown that science is not a cumulative building of truth. Rather, it proceeds as a series of shifts in conceptual focus or assumptions about the nature of its subject matter. Each focus, when it is in vogue, is monolithic and persists in the face of falsifying evidence. As another example, Baysian statistics takes the radical position that one enters contexts with a particular prior hypothesis or focus that determines the kind of sense one makes of evidence. Despite Kuhn, Bayes and others who have questioned the rationality and usefulness of science as actually practiced, there is little in the conduct of social science to suggest that mainstream social scientists are ready to enter into an egalitarian relationship with the range of new perspectives, concepts, roles or obligations that would make our science more vital, ethical, and focused on the real and urgent matters that face humankind.

The emerging ethical issues are questions one would ask if one thought to go beyond the political boundaries that each discipline sets for itself. These include questions about choice of theory and method, one's relationship with those studied, and effective dissemination of findings. Social scientists who desire to examine these questions typically find themselves in unconscious conflict with colleagues who desire to maintain their traditional ground rules, philosophy of science, or roles. In contrast, a dialectical relationship could exist within social science in which competing ideas and styles of doing science are given something approximating a fair hearing, and scientists would learn to choose or to synthesize methods and approaches from among them.

The taxonomy of issues that has guided me in my literature search provides a context for discussing what seem to be the emerging ethical issues. The taxonomy begins with issues that precede the research process, such as epistemological and methodological issues, and ends with issues that follow from the research process such as issues of dissemination, application and feedback from practice to theory and research.

Table l. Taxonomy of Ethical Issues in Social and Behavioral Science

I. Theories, methods and procedures: Their political, moral and scientific underpinnings and consequences.

A. *Values and epistemology.* Views on how data should be collected, used and disseminated are closely related to a researcher's beliefs about the nature of knowledge and reality. When knowledge, *per se*, is considered an unlimited good, then issues of potentially harmful application become somewhat tangential to the research enterprise. But, when knowledge is considered as a kind of power, then the question of access to that power becomes a crucial ethical issue. The way researchers define reality and their relationship to that reality affects both theory and methods. When reality is believed to be something "out there," that should be studied objectively without interfering with it, then deception may be considered the most "scientific" method of social research, since it least interferes with that reality. If, on the other hand, reality is believed to be a construction, composed of interaction between investigator and investigated, then scientific method consists of taking into account rather than ignoring the effect of the investigator on the investigated. Works concerned with the nature of beliefs about knowledge and reality and the effect of each set of assumptions on the method and product of research are pertinent to this category.

B. *Validity and ethics: Implications for choice of theories and methods*. These are normally thought of as scientific, rather than ethical, issues. However, in order for research to be ethical, it must be valid. Research done with faulty design, method or interpretation is not an ethically justifiable use of human resources and yields false information as well. Clearly, not every work dealing with issues of design, methodology and interpretation are included in this category. Included in this category are works dealing with issues of validity that have important ethical consequences.

C. *Ethical socialization.* Social scientists and others are often unaware of the ethical implications of their actions and policies, or of the alternatives that exist for making science and its applications more ethical. Ethical socialization refers to the teaching or training of scientists (a) to be more ethically aware and (b) to cultivate more ethical scientific practices. Works categorized under ethical socialization are ones that raise an issue about which social scientists need to become more aware, or that suggest ways in which social scientists might behave to reduce possible harm or wrong, or to increase benefit.

II. Who defines the good, goals and prohibitions in social science?

A. *Scientific freedom.* Both scientists and subjects have rights and responsibilities. The right of the investigator to conduct research must be balanced against the rights of those studied. The responsibility of the scientist not to injure those studied should also be balanced against the responsibility of citizens to contribute to knowledge which may benefit themselves, others and society. Where the balance lies and by what mechanism it should be determined is problematic.

B. *Values, ethics and politics, social policy and support for research.* Values and distinctions between moral and immoral behavior are frequently based on political criteria. When we approve of a particular cause, group or government we typically regard as moral research that supports its aims (e.g., research that aided the United States during World War II), but when we disapprove of a cause, group or government we typically regard as immoral any research that supports its aims (e.g., research that aided the United States during the Vietnam conflict). Charges of scientific irresponsibility or immorality may mask profound political disagreements; those who work for causes one disapproves of are accused not only of being wrong, but of being immoral. The issues of whom an investigator works for and how the data are used raise ethical and political questions that often are not separated from one another.

C. *Questionable, forbidden or controversial topics of research.* While science and society value freedom of inquiry, there is some question as to whether social scientists should study certain questions, particularly when supported by public funds. Two concerns are: (1) will the truth cause serious or irreparable social harm, and (2) will scientists produce misleading or invalid results that will then be misapplied? For example, the issue of whether research should be done on race and IQ can be cast in terms of (1) whether it would be harmful to society to have proof positive that one race has a few less IQ points than another on the average, and (2) whether such research can be performed and interpreted validly. A related issue is whether the truth will be used in ways that are politically or personally harmful to some groups or individuals, or to society at large.

If society agrees that certain topics should be avoided, who is responsible for the decision: researchers individually or collectively, pressure groups, those studied, federal agencies, or review boards? What are the likely consequences of restricting versus not restricting inquiry?

D. *Government regulations.* A large body of local, federal and international law pertains to or affects the conduct of social research and application.

E. *Human subjects committee activity, institutional review processes.* Any work dealing with the nature or conduct of IRBs falls into this category. Many works dealing with Human Subjects Committees also fall under Regulations, but many do not. In the latter category are many informative works describing ways in which IRBs actually function and the ways in which they might be improved.

III. Risk and Benefit.

A. *Risk, wrong and harm.* What forms of harm are considered in evaluating whether a research procedure is ethically warranted? How does one weigh moral wrongs that do no harm? How are degrees of risk assessed? How can procedures be made safe, and how is safety judged? Risk assessment has become a field of great importance in recent years. Its application to the social sciences is only now becoming rigorous.

B. *Benefit or promise of research.* The ethical justification for research is that it is beneficial. What the benefits of specific research may be, how these may be estimated or maximized ahead of time, and how they may be measured or maximized after the research or application has occurred needs to be considered if research planning is to be ethical (i.e., to optimize benefit over cost in a satisfactory manner). Included in this category are works that focus on the nature, measurement, and maximization of benefit of social research and research application. The recipients of the benefit may be any individual or collective, e.g., the scientist, the subject, society at large, Native American children, etc. *Benefit* may refer to any form of good, e.g., physical, material, spiritual, intellectual, aesthetic, or legal benefits. It could refer to freedom of inquiry on the part of science; affection, friendship or cooperation among friends who participated together in a study; health, strength and activity of senior citizens; adventure; security, peace and privacy. Many works clarify notions of benefit in social science without dwelling on risk/benefit assessment; such articles are included in this category. Articles that focus on risk/benefit assessment without detailed examination of the nature, measurement or maximization of benefit would appear under risk/benefit assessment; articles that focus on both areas would appear under both categories.

C. *Risk/benefit assessment.* It is recognized that the price of scientific knowledge may be some risk of harm or some wrong to an individual or a group, as well as some economic cost to some sector of society. When is the price ethically justified? All works that deal with the question of how to weigh some promised or actual scientific benefit against a possible or actual cost are included in this category. Costs include intangible wrongs such as injury to one's autonomy, and treating persons as objects rather than individuals, or treating them solely as means to the researcher's ends.

D. *Justice or equity of the relationship between scientist, subjects, populations, gatekeepers, sponsors and society.* Procedural and distributive justice arise as issues in many parts of the research and application process in social science. Who sponsors and pays for research? Who benefits? How are research subjects selected? How is the power of the scientist balanced against the powerlessness of the subject?

IV. The relationship between investigator and investigated.

A. *Informed consent.* This broad category goes far beyond the legal requirement of informed consent. It includes any work that deals with the understanding between the researcher and the subject about the purpose, procedure and intended outcome of the research, and with the various ways in which this understanding is conveyed, comprehended and used, or not conveyed, not comprehended or not believed. It is concerned with a continuum from highly informed consent at one pole to deception or concealment at the other. It includes works dealing with research relationships that do not use the legally required informed consent procedure but which convey some agreement about the researcher-subject relationship, including implicit agreements.

B. *Deception.* Deception includes concealment, intended deception, mental reservations, perceived deception, and the use of devices intended to take one's attention off of the main purpose of an activity in order to evoke spontaneous behavior. The placement of a procedure into this category does not assume that it is an unethical procedure. It is recognized that deception in social science ranges from management of the perceptions of others using tact and body language—forms of deception that we naturally expect to encounter—to lies which may undermine the confidence of persons in themselves and others, leave persons seriously deluded, and reveal to students of social science the high degree of disrespect for others that occurs in the name of science.

C. *Creating and using relationships as sources of qualitative data.* "Qualitative" social research often involves getting to know a person and then reporting on some aspect of the person's life. This is particularly true in cultural anthropology or fieldwork, but it applies to all varieties of social research. The nature of the relationship between the investigator and the investigated affects many aspects of most kinds of social research: the definition of the research problem, the collection and organization of the data, the framing of research reports, the dissemination of results, and the utilization of the findings. The model of research used is based, in part, on the way one weighs the power between the investigators, investigated, sponsors and gatekeepers (those who control access to the investigated). These relationships affect not only the findings but also the salient ethical issues associated with research. What are the ethical implications of using a relationship to obtain scientific data and professional power? All works that deal with the dilemma posed by gathering information about a person in the course of a relationship, then using the data for scientific or other purposes are pertinent. Of particular interest are works dealing (a) with situations that involve very intense or personal relationships between the investigator and the subject, and (b) with contexts where the information reported is cast in a critical or analytic way that is inconsistent with the way the informant would wish to be represented to the world, or that is given to parties who can use the information to exploit the informant.

V. Acquisition and use of information.

A. *Privacy*. Privacy refers to a person's interest in separating him or herself from others, or to a person's being somehow separated from others. As explained under Confidentiality (Cf., Confidentiality), privacy refers to persons and not to data, though the two are intimately connected. Privacy is not necessarily something that is sought or protected. It may in some cases be intolerable; a subject who feels a great need to share personal information with a sympathetic listener may disclose more to an investigator than the investigator would wish to know or would wish to be responsible for knowing. As a behavioral phenomenon, privacy refers to certain needs to establish boundaries. These needs seem to be universal, but are manifested differently depending on learning, culture and developmental factors. Thus, the social scientist's views on privacy may be inadequate for judging what privacies another might expect, what devices another would use to guard privacy or how to create rapport so that the subject would not consider privacy to be invaded. As a legal term, privacy refers to those privacies that persons want to have and to protect, and particularly to those privacies that are regarded as basic to our form of government and society. Certain constitutional and federal laws indicate basic rights to privacy that scientists must respect, and statutory and common law provides mechanisms under which persons might take action against an investigator who was alleged to have invaded privacy. The law expects scientists to be sensitive to persons' individual claims to privacy but recognizes that there are situations where claims to privacy must yield to competing claims. Works pertaining to any aspects of privacy fall into this category.

B. *Confidentiality*. Confidentiality means limiting access to information that has already been acquired. Privacy and confidentiality refer to states of persons and of data, respectively.(Cf., Privacy.) The concepts are closely related, however. An individual may hold certain information as private, yet be willing to disclose it to another person if it is clear that the second person will limit others' access to the information in appropriate ways. Under those conditions, the second person would not be said to have invaded the first person's privacy by knowing the private information, but rather by failing to keep that information confidential.

After the social scientist has discovered what matters relevant to the proposed research are held as private by members of the prospective population of research subjects, the next step is to discover the conditions under which subjects would disclose that information willingly to the investigator and whether the investigator can meet those conditions. A promise of confidentiality in good faith by an investigator does not necessarily mean that the investigator (a) understands the implications of the promise, or (b) can keep the promise under all conditions. There are various classes of risks to confidentiality which the responsible social scientist must recognize, taking steps needed to reduce or eliminate these risks. Moreover, scientists need to recognize that, unlike reporters, they have no shield laws to protect their data, and no First Amendment rights to exchange information (in the name of research). The scientists' assumption that she or he owns the data collected may be challenged in a variety of ways. Included in this category are works that discuss forms of confidentiality, risks to confidentiality, procedures to protect confidentiality, desires and promises of confidentiality, breaches of confidentiality, and laws governing confidentiality or threatening confidentiality.

C. *Dissemination, publication, and application of information.* How scientific information is disseminated, and what is contained (or omitted) in the reporting has ethical implications: Who is benefited? Who is harmed? What misinformation or misunderstanding is conveyed? Should one conceal or suppress potentially harmful data? What are the likely consequences of disseminating the information in a particular way? What do social scientists need to know about the dissemination process? How can social scientists participate in that process in a more responsible way? What kinds of groundwork and relationships are needed to make applications of social science successful? What feedback between research and application is desirable? What is the proper role of the mass media in scientific reporting? What are the social scientist's obligations to contribute to the social scientific literacy of the layman, including subjects and persons to whom the social sciences are applied?

The issues that seem to be emerging now in social science, and are as yet unrecognized in the mainstream of social science, are ones that lie at the extreme ends of this ordering of issues. They are:

1. *Issues of epistemology*. What is social science? What are the scientist's proper roles, ways of arriving at "truth," ultimate aims, modes of inquiry, and personal characteristics? How does the scientist relate to the world at large? What does the scientist consider to be the proper realm of science, and what is regarded as an ethical issue within this realm? Of particular interest here is the work of Ian Mitroff and Ralph

Kilmann (1978) who present a four-fold table of distinct styles or definitions of social science. They show that important work has emerged out of each style, and that, in order to be truly ethical and to use the full power of social science, one needs to be able to move flexibly through these styles of social science. Yet, only one of these styles is "in fashion" and is represented in mainstream journals. Also of interest is that when Mitroff and Kilmann's work is presented to students, they experience powerful "Aha's!" and ask why they haven't been given this liberating experience earlier in their education. Interestingly, students recognize that most of their professors would regard this broadening of the "standards" of science as unacceptable.

2. *Issues of validity and ethics.* Current methodology is rather inflexible or unresponsive to matters of ethics. It follows from the comments on epistemology that science plays favorites in the kinds of models of man and methods of pursuing knowledge that it sanctions. For example, the perception that a more collaborative approach between researcher and researched might yield a better defined research problem, more candid responses, or a greater likelihood that the knowledge will be used in constructive ways is often "cut off at the pass"—utterly ruled out because a collaborative approach would violate deterministic fashions that deem science more objective when persons are treated as things. Of particular interest here is the work of Argyris (1968) who has presented extensive evidence that some deterministic methods yield not only superficial ideas, but also destroy the social structures by which nonsuperficial social science might be effectively disseminated or developed in society. Argyris shows that deterministic and humanistic methods may be blended with no loss of rigor. If researchers will go beyond the traditional tenets of "rigor" to methodological flexibility, and beyond the usual perception of ethical issues to a systems model that asks more of social science, they may embark on a more useful and scientifically profound undertaking.
3. *Ethical socialization of social scientists.* "Ethics" in science often means adherence to a Procrustean professional code. Adherence to a code is likely to be done either resentfully or with an unimaginative, uncreative and self-righteous sense of knowing right from wrong. A more intellectually and aesthetically sound approach is needed. "Ethics" needs to grow beyond professional codes and beyond what is taught under the rubric of "ethics" in philosophy. Ethics in social science needs to merge with epistemology and methodology to focus on very specific technical and theoretical issues. Finally, ethical socialization needs to begin, explicitly, early in the social science curriculum. Of particular interest here is the work of Donald Warwick (1980) who chronicles the meagre history of ethics in social science.
4. *Scientific freedom.* Now that we recognize that freedom must be mixed

with responsibility, we must inquire into the possible ingredients of this mixture. Of special interest here are the ideas of John Dewey spoken over 80 years ago, and almost totally ignored, and the ideas of Seymour Sarason (1979), who has profited greatly from reflection on Dewey's ideas. These people have thought critically about our duty to work in collaboration with those we seek to study, to define problems in the community, to train persons who will apply ideas both in science and in public service so that they will operate as ethical professionals, and to build in feedback loops so that the scientist can be maximally sensitive to the flaws of applied research and development and can use this as information to improve the validity and value of scientific contributions. In other words, theory and research should not be more important than practical results of the application of science; rather they should guide and correct one another. The working out of this relationship is of crucial importance and at present is all but ignored in social science.

5. *Ethics and politics.* John Doris (1982) has documented that social scientists have no special ability to distinguish between a scientifically based idea and an emotionally based idea when it comes to major social and political ideologies. Doris has forcibly demonstrated—in a review of the history of eugenics and of the institutionalization and the subsequent deinstitutionalization of the mentally retarded—that it is values, not science, that dictate (a) what we take to be socially relevant facts and (b) whether these "facts" can successfully guide social policy. Most social scientists are not trained to examine the interactions between knowledge, action alternatives and values, to communicate constructively and openly with politicians and the general public about the practical application of social science to social problems, or to select and design applications that solve social problems without creating new ones. Indeed, given the current epistemological "styles" in social science, many academic social scientists hold that such activities and the values they imply are antithetical to "real" or "rigorous" social science, and hence are to be eschewed.
6. *Dissemination and application of science.* At the other end of the taxonomic continuum is the question of how we present our results and what we do with them. Not surprisingly, we anticipated these issues at the beginning of the taxonomy: Specifically, do we acknowledge the range of theoretical and methodological approaches that we might have employed, and consider the implications of our choices? In the expression of scientific ideas, do we hide behind a mask of supposed objectivity or do we acknowledge our biases? For whom do we write and what is our aim in writing or in choosing another medium of communication? To come out of our ivory tower and

> write, speak or make films for the general public involves different models and aims than those dominant in present social science. Of particular interest here is the work of Kirsch (1982) who has examined the difficulties of "going public." How does the use of public media impact the career of the scientist? What new ground rules may pertain when one is presenting evidence to the general public for their practical use as opposed to presenting evidence to one's scientific peers for their critical evaluation? Should the scientist advocate or merely inform? What are our obligations to forewarn of misuses of ideas? What are our obligations to make our research useful and used? How do we fulfill these obligations?

In short, I am proposing that social scientists need to work out ground rules for getting along in the real world. I am also proposing that these ground rules be flexible and dialectical. They must embrace many systems of inquiry so that social science can work more creatively and be able to move in humanistic directions when that is the ethical and productive way to move. They must also embrace the ethics of working in multiple ethical systems, for the social scientist must operate in multiple roles. Each of these roles has its own ethical rules. For example, the social scientist must seek to be highly objective, while the social advocate may need to gerrymander information to make a point with the greatest possible political force. Somehow, rules must be forged for the merging of such conflicting roles.

REFERENCES

Argyris, C. Some unintended consequences of rigorous research. *Psychological Bulletin*, 1968, *70*, 185-97.

Churchman, C.W. *The systems approach and its enemies.* San Francisco: Jossey-Bass, 1979.

Doris, J. Social science and advocacy. *American Behavioral Scientist*, 1982, *26*, 199-234.

Kuhn, T. *The structure of scientific revolutions.* Chicago: University of Chicago Press, 1962.

Mitroff, I., and Kilmann, R. *Methodological approaches to social science.* San Francisco: Jossey Bass, 1978.

Saranson, S. *Psychology misdirected.* New York: Free Press, 1979.

Warwick, D.P. *The teaching of ethics in the social sciences.* Hastings-on-Hudson: Institute of Society, Ethics and the Life Sciences, 1980.

23. ETHICAL CONSIDERATIONS IN PROTECTING HUMAN SUBJECTS IN SOCIAL AND BEHAVIORAL RESEARCH

Eleanor S. Kohn

The overriding ethical issue facing researchers in using human subjects in behavioral and social research is one which is generic to the entire research field. How does a society best balance its need for increased knowledge against the moral imperative to protect the rights and human needs of those research subjects who are used in the advancement of science?

I will focus on some issues germane to this question which have major implications for all research using human subjects as well as on some problem areas unique to the social and behavioral field.

As a volunteer in a research advocacy role for many years, I have participated in countless acrimonious meetings in which human rights defenders have complained bitterly that various populations were suffering an abrogation of their rights in the name of scientific research. At the same meetings, researchers have contended that scientific inquiry is being hamstrung by regulations, red tape, and paperwork. Public comments to the National Commission for the Protection of Human Subjects in reference to the utilization of the mentally infirm as subjects, offer ample examples of the opposing views (U.S. Department of Health, Education and Welfare, 1978). There are ongoing efforts on the part of mediators of many stripes to bring these opposing views into some proximity. I believe that may not be in the best interests of the research world, the subjects, or the public at large. The tension which exists between scientists and civil libertarians may be the most positive mechanism we have to assure the maintenance of the balance I alluded to.

That relationship will be subject to additional strain in the near future for there are societal changes upon us which auger an increased possibility of subject misuse, if not abuse, and which warrant further discussion by any group concerned about ethical values in the scientific world.

Among those changes is our growing love affair with high technology. There is certainly evidence of increasing governmental commitment to a technology which is remote, if not divorced, from concern for the individual. That commitment has been described as a prerequisite for our continuation as a democratic society. But let us examine its implications for research from both an historical and future perspective. It is obvious that researchers are chafing under the burden of IRBs, informed consent procedures, and risk-benefit assessments. The system is onerous and costly to the researcher, the institution, and the public. However, we cannot easily brush aside the fact that the concept of protecting human subjects, for the most part, was a direct response to abuses by overzealous, dogged, and frequently well-intentioned scientists so intent on gathering knowledge that they were blind to the human cost of the search. Blatant examples of that irrational quest for knowledge are obvious in the Willowbrook hepatitis study, the Tuskegee syphilis project, and the ultimate example of science gone insane, the Nazi medical atrocities (Ramsey, 1970).

I recognize that it is an affront to raise these spectres before a group which has come together out of deep concern for a matter of ethical significance. I do so because I see around me the disturbing evidence which I referred to, of a society so caught up with technological advances that it has become increasingly deaf to human needs. We must be concerned about what that portends for human research. Our nation's research investment in destructive methodology dwarfs its research investment in easing human suffering and enhancing human potential. The Administration has proposed for 1984 a defense research budget of almost 30 billion dollars. The recommended research budget for HHS is 4.4 billion dollars (*Congressional Quarterly*, 1983). That single fact raises disturbing ethical questions about the priority which the protection of human rights and human dignity may come to have in a research world increasingly invested in improving methods of destruction.

Additionally, demographics point to projected increases in those populations traditionally most vulnerable to research abuse—the poor, the elderly, prisoners and the mentally disabled. The social climate is becoming noticeably hostile to these groups as evidenced by the heightened stridency from both the public and government in calling for decreased services, fewer benefits, harsher punishments and diminished rights for various of these groups.

At the same time, public expectations of science are growing and in order to satisfy those expectations, it may be convenient to justify a stretching of the protection limits in the name of the benefits it will bring to society as a whole and to these groups in particular. There is certainly an argument to be made against overprotection. Ratzan writes, "If we do no research on senile dementia for ethical reasons, we may be in danger of protecting our patients to the extent that while nothing bad may happen to them as a result of the experimentation, nothing good will happen either" (Ratzan, 1980). Statements such as this simply highlight the basic dilemma inherent in any discussion of ethical issues in research. There are obviously competing values to be considered, all of which can lay legitimate claim to being the primary or overriding justification for a particular decision. Thus far, despite valiant efforts from many directions, our society continues to struggle with an appropriate means of solving the dilemma. It becomes increasingly obvious that the factors which are the basis for deepest concern in any compendium of ethical issues in research with humans are not likely to appear on the agendas of an IRB meeting. Rather they are factors outside of the realm of scientific inquiry and unrelated to the advancement of knowledge. Because political rather than research needs may carry inordinate weight in future decision making, ethical considerations call for increased rather than diminished vigilance, in maintaining protective oversight. London contends that "...a decent society regulates all technology that is powerful enough to affect the general welfare, at once restricting the technicians as little as possible and as much as necessary" (London, 1974). It is the definition of those parameters which engenders meetings such as this.

Another source for concern which warrants attention is the apparent intent of the federal government to withdraw as rapidly and completely as it possibly can from responsibility for many kinds of oversight. Review of recent HHS regulations, readings of the *Federal Register*, and news reports of Congressional activity are replete with examples of this deregulation fever. On whom, then, will the ultimate responsibility fall for monitoring the protection of human subjects? The 1981 regulations on protecting human subjects were characterized in *The Hastings Center Report* as essentially cutting back on the oversight of social science research which, in the words of the regulations, "presents little or no harm" (Veatch, 1981). *The Hastings Center Report* goes on to suggest that this action puts more responsibility on individual researchers' moral integrity (President's Commission for the Study of Ethical Problems, no date). The question must then be asked— who will be the judge when the personal principles of the researchers are not shared by society or the subject?

Is there any way that public oversight can be expected to adequately monitor the protection of human subjects given the fact that there are multiple publics with shifting allegiances? If the public is to be the final arbiter, what of the possibility that small but vocal interests could successfully discourage research on important social problems simply because that group does not share the researcher's social and ethical framework?

Does the media have a role to play since it has frequently been the whistle blower in other arenas? I believe that public participation and the press can be important adjuncts to the regulatory process, but realistically they cannot provide an appropriate mechanism and the authority to carry it out.

If the federal government continues to opt for less rather than more responsibility, if researchers' vested interests sometimes collide with the provision of adequate subject protection, and if the public and press are not in a position to do the job, what other options exist? Can the responsibility be entrusted to the state legislatures or the courts? As for the states, few have the resources, expertise or power to question the adequacy of protection provided to research subjects. On the other hand, if the protection mechanism were to ultimately be answerable to the court system, it is not difficult to envision a scenario involving adversarial contests which are a costly and time consuming way of responding to the needs of science and its subjects.

And what of the research institutions with their already functioning IRBs? Can they be expected to assume the role of the final monitor? A recent report from the President's Commission found that "great diversity exists in the manner in which grantee institutions implement the regulations, that most funding agencies know little about institutional compliance with the regulations, and that few funding agencies have clear procedures for responding to reports that the regulations may have been violated or that human subjects may have been placed at risk. . ." (p. 54). The Commission goes on to recommend the establishment of an office at the federal level to coordinate and monitor government-wide implementation of the regulations. That is a recommendation which deserves serious attention. I believe it is a responsibility which ultimately and appropriately belongs at the federal level.

Support of the research enterprise, especially in the area of social and behavioral research, is dependent on public confidence in the integrity of such research. Maintenance of that confidence is, in turn, dependent on the public's perception of scientific research as a beneficial enterprise. We are beginning to see indications of an incipient public mistrust of the world of science—anti-nuclear demonstrations and the furor over genetic engineering, as examples, point to public uneasiness about the scientific mission. Finding ways of reinforcing public confidence in the moral values which motivate the scientific world should be an agenda item in any discussion of ethical considerations in the field. This question of values raises a variety of issues which relate to the integrity of social and behavioral research in particular. Identifying some of the questions is the easy part of the exercise. It is finding appropriate answers which promises to perplex the field for some time.

The first matter has to do with the use of deception and concealment in some research protocols. This is a thorny issue. Sissela Bok (1982) comments that the physician-patient relationship (and I can assume that she includes members of all the helping professions in that category) is predicated on trust, and anything that undermines that basic relationship damages care of the patient. It follows that deception in research, no matter how sensitively the debriefing is handled, destroys that trust.

Another writer suggests that if one rationalizes deception for the purposes of research, inevitably it can be rationalized for other purposes (Weiss, 1980). Unfortunately, the issues are not as morally clear as these writers suggest. To quote *The Hastings Center Report* on deception:

> We are faced with a moral dilemma. Since the search for knowledge is at least morally permissible (if not to a certain extent, morally obligatory), and since the use of deception is morally unacceptable (at least on a prima facie basis), in some situations, both moral desiderata cannot be satisfied. And it is not clear which moral value ought to be sacrificed for the sake of the other (Soble, 1978).

A second issue of ethical consideration in this social context regards research which presents subjects with severe conflicts and emotional stress, as exemplified by the Milgram study (Milgram, 1974). In much social research, measurement of minimal damage or harm is so elusive that one has to wonder how valid a protection criterion that can be and on whose judgment will the degree of damage and/or harm be evaluated.

Another question to be asked is what protection is and should be afforded subjects of research on organizations, institutions, and social classes? There appears to be considerable diversity in the way in which IRBs handle the question of informed consent in relation to a community and in the consideration that is given to the community's perceptions and objections. This is obviously an area in which value systems and public attitudes may collide with society's need for knowledge and the right of free inquiry. Basic to all these examples of troubled ethical considerations is the question once again of where the ultimate decision making authority should rest.

Finally, an additional non-scientific phenomenon raises another issue of ethical concern. If public funding of social and behavioral research continues to lag, it is highly probable that we shall see an increase of interest by academia in alternative sources of funding, such as the corporate business world.

A recent *New York Times* article reported on efforts by Harvard and Yale to adopt rules limiting the influence which commercial interests bring to bear on laboratory studies which they sponsor. Other universities are moving in the same direction (*New York Times*, 1983). Conflict of interest questions are also being raised about faculty involvement and investment in private industry. There is obvious ambivalence on the part of universities about the appropriate role of business in academic research.

My concern extends to the level of protection which subjects can expect should major research funding be derived from corporate grants. I believe the concern is warranted. Universities, lured by the prospect of corporate funding which will enable them to continue hard pressed research programs, may find themselves having to choose between enforcing strict IRB standards or acceding to a less stringent review should commercial interests demand such leniency.

It is disconcerting to learn that General Counsel has advised HHS that there is no clear statutory mandate in the National Research Act to support a requirement of IRB review of other than PHS funded research. The Department has asked its grantees for a "statement of principles governing the institution in the discharge of its responsibility for protecting the rights and welfare of the human subjects of research conducted at, or sponsored by, the institution regardless of the source of funding" (U.S. Department of Health and Human Services, 1981). If business will indeed become an important source of dollars in the near future, such a statement of principles will hardly suffice. The track records of some for-profit organizations in both influencing public policy and protecting individual rights have been something less than exemplary, measured by ethical standards. A *Hastings Center Report* on the federal government's role comments, "If researchers are shrewd enough to conduct research without HHS funds, their experiments will escape the body of regulation that has improved the moral and scientific climate of research involving human subjects" (Veatch, 1981).

In summary, examination of the ethical considerations involved in using human subjects must move beyond the confines of the research lab and the IRB meeting room. There are powerful and pervasive influences having little to do with scientific inquiry which may have major impact on the quality of protection offered. A realistic evalution of the weight of those influences must be included in any balanced consideration of this subject.

REFERENCES

Bok, S. *Secrets: On the ethics of concealment and revelation.* New York: Pantheon, 1982.

Congressional Quarterly Weekly Report. February 1983, *41*, No. 5.

London, P. Behavior technology and social control—Turning the tables. *APA Monitor*, April 1974, p. 2.

Milgram, S. *Obedience to authority.* New York: Harper & Row, 1974.

President's Commission for the Study of Ethical Problems in Medicine and Biomedical and Behavioral Research. *Summing up: Final report on studies on the ethical and legal problems in medicine and biomedical and behavioral research.* Washington, D.C. pp. 53–54.

Ramsey, P. *The patient as person.* New Haven: Yale University Press, 1970.

Ratzan, R.M. Being old makes you different: The ethics of research with elderly subjects. *Hastings Center Report*, 1980, *10*(5), 32–42.

Schools study ethics of business-aided research. *New York Times*, April 8, 1983. p. A20.

Soble, A. Deception in social science research. *Hastings Center Report*, 1978, *8*(10), 40–46.

U.S. Department of Health, Education and Welfare. Research involving those institutionalized as mentally infirm. Report and recommendations for public comment. *Federal Register*, March 17, 1978.

U.S. Department of Health and Human Services. Final regulations amending basic HHS policy for the protection of human research subjects. *Federal Register*, January 26, 1981. p. 8366.

Veatch, R.M. Protection of human subjects: The federal government steps back. *Hastings Center Report*, June 1981, 11(3), 9–12.

Weiss, R.J. The use and abuse of deception. *American Journal of Public Health*, 1980, 94(4), 219–22.

24. ANIMAL WELFARE ISSUES

Perrie M. Adams

Recent media coverage of the incident in Silver Spring, Maryland concerning the confiscation by animal welfare activists of a number of primates used in a research laboratory has served to raise the level of awareness of both the layman and the scientific community to the issue of animal use in research. The issues raised in the subsequent legal and congressional hearings included:

(1) the rights of animals as organisms capable of conscious awareness and suffering,
(2) the adequacy of care and laboratory management,
(3) the appropriateness of the research itself,
(4) alternative approaches to the use of live animals,
(5) the adequacy of the NIH review process relative to the use of animals in research,
(6) the role of animal care committees at research facilities.

These are only some of the issues raised in the numerous debates that have occurred in recent years on the use of animals in research. While the content of the debate is not particularly new with regard to the issue of whether animals should be used in research, there does appear to be an increased responsiveness by members of Congress, the NIH, scientific societies, and the general research community to the concerns raised by the animal welfare activists.

Historically, the concern for animals used in research in the United States stems from the antivivisection movement in Europe, an effort which is still very visible in Europe, particularly in Great Britain. In the United States the use of animals in research had become quite acceptable by American society by the early 1900s. Significant medical advances were accomplished during the first forty years of this century due, in large part, to the contributions of animal research.

By the beginning of World War II there were major research programs utilizing animals in this country and a significant investment was being made in animal care facilities. Post-World War II there was an increase in funding of research, much of which was with animals, and a growth in the development of laboratory animal science. Thus, not only was there an increase in the number of animals used in research, but an increase in the attention being paid to the management and care of laboratory animals as well.

Perhaps the single event in medicine that most impacted on the number of animals used in research was the thalidomide tragedy. Following the discovery of a high incidence of birth defects in association with gestational exposure to thalidomide, a major screening program was begun utilizing large numbers of animals across a variety of species to determine drug and chemical toxicity. In addition to the research on the toxic effects of drugs which utilized large numbers of animals, new federal regulations have required extensive animal testing using a variety of models to assess the toxicity, pharmacological action, and potential therapeutic benefit of drugs before testing the drug on humans.

Stimulated by the large numbers of animals used and the nature of the animal models frequently used in toxicity testing, the animal welfare activists groups have put more and more pressure on Congress and the scientific community to seek alternatives to the use of live animals. Particular attention has been focused on primate centers as evidenced by the Taub case in Maryland and the recent demonstrations at the regional primate centers. In addition, considerable pressure has been placed on reducing the use of dogs and cats in experiments and in medical school teaching.

There has also been considerable attention directed at the elimination of specific tests which they consider unnecessarily cruel to the animal (e.g., the Draize test used in the cosmetic industry and the LD50 test used in screening toxicity of drugs which by definition results in the death of at least half the animals used in the experiment). As a result of the debate over these issues, the cosmetic industry is funding a major effort to find alternative ways of assessing the toxicity of new products with the hope of replacing the Draize test as the major screening test. Whether the effort will be successful in eliminating such a screening test, while still meeting federal regulations for safety, remains to be seen.

It is important to point out that while the increase in the utilization of animals was occurring it did not proceed without concern by the scientific community for the care and appropriate use of animals in research. Evidence for this concern is perhaps best demonstrated by NIH. In 1963, under contract with NIH the Institute of Laboratory Animal Resources (ILAR) established the primary reference on the standards of animal care, the *Guide for Laboratory Animal Facilities and Care*. This publication has served as a model for many of the scientific societies in developing guidelines specific to their particular discipline. Within the past five years major organizations including the American

Psychological Association, American Physiological Society, the Neuroscience Society, and the Federated Societies have developed or updated their guidelines for the care and use of animals in research.

In addition to the effort by the scientific societies to define the proper conditions under which animals can be used in research, considerable attention to the issues has occurred in the form of symposia and conferences on the subject. A review of the contents of these meetings clearly demonstrates that there is a heightened awareness by the scientific community of the issues and that it is their responsibility to insure that progress in research also includes paying close attention to the care and welfare of the animals employed.

As pointed out at a recent conference, responsibility for protecting the welfare of the animal research subject (and the human as well) must be shared among the investigators, the institution(s), funding agencies, and editorial offices. While I concur with the necessity to share these responsibilities, I think there is one area where we as scientists must accept the major role. That is the education of our students as to what constitutes good laboratory practice. This education should include not only establishing good technique, appropriate design, and a logical interpretation of the results, but must also attend to the issues of appropriate species, consideration of care and health statutes, and relevance of the design to the scientific information being sought. Finally, we must educate others, both inside and outside the scientific community, to the relevance of animal research within our discipline. Perhaps in this age when molecular biology is making such tremendous strides it is more difficult to evaluate the accomplishments of psychological and more behaviorally-oriented research. It is important that the scientific community stand unified in its support of all animal research, not only of that which appears in vogue or to be the most applicable to today's needs.

At the present time there is considerable legislative activity on the subject of animal research. In 1982, Congressman Walgren introduced HR 6928, a bill designed to promote the development of nonanimal alternatives for research and to insure the humane care of animals used in research. A similar bill was introduced in the Senate (S 2948) by Senator Dole. Both of these bills included specific authorization to find alternative methods to the use of live animals to address research questions. Secondly, federal support of animal research would only be allowed in accredited research entities. The accreditation procedure would include assurances by the research entity that research involving animals will be reviewed and approved by an animal studies committee and that periodic inspections of animal facilities will be held by the committee and any evidence of unacceptable conditions will be reported in writing to the Department of Agriculture, the Federal agency responsible, and the applicable accrediting agency. A ten year grace period to achieve accreditation was included in the bills.

While both of these bills received considerable discussion in both houses of Congress, neither passed. It is anticipated that both will be introduced again in 1983 with some modification in the language, but with comparable recommendations for improving the welfare of animals used in research.

In addition, bills have been introduced into both houses which call for a study to assess current animal protection activities in federally funded biomedical and behavioral research facilities. The intent of these bills is to provide Congress with the necessary information upon which to develop new legislation. These bills appear to be a reasonable approach to establishing an accurate data base for future deliberations.

In summary, as noted by Dr. Thomas Malone in a recent address on the subject of animal welfare, we need to move toward replacement, reduction and refinement in the care and use of animals in research. I would add a fourth "R," that of reeducating the scientific and lay community that the principles of scientific inquiry include an awareness of the welfare of our research subjects. However, we should move cautiously in our development of new regulations, and of, perhaps, unwarranted restrictions on animal research for fear of reducing the benefits of such research to mankind.

PART 8
FEDERAL REGULATIONS

25. FLEXIBILITY FOR BEHAVIORAL AND SOCIAL SCIENCE RESEARCH IN REVISED HHS HUMAN SUBJECTS REGULATIONS

Michele W. Applegate

While any regulations carry some burden with them, I believe that the human subjects regulations of the Department of Health and Human Services (HHS, 1981) can facilitate behavioral and social science research. My discussion of this subject represents my personal views stemming from participation in the development of the Department's human subjects regulations over the past 10 years, as well as my experience in the Alcohol, Drug Abuse and Mental Health Administration (ADAMHA) which funds a great deal of behavioral and social science research.

The Nuremberg Code and subsequent ethical codes underline the responsibility of the individual investigator for ensuring that human subjects are treated with dignity and respect for their rights and welfare. In funding human subjects research, the federal government also is held accountable for ensuring that high ethical standards are observed in the research it supports.

It is important to note that federal regulations in the human subjects area have not been issued merely in response to a handful of offensive incidents in the treatment of subjects. Other factors have included increasing public demands, articulated through Congress, special interest groups, and the press, for protection of individual rights, and for accountability for how public funds are spent.

Another historical point to note is that behavioral and social research have been covered under Public Health Service policies on human subjects since the mid-1960s. While these policies were designed, until recently, primarily with biomedical research in mind, it is my perception that the Alcohol, Drug Abuse and Mental Health Administration and our colleagues in the National Institutes of Health have been able to apply these policies and regulations to health-related behavioral and social science research with little difficulty or hindrance to research. Also, over the last decade, I have noticed a significant change in the sensitivity and sophistication of investigators in these fields in addressing human subjects protections, including informed consent, privacy and confidentiality.

References in various ethical codes, as well as in human subjects regulations, to "protection of the rights and welfare of subjects" illustrate the obligation not only to protect against harm but also to safeguard subjects' rights. The most fundamental right that must be protected in research is the right to consent—that is, the right of an individual to decide, on the basis of adequate information, whether to participate in a research project. This concept is similar to the concept of "respect for persons" which the National Commission for the Protection of Human Subjects of Biomedical and Behavioral Research identified as one key ethical principle which should underlie federal regulations dealing with human subjects (HEW, 1979). This right is not inherently limited, nor should it be in my view, by the particular scientific discipline of an investigator. Nor should it be limited by the methodology of a study, e.g., whether it involves administration of an experimental drug or a survey seeking information about an individual's behavior.

While investigators have a general moral, if not legal, obligation for obtaining informed consent in all types of research, there are legitimate public policy concerns (such as workload burden and the need to avoid undue stumbling blocks for research) which have been considered in developing human subjects regulations. As a result of these considerations, the 1981 revision of the Basic Human Subjects Regulations of the Department of Health and Human Services (HHS) contained provisions aimed at facilitating certain types of research, including some kinds of behavioral and social research.

One such provision, 45 CFR Part 46.101(b), is for exemption of five categories of research, which are all at least in some measure behavioral or social science, from coverage under the regulations. Certainly such exemptions can reduce paperwork and expedite the process of preparing research proposals in various behavioral and social science areas.

To date, however, not many exemptions have been claimed in applications submitted to ADAMHA. This is in part due to the nature of research applications submitted to our agency, most of which clearly fall under the regulations. Nonetheless, in areas where exemptions might be claimed, so far they usually have not been. This may be due to the relatively short time institutions have had to implement these provisions, and the lack of a place on the application form, until recently, to claim an exemption. It might also be due to institutions deciding on their own that they want to continue to review all or most of this type of research.

Even where a legitimate claim might be made for exemption, this does not mean that there are no risks or special protection issues which must be addressed. For example, an interview study assessing reactions of rape victims might be exempt because no identifying information is being recorded. However, clearly one would have concerns about ensuring that the interview would not increase the already great trauma experienced by such persons and that subjects would not feel coerced to participate. Similarly, while a study of illegal drug use might involve an interview where no identifying information is recorded, there would be a need to ensure that subjects are approached and their responses provided in a confidential setting.

Given such situations, it is important to acknowledge the responsibilities of various parties in regard to exempt research. Clearly, investigators have a responsibility for treating subjects in accordance with the ethical standards of their profession. Institutions also have an interest in the ethical behavior of their faculty or staff. Accordingly, they may decide, although not required by regulation, to adopt ethical principles for all human subjects research at their institutions or to require some reporting process for exempt research. The federal government, on its part, also must ensure that there are adequate plans to protect subjects' rights and welfare in all projects for which it provides funding.

A second provision of the HHS regulations (Section 46.110), which should facilitate some behavioral and social science research, is expedited review. Two types of behavioral and social science research for which such review is permitted are minimal risk research involving studies of (1) "...existing data, documents and records...," and (2) "...individual or group behavior or characteristics of individuals... where the investigator does not manipulate the subjects' behavior and the research will not involve stress to subjects." While I have no direct information, I would expect that expedited review is helping to reduce the work load and increase efficiency of review for both investigators and IRBs.

A third set of changes in the Department's regulations which might facilitate some behavioral and social research provides for flexibility in the consent process. One change is a provision under which an IRB can alter or waive some or all elements of consent under certain conditions (Section 46.116 (d)). In addition, the IRB can waive the requirement for documentation of consent in certain specified circumstances (Section 46.117(c)).

While I believe that the IRB should start from the principle that regulatory requirements for consent are appropriate, there are legitimate circumstances where alterations or waivers might be justified. In considering such action, the IRB should weigh, among other things, the nature and degree of risk to subjects, potential significance of the knowledge to be gained, whether the research could reasonably be carried out otherwise, special issues of vulnerability for certain population groups, and the adequacy of protections for subjects' welfare.

In regard to the overall regulatory process for human subjects research,

I would add the observation that procedures which seem to hinder research may actually facilitate them. For example, an IRB or a federal agency may require certain procedures for protecting confidentiality, and the explanation of such procedures to potential subjects might convince subjects to participate or encourage agencies to cooperate. Also, while the process of IRB review may be time-consuming, a considerable burden in carrying out a proposed research project might be avoided by having the IRB approve a procedure (such as waiver of consent documentation) which ordinarily an investigator might be concerned about doing on her or his own.

In sum, the 1981 revised HHS regulations on the protection of human subjects contain provisions which should facilitate behavioral and social research by providing various exemptions and waivers where appropriate, while upholding the general principle that research subjects are entitled to protection of their rights and welfare in federally funded research.

The opinions expressed in this paper are those of the author and do not necessarily represent the views of the Alcohol, Drug Abuse and Mental Health Administration.

REFERENCES

U.S. Department of Health, Education and Welfare. *Belmont report:* "Ethical principles and guidelines for the protection of human subjects of research." The National Commission for Protection of Human Subjects of Biomedical and Behavioral Research. *OPPR Reports*, p. 3, section B, April 18, 1979.

U.S. Department of Health and Human Services. Protection of Human Research Subjects, 45 CFR Part 46. *Federal Register, 46*, No. 59, p. 19195, March 27, 1981.

26. FLEXIBLE REGULATION: A BOON TO SCIENTIFIC FREEDOM AND RESPONSIBILITY

Joel Cooper

Any form of regulation brings with it the fear that that which is being regulated will become diminished, changed or eliminated in the process. When the Health and Human Services guidelines for the protection of human subjects were first promulgated, they struck many behavioral researchers like a thunderbolt. Was the government going to tell researchers what to do, how to conduct their inquiries and how to handle their data, even to the point of indicating how to lock their data files?

The issue is more complex than the old adage, "He who pays the piper calls the tune." When we, as a research community, accepted the idea that the government would pay the bills for a vast array of research, we accepted a principle that indicates that the public has a vital interest in research. Having a vital interest in research does not mean that the government should tell researchers how to conduct scientific inquiry. To the contrary, it means that the public invests in the scientific community its faith that the persistent dedication to scientific inquiry will ultimately be in the public interest. Through its funding, the public puts its faith in the idea that the cumulative compiling and integration of research findings will lead to greater understanding of behavior, of medicine and of technology. This, in turn, may pay off as a discovery of a new vaccine, a new form of psychotherapy or a new way to help astronauts gain their perceptual balance in space. Alternatively, the research may lead us to the discovery of "truth" which the public tells us is an enterprise also worthy of support.

The rub is that the public also needs to protect other basic human values. The goals of research need to be consistent with those values if they are to enjoy the public's support. If research were ever to interfere with basic human values, then the public has an obligation to attempt to protect those values. My point is that regulations need not be perceived as an attempt by a governmental agency to tell researchers how to limit their endeavors. Rather, establishing the principle of regulation only implies that the public's historic support for the freedom of scientific inquiry has to be tempered by the public's more historic concern with basic human protections.

There is nothing new here for the research scientist. Indeed, the research community has never seen its freedom as unlimited. Individual researchers as diverse as Sigmund Freud and Werner von Braun have worried about the ethical implications of their investigations and have limited their own activities to be consistent with their views of individual and societal liberties. Professional research societies have been still more clear in their enumeration of facilitating research while protecting the human beings who donate their time to the research endeavor. Indeed, my own discipline of psychology had an elaborately delineated set of ethical principles for the protection of human subjects even before the HHS guidelines.

Why, then, were researchers thunderstruck at the notion of governmental regulations and why did they fear that these regulations would hinder the research effort? I believe that the answer lies only minimally in philosophical disagreements over the proper role of government, and more in the pragmatic question of the imminent consequences that might accrue to the research that was not in accordance with the guidelines. This can be seen most particularly from the national attention that was focused a few years ago on one of the branches of the State University of New York. Through a series of unforeseen events, it came to light that a particular research project (one that was not funded by government money) had not been reviewed by an IRB. Both state and federal agencies expressed their dismay and threatened sanctions. Sanctions were, in fact, imposed by the State of New York and the resulting turmoil brought the question of governmental regulations to the forefront in the attention of the research community.

This perspective on governmental influence on research is a prelude to answering the question with which we are faced: Do the regulations hinder research in the behavioral sciences? Have we been deflected, through our government regulations, from our mission as researchers? Have the rules and regulations with which we must live caused us to limit or alter the research activities that we would have liked to follow?

It is fashionable for researchers to object to governmental regulations and to decry their adverse impact on research. I would like to take the theoretical position that the answer to the questions we are dealing with is "No"—that the governmental regulations have not caused us to alter our tasks as researchers. First, the argument that governmental regulations are an infringement on academic freedom and thus detrimental to research is not compelling. The premise of this argument, that it is the right of investigators to pursue their interests independent of any other considerations, is a caricature of the principle of academic freedom—a caricature to which almost no one subscribes. My previous remarks were intended to indicate that our research community has always recognized the very real rights of people who are affected by our research and has recognized the need to find ways of welding academic freedom with the protection of individual liberties.

My second point is more pragmatic than it is philosophical. I see the guidelines laid down in the most recent set of regulations as flexible enough to allow research to proceed. I view regulations as encouraging investigators to think of the major responsibilities they have toward research participants: Are they being informed of what they are getting involved in when they volunteer for research? Are there risks involved that the participants should be informed of? Are individuals being coerced into participation by their institution or, more insidiously, by payments and rewards that their economic situation may make difficult for them to refuse? Are their responses being kept confidential as they have reason to trust they will be? When questions such as these are considered, research is almost always improved. As an investigator, I have never found myself in the predicament of not being able to test a research question because of the human subjects regulations. And I am one of those social psychologists whose methodology often requires us to withhold some information from our participants. I have found that the guidelines help me to design studies that meet my objectives in a way that gives a bit more attention to my subjects than I might have done in the absence of the regulations.

The real value of the human subjects regulations is that I not only have to convince myself that I have protected the welfare of my participants and that my research is worth the risks I might be generating, but I also have to convince a panel of my peers.

It is this feature of the regulation and review process that enables me to respond more fully and pragmatically to the question with which we began. If the human subjects review process is not a hindrance, is it possible that it is a help? I have found the answer to this question to be affirmative. It is often the case that we have to ask people to volunteer to be in our research. Sometimes, we must ask parents to consent to bringing their children to our laboratories. Can they trust us when we say that they will not be at risk in our studies? Can they rid themselves of the stereotyped image of Boris Karloff in his basement laboratory conducting experiments as Dr. Frankenstein? The peer review process that goes hand in hand with the HHS regulations assures the public that our research has met the criteria for the protection of human subjects as assessed by other scientists and community representatives. The public, then, can be assured that it is not merely the researcher's own view that a participant will not be hurt but rather is the view of a broad-based human subjects panel.

Researchers at my institution have also found the existence of the regulations to be a boon in convincing schools, hospitals, and other institutions to cooperate with behavioral research projects. How can a school system, for example, convince its potentially worried parents that a project on the impact of television viewing is sufficiently safe and worthy to be conducted during school time? Having the reassurance that the project was proposed to an interdisciplinary IRB and that the IRB found it to comply with basic rules for the protection of the children is a definite advantage for obtaining the cooperation of the school system. It is not that IRBs absolve school systems, institutions or individuals from making their own assessment as to the worthiness of the research and the safeguards provided in a particular project. However, I think it is clear that merely having the added protection of an institutional peer review is a safeguard that facilitates cooperation with research.

We have all gone through a stormy period with regard to governmental regulations. As was pointed out earlier, any imposition of regulation arouses suspicion and hostility because it signals a potential limitation of the research community's academic and personal freedoms. But flexible regulations, when applied with reason by the peers who serve on IRBs, place in juxtaposition the many overlapping rights and responsibilities that we share as citizens and researchers. The result of governmental regulations on institutions and citizens is not always a happy one. But in the case of human subjects regulations, the marriage of governmental concern and research response has been productive.

27. GOVERNMENT REGULATIONS: DO THEY FACILITATE OR HINDER SOCIAL AND BEHAVIORAL RESEARCH?

Richard T. Louttit

Under the leadership of the Office for Protection from Research Risks, federal regulations for the protection of human subjects have evolved since 1966. The purpose of such regulations has been to assure fair and ethical treatment of the persons who provide the data to advance behavioral and medical knowledge.

The establishment of Institutional Review Boards (IRBs) allowed issues to be addressed and resolved in a local context, where concrete problems and differences of opinion could be resolved directly between IRBs and investigators.

This was a good idea and, in general, has worked well. However, in some institutions problems arose regarding the interpretation and implementation of the then existing regulations, especially regulations governing research in the behavioral and social sciences. In institutions where, for example, the university IRB was in the medical school, little or no behavioral or social science expertise existed on the IRB. As a result, instances arose in which behavioral science projects were rejected or a confrontation resulted between the IRB and a principal investigator because the medical members of the board didn't think the research important or worthy of even minimal risk or inconvenience to subjects. In one study (Seiler and Murtha, 1979) 25% of IRB chairpersons surveyed reported that their board had banned at least one survey study. Some IRBs went to extremes which were not required by the regulations and were never expected by the authors of the regulations. The following memorandum was circulated by the IRB chairman of a major research university in April 1976:

> All studies funded or not funded must be reviewed with or without risk, whether or not risk is involved. Every experiment involving human subjects (including questionnaires, surveys, unobtrusive observations and experiments, and the use of public information) must be reviewed.

It is this level of detailed nonsense which led to much consternation in the social science community, and to the revisions implemented in July 1981 under which universities now operate.

At the National Science Foundation, we do not support "clinical" research, that is research focused on diseases. Therefore, most of our involvement with the human subjects regulations is with behavioral and social research. Since 1978, the NSF has accepted the HHS human subjects regulations and has worked closely with the Office for Protection from Research Risks. In 1980, the NSF was represented in the working group which developed the current regulations.

The rewriting of the regulations took many meetings and discussions. The receipt by OPRR of over 400 comments on draft regulations published in the *Federal Register* caused controversy within the Committee. The concerns of the late 70s raised by the social science community were most forcefully stated by Ithiel de Sola Pool (1980). These were all taken into account and resolved. I believe that the current regulations, if read correctly, do *not* hinder research in the behavioral and social sciences. Nevertheless, I expect they only facilitate research in an abstract sense—by assuring that seriously-damaging research, which would be harmful to the image and reputation of the field is not conducted, at least not with taxpayer support.

Much research of minimal risk was exempted from IRB review in order to reduce the IRB workload so that research involving ethical questions could get more than cursory review. But some institutions have decided that the IRB, or its chairperson, must *review* proposals to decide if they are exempt from review. If this seems contradictory, it is. And this was not envisioned by the staff group which worked out the exemptions. Proposals to HHS or to NSF are signed by the principal investigator and a designated institutional official. If they state that the research proposed is exempt under these regulations, that should be enough at the university level. If NIH or NSF staff disagree, we can always call up and request an IRB review. The responsibility of NIH and NSF staff for assuring that research we support is conducted with appropriate ethical considerations was never meant to be abrogated by the assignment of human subjects review responsibilities to IRBs.

A few areas of behavioral and social research remain subject to the regulations and to IRB review. These include clinical psychological research, especially if it involves vulnerable populations—including the mentally ill and the mentally retarded. Areas not exempt are those survey, interview or observational projects which deal with especially sensitive or illegal aspects of behavior, where the individual subjects can be identified, and research involving deception of the subjects in order to accomplish the research purposes.

As a result of the revised regulations, with minor exceptions, basic research in the following fields is exempt from IRB review: anthropology, economics, education, linguistics, political science, sociology, and much of psychology.

These regulations should not hinder social research.

REFERENCES

Pool, I.S. The new censorship of social research. *The Public Interest,* Spring 1980, 57-66.

Seiler, L.H., and Murtha, J.M. *Freedom at Issue*, November/December 1979.

28. RESEARCH WITH VULNERABLE POPULATIONS: ETHICAL CONSIDERATIONS AND FEDERAL REGULATIONS

Natalie Reatig

The only reference to "vulnerable" populations in the body of the DHHS regulations is found at 46.111 (b) describing research subjects "who are likely to be vulnerable to coercion or undue influence, such as persons with acute or severe physical or mental illness, or persons who are economically or educationally disadvantaged." IRBs are asked to ensure that "appropriate additional safeguards have been included in the study to protect the rights and welfare of these subjects."

The preamble to the January 26, 1981 *Federal Register* promulgation of the regulations includes some additional advisory statements (at page 8378): "HHS believes that the proposed involvement of hospitalized patients, other institutionalized persons, or disproportionate numbers of racial or ethnic minorities or persons of low socioeconomic status should be justified." And..."(A)s the vulnerability of patients increases, it becomes more important to evaluate risks of harm and possible benefits and to require a reasonable relationship between them. Therefore...in risk assessment, the IRB should look at the context in which the research is conducted. Someone known to be under physical or emotional duress may be subject to greater risk, as a participant, than someone who is not under duress."

The Belmont Report speaks about "persons with diminished autonomy" and their entitlement to protection. It defines an autonomous person as "one who is (both) capable of deliberating about personal goals and of acting under the direction of such deliberation."

Vulnerable subjects are those who are diminished, to varying degrees, in their capacity for self-determination. They can be identified as belonging to one or more of the following groups:

A) Those whose actions are restricted by their socio-legal status—children, the adjudicated mentally incompetent, prisoners, lawbreakers, persons engaging in criminal or other types of socially uncondoned activities, victims of discrimination, or those forced into a state of dependency by economic circumstances;

B) Those who are restricted in their physical freedom of movement—persons with serious illness, injury, or physical handicaps; prisoners and others detained involuntarily;

C) Those who are limited by some form of cognitive impairment or "estrangement"—those whose ability to think is interfered with by pain, illness, brain injury or immaturity, and also those whose language, perceptions, or cultural values differ to the extent that their understanding may be questionable.

What should the IRB look for when reviewing research involving vulnerable populations? First of all, when applicable, attention must be paid to the special sections of the regulations dealing with pregnant women and fetuses, prisoners and children. (45 CFR 46 Subparts B, C, and D.)

The following items should be scrutinized for all vulnerable populations.

1) Selection Criteria: Determine that the population has not been selected for their easy availability or manipulability. The research generally should be related to the subjects' special status or condition although it need not necessarily be 'therapeutic' in its intent. Specific diagnostic, symptomatic, or demographic inclusion criteria should be described to enable IRB assurance that the subjects are appropriate for the study. Risks should be reasonable in relation to the potential benefits and knowledge to be gained; safeguards should be developed to accommodate any special needs characteristic of the population. Appropriate medical and psychological screening should be included to prevent or reduce the chances of adverse reactions. Subjects should be selected equitably. One group should not continually be offered opportunities to participate in research involving procedures or therapies from which they may derive benefits to the unfair exclusion of other equally suitable groups. Nor should one group continually be exposed to the risks and discomforts of research participation when other, equally suitable groups of subjects exist.

2) Voluntariness: Determine that consent is negotiated in an environment and by persons not intimidating. To ensure absence of coercion or undue inducement IRBs should scrutinize not only the words of the consent form but also the process and setting of the consent negotiation. Vulnerable persons may be physically, financially or emotionally dependent on their care providers and thus constrained in their ability to resist requests for their "cooperation." Persons who are totally

dependent on an institution may submit to perceived or actual pressures to conform with institutional requests out of fear of being denied services or privileges. If the quality of medical care, staff attention, or living conditions are poor, an invitation to move onto a special unit or research ward may be irresistably appealing. Nevertheless, no prior assumptions should be made as to the effect on an individual of an institutional setting; people do not automatically become incapable of voluntary consent the moment they enter an institution.

3) Comprehension: Determine that the language of the consent form and the verbal explanation is comprehensible to the subject population, that there is adequate and appropriate information and that the timing, setting and presentation provide subjects sufficient opportunity to ask questions and thoughtfully consider their decision. IRBs should assure that investigators have included an appropriate method for identifying potential subjects whose competency is uncertain and a reasonable procedure for determining when and whether such subjects are not competent to consent for themselves. When subjects are not competent or when rationality fluctuates, IRBs should ensure that a plan is developed for involving other participants; the plan should state who the person(s) might be and what role they would be expected to play (e.g., legally authorized proxy consentors, supportive consultants, auditor/witnesses, consent monitors, etc.)

IRBs should encourage investigators to develop consent procedures that will enhance the possibilities for subjects to consent for themselves. The DHHS regulations allow waivers or alterations of required consent elements in minimal risk research "if the purpose is to ensure that. . . subjects receive information they can reasonably be expected to understand in order to make a knowledgeable decision regarding their participation in the research. . . " Procedures and criteria for determining valid consent may vary in accordance with the degree of risk or discomfort attendant on the research procedure.

With respect to persons of "uncertain competence," e.g., persons with chronic or acute mental disabilities, victims of accidents, persons being treated with drugs which impair mental functioning, aged persons with diminished capacity, or persons of limited intelligence, HHS recognizes that "individuals possess varying degrees of capacity to understand, and that a particular individual's capacity can vary from time to time. Allowance for alteration or waiver of the elements of informed consent in research involving minimal risk (46.116.d.) can serve as a justification for tailoring the amount and complexity of information to be provided in the consent process where potential subjects are likely to have somewhat impaired or limited capacity to understand." (See *Federal Register*, January 26, 1981. Preamble, page 8383.)

The option to tailor the content and presentation of information is intended to expand the opportunities for vulnerable persons to make their own decisions and to enhance their autonomy by avoiding, whenever possible, the necessity for adversarial or judicial proceedings to obtain third party consent for minimal risk research.

PART 9
FOSTERING INTEGRITY IN RESEARCH

29. FOSTERING INTEGRITY IN RESEARCH: A COLLECTIVE RESPONSIBILITY

Thomas E. Malone

I am pleased to have the opportunity to discuss the topic of fostering integrity in research. Lest I be accused of plagiarism, let me say at the outset that my remarks today are essentially a reiteration and updating of a similar talk given by Dr. Edward N. Brandt, Assistant Secretary of Health, at an educational seminar such as this one, held last Fall in Atlanta.

It is particularly appropriate that we address the subject of integrity in research today. It follows a very fruitful discussion of issues arising from the shared responsibility of awardee institutions, investigators, and funding agencies for protecting human subjects. This is only one of the important ways in which the private and public sectors collaborate to improve our understanding of health and disease for the ultimate benefit of all people. What began as primarily a fiscal partnership has evolved into a complex network in which all participants—funding agencies, institutional officials, and individual investigators—share responsibility for the continued well-being and productivity of the entire enterprise. The success of that endeavor, in turn, accounts for the extraordinary support enjoyed by biomedical and behavioral research in this country.

This seminar, focusing on protection of human subjects of social and behavioral research, exemplifies the finest elements of the partnership. The policies and implementing regulations you have been discussing reflect substantial consensus about a key element in the governance of science. Responsibility for ensuring compliance with those requirements is vested first and foremost in the awardee institutions with the guidance of our Office for Protection from Research Risks. Individual investigators—both in the institutions and in PHS intramural programs—are in turn responsible for becoming informed about requirements for human subjects protection and observing both the letter and the spirit of the regulations.

If one examines the history of these regulations, it is clear that they reflect well-founded concerns about the rights and the welfare of those who voluntarily participate in research projects. Their development, modification, and acceptance offer positive evidence that the research community can balance the demands of scientific inquiry with the expectations of society as a whole. Let me now discuss some related issues of accountability that present similar challenges to scientists and their supporters.

We have heard a great deal in the past five years about misconduct in research programs funded by the Public Health Service. We are only too familiar with recent examples of falsification, fabrication, intentional misrepresentation or mishandling of data. We have seen instances of misuse of research funds and failure to comply with the terms and conditions of awards—including requirements for protection of human subjects and animal welfare.

A recent NIH review showed that 45 cases of alleged or suspected misconduct came to our attention between October 1, 1980 and September 30, 1982. Fewer than half of these proved to be factual, and some could be attributed to correctible deficiencies within the awardee institution.

Viewed against a denominator of more than 20,000 NIH awards, these numbers are small, almost insignificant. Viewed in the context of the ethics of science, the public's faith in research, and the unknown dimensions of possible unreported incidents, they are profoundly disquieting. These incidents have given rise to well-founded concerns about the efficacy of traditional practices often cited as safeguards against misconduct. Those practices, which include peer review of research proposed for funding or publication and replication of significant findings, are based on the assumption that individual investigators, while perhaps erring in methodology and theory, are honest and well-intentioned. They are not designed to detect clever, systematic cheating.

The realization that traditional safeguards of science cannot entirely prevent misconduct has been accompanied by increasing evidence that awardee institutions and funding agencies are often ill-prepared to deal with allegations or evidence of wrongdoing. We have, of course, always had audit and investigative units to pursue cases involving misuse of funds or criminal activities. More recently the Office for Prevention from Research Risks (OPRR) has played an important role in detecting and dealing with failure to comply with human subjects and animal welfare requirements.

Until recently, we have been able to treat such incidents as isolated events, employing *ad hoc* procedures for each case. In the past few years, it has become apparent that more explicit and predictable procedures are needed to enable the funding agencies to deal with the increased number of cases of alleged or actual misconduct. It is clear in retrospect that the lack of policies and procedures resulted in a number of false starts and inordinate delays. As research administrators, we were ill-equipped to deal with the conflicting demands of accountability and fiscal stewardship on the one hand, and due process and protection of individual privacy on the other. We have benefited greatly from the public and Congressional debate engendered by some recent cases, but continue to find these conflicting considerations to be among the more troublesome issues we face.

Let me summarize some of the actions undertaken by the Public Health Service (PHS). In the Fall of 1981, Secretary Schweiker identified as a major management priority the development of improved policies and procedures for dealing with misconduct in science. Major research agency initiatives included the following:

- Conducting regional seminars such as this one for investigators, academic officials, and institutional review board members regarding protection of human subjects and related regulations and policies.
- Discussing with members of NIH advisory councils and peer review groups their responsibilities related to misconduct in science.
- Improving internal NIH procedures for identifying incoming grant applications and contract proposals from individuals or institutions under investigation or subject to post-investigational sanctions.
- Modifying the coding and processing of competing grant applications to ensure that all requirements for protection of human subjects are met.
- Developing a uniform procedure for documenting the results of agency staff review of annual progress reports.

NIH also undertook an intensive review of its policies and procedures to identify the need for improved guidance to agency staff and awardee investigators and institutions. In August 1982, Dr. Brandt directed NIH to take the lead in developing policies and procedures for all PHS research programs, and to include in that effort mechanisms for communication and collaboration among the PHS agencies when appropriate. An interagency committee has undertaken the development of the following documents:

1. *General Policies and Principles*—a brief statement of policy, intended to underscore the commitment to integrity in all research funded, conducted, or regulated by the PHS.
2. *Policies and Procedures for Awarding Agencies*—a step-by-step guide for agency staff covering the "life cycle" of an incident. It outlines procedures for evaluating the significance of allegations, conducting an investigation, taking interim administrative actions when appropriate, and imposing post-investigational sanctions when warranted. It emphasizes the need to protect the rights of accused individuals and "whistleblowers" and to provide an adequate public record of

the agencies' actions without violating the privacy of individuals. An important section of this document is a statement of expectations for awardee institutions that underscores the institutions' responsibility to take prompt and appropriate action when misconduct is known or suspected and to inform the funding agency when the matter is judged to be serious enough to warrant an investigation.

3. *Policies and Procedures for Intramural Research Programs*—guidance for agency research managers who may confront allegations or evidence of misconduct in an agency's in-house research program. It embodies many of the same principles enumerated in the extramural document, adapted to take into account the employer-employee relationship. We view it as the PHS internal counterpart of procedures now in place or being developed at many research institutions.
4. *Policies and Procedures for Regulatory Agencies*—a compendium of regulatory procedures, primarily those of FDA. It differs from the preceding two documents in that it is primarily a distillation and summary of well-established procedures used by the agencies to ensure the integrity of regulated research, with special attention to the interface of regulated research and funded research (both extramural and intramural).
5. *Interagency Collaboration and Communication*—establishes mechanisms for ongoing consultation on matters of policy and for collaboration on specific investigations of concern to more than one PHS agency.

The biomedical research community has been quick to recognize that new federal policies, while necessary, are not sufficient to deal with the problem of misconduct in science. Both the Association of American Medical Colleges (AAMC) and the Association of American Universities (AAU) have developed statements of principles and model procedures for the guidance of their member institutions. Several institutions have developed their own guidelines, or are in the process of doing so.

The institutions' efforts are particularly noteworthy because they represent more than a simple elaboration of existing internal procedures for investigating and adjudicating alleged misconduct. At a more fundamental level, many institutions seem to be concerned about whether the mores of academic science may be contributing to the problem, as has often been asserted. In that vein, some are urging less emphasis on quantity of publications and more attention to the quality of research. Although the institutions have not achieved consensus on when or how the funding agency should be notified of a matter under investigation, they clearly recognize their obligations as recipients of public funds.

The scientific journals have similarly begun to consider whether changes in editorial policies may be needed. Some journals, for instance, do not publish retractions or do so only when authors request it. Perhaps this policy needs to be modified in order to deal with documented but unacknowledged misconduct on the part of one of the authors of a manuscript.

Individual investigators also need to re-assess their own behavior, and many are doing so. Some have learned—the hard way—that their position as co-author or project director carries with it responsibility for the veracity of the final results. No one has any desire to police the laboratory or otherwise stifle the open atmosphere necessary to creative scientific research, but it seems clear that more caution and rigor in collaborative efforts may be warranted.

I am particularly pleased at the way in which individual scientists have contributed to our efforts to deal with the problem of misconduct. Members of NIH peer review groups and National Advisory Councils have offered helpful insights, cautions, and suggestions. Especially gratifying has been the response of those who have been asked to lend their expertise to agency investigations. Despite the arduous and often unpleasant nature of this task, we have been fortunate to obtain the assistance of some of the most eminent scientists in the country, who clearly recognize and accept the community's collective responsibility for the well-being of the research enterprise.

We are pleased with the progress being made in the development of improved policies and procedures for the PHS. I am confident that research institutions will continue to develop and refine their procedures as well. More than likely, we will continue to learn of new incidents of misconduct in science. I believe, however, that this unfortunate trend soon will change direction as all partners in the research enterprise learn to deal with real or apparent misconduct in a prompt and equitable manner. Thus, I would urge greater attention to preventing misconduct through educational efforts, a re-examination of our values regarding what constitutes appropriate scientific endeavor, and commitment to dealing firmly with documented instances of misconduct. Our ability to follow through on these commitments is critical if science is to enjoy the continued support of the American people and thereby give society the full measure of benefit in return.

30. THE RISKS OF GOVERNMENT ACTION AND UNIVERSITY INACTION

Joel Cooper

Addressing the problem of academic fraud at a conference of researchers and government officials is entirely appropriate. No one would deny that we need to worry about academic fraud; no one would deny that we need to sharpen our procedures for dealing with the problem. In examining Dr. Malone's address, I would like to take the role of the skeptical critic, looking for problems that may be hidden not too deeply below the surface. Until now, we have had a sometimes stormy but generally successful marriage between the research community and the federal government. A careful examination of Dr. Malone's remarks suggests that there may be trouble on the horizon.

In his address, Dr. Malone talks about the "governance of science." Who "governs" science? Science, by its very nature, needs no governance. Science is a process, a method of inquiry. Science needs funds, and the use of those funds should be watched. Science needs cooperation from human participants, and we know well that we must protect their well-being. Science may also need to protect itself from imposters who engage in the antithesis of science—academic fraud. But the process of science needs no governance.

Dr. Malone's remarks link the governance of science to the control of funds. This strikes me as a dangerous link. The control of funds has placed agencies such as FDA in an investigative relationship with university communities. Inspectors and auditors are among the cast of characters in the relationship. When we link the conduct of scientific inquiry to the way in which certain agencies exercise fiscal control, then we open the door to the possibility that scientific inquiry will be overseen in the same way. In this context, the phrase "governance of science" takes on ominous implications.

As a partial response to the appearance of academic fraud, the Public Health Service has established an interagency committee which is drafting guidelines to cover the life cycle of an alleged incident. The description that Dr. Malone provides concerning the main thrust of these guidelines provides some further areas of concern. The guide is to discuss: conducting investigations, invoking interim administrative actions, post-administrative sanctions and the creation of a public record.

It is conceivable that what is being referred to is a govenmental investigative system with the power to invoke sanctions both concurrent with and subsequent to an investigation. Dr. Malone raises appropriate concerns about the public nature of the investigation. How will the "whistle blower" be protected? How will an accused but exonerated researcher be protected? It is not clear how this task can be accomplished in the context of a governmental investigation with public documentation.

The interagency committee is also charged with establishing expectations for awardee institutions concerning integrity and the stewardship of public funds. Few can really doubt the government's right to link regulations about integrity with the acceptance by institutions of public funds. But its wisdom can be doubted. The notion that "expectations" or "regulations" promulgated by the Public Health Service belongs in research institutions because of the government's obligation to monitor public funds should be thought about very carefully.

If there is danger in the government's playing a role in dealing with the problem of academic fraud, then what should be done? It is clear that the problem exists, and that the research community must do something about it. Institutions must voluntarily put procedures in motion for dealing effectively with suspected cases of academic fraud. Unfortunately, the clever, systematic cheater—if he or she is truly clever—may never be caught. But, as we know, isolated cases do come to the attention of their colleagues and these cases must be dealt with quickly and efficiently.

It is the function of universities or research institutions to establish their own procedures consistent with the administrative hierarchy of those institutions. Chairpersons and deans cannot escape responsibility in the procedure. It is not possible to prescribe the precise system that any single institution should use. However, prototypes do exist. The Association of American Medical Colleges, for example, has outlined a sample procedure involving faculty, chairpersons and administrators that appears to be an admirable model from which procedures can be built.

Whatever procedures are established, there are two points that need to be emphasized. One is that it should be superfluous for the government to generate these procedures. They can and should be constructed by the institutions themselves. Second, any procedure should be outside the province of IRBs. I raise this point because Dr. Malone has placed in close juxtaposition our responsibility to human subjects and our concern with the integrity of research. I also raise this concern because we are, today, considering the response to academic fraud on the same program that we consider vital questions concerning IRBs. My position is that IRBs are precisely the wrong bodies to investigate fraud. IRBs were never established as investigative bodies. They do not typically involve the chains of command of the institution. The IRBs require the trust and good will of the faculty if they are to do successfully the job they were set up to do. And finally the method of selection of IRB members pertains to their expertise at evaluating research projects and their sensitivity to professional and community concerns about the treatment of human beings in research projects.

I also believe that the crux of the matter in curtailing academic fraud does not lie with the procedures for reacting to the allegation of wrong-doing. To the contrary, the crux of the issue lies with establishing a research environment which is conducive to integrity in science. In many ways, such an environment does not always exist today. The fact is that scientific publications take on the value of an economic commodity. They have professional and economic value for their owner. In the publish-or-perish mentality that exists in many institutions, the "publication" is the ticket to promotion and the ticket to raises in salary. The "publication" makes its owner marketable to other institutions and once again increases his or her economic value. In short, there are real and tangible rewards for turning out publications. If an investigator's data do not cooperate, there is an economic temptation to fraudulently create the data that will lead to a significant publication.

Now, it goes without saying that investigators who misrepresent or fabricate data are not engaging in science at all. Rather, they are engaging in grand larceny. As with other forms of grand larceny, the perpetrators who are caught must be punished. But is is also true that society should do whatever is in its power to reduce the temptation to enter into grand larceny. The academic institutions here have a major responsibility. The emphasis or perceived emphasis on the number of publications can be lessened. Quality can replace quantity as the criterion for advancements in prestige, promotion and income. Emphasis can be placed on the *process* of scientific inquiry rather than merely on the outcome. As universities, we must stop thievery. Simple punishment will not do the job as effectively as reducing the root causes of that thievery.

The government and the research community have been able to find compromises in dealing with the joint question of academic freedom and concern for the rights of human participants. Regulations have been applied with flexibility and wisdom by the Office of Protection from Research Risks. I fear that we are nearing the brink of yet a new series of governmental regulations for dealing with academic misconduct that may create a more stormy period than anything we have seen before. The universities, for their part, should seize the opportunity to move effectively and quickly to establish the procedures and the environment that will move toward a diminution of the problem. If they do not act, then, for better or for worse, the government surely will.

31. COMMENTS ON "FOSTERING INTEGRITY IN RESEARCH: A COLLECTIVE RESPONSIBILITY"

Herman S. Wigodsky

The following comments relate to some key statements (shown in quotes below) in Dr. Malone's paper.

1. "What began as primarily a fiscal partnership has evolved into a complex network in which all participants share responsibility for the continued well-being and productivity of the entire enterprise."

It is true that a complex network has evolved which, including the Institutional Review Boards, emphasizes the relationship between the PHS on the one hand and the institutions on the other. The partnership is real and effective based upon mutual respect. It should be remembered that the early IRB regulations appeared to attempt to allow the PHS and FDA to reach down into the interior of the institutions and make IRBs agencies of the NIH and FDA when the IRBs actually are agencies of the institutions. Recognition of the latter and emphasis upon the PHS-FDA relations with the *institutions* in the final IRB regulations resulted in the real partnership and network.

2. "The policies and implementing regulations you have been discussing reflect substantial consensus about a key element in governance of science."

Reference to the governance of science is inappropriate. Regulations are based upon *policies* and their implementation on the better definition of license. Governance of science is dependent upon *principles*. The governance of science is an inherent part of scientific societies and other scientific organizations and is not a matter for government regulation. Where governmental governance of science has been attempted, science has failed to thrive and even, in some instances, has led to national disasters.

3. "Their (regulations) development, modification and acceptance offer positive evidence that the research community can balance its behavior with the expectations of society as a whole."

It is inherent in science that it will respond to the expectations of society as a whole as science is international in scope and prospers when international exchange of knowledge is unlimited. The translation of scientific discovery into real benefits for mankind are a part of the scientific endeavor.

4. "A recent NIH review showed that 45 cases of alleged or suspected misconduct came to our attention between October 1, 1980 and September 30, 1982. Fewer than half of these proved to be factual, and some could be attributed to correctible deficiencies within the awardee institutions; these numbers are small, almost insignificant."

Falsification, fabrication, intentional misrepresentation or mishandling of data are the most serious kinds of violations of the scientific method and are, therefore, highly unethical. These are quite different from misuse of research funds and failure to comply with the terms and conditions of awards which are contractual violations involving illegal acts. The two should not be confused and their juxtaposition in several places in Dr. Malone's paper causes great uneasiness in the scientific community because they demand different responses. Laws and regulations may spell out punishments for contractual violations but are inappropriate for violations of the scientific method. The 45 cases which came to the attention of NIH appear to be a mixture of violations of the scientific method and contractual obligations. Since fewer than half proved to be factual, and assuming that the remainder were about evenly divided into one or the other of the two groups of violations, the incidence of violations of the scientific method at NIH (not FDA) is of the order of 11 or 12 per 20,000 NIH awards. This incidence of 0.06% is remarkably small and cannot help but make one wonder why "they are profoundly disquieting." Could it be that this is a political reaction? There are in place adequate means of detecting and dealing with contractual violations but it is highly unlikely that the methods used to detect, correct, and punish contractual violations will work in dealing with violations of the scientific method.

5. "—well founded concerns about the efficacy of traditional practices often cited as safeguards against misconduct—are based on the assumption that individual investigators, while perhaps erring in methodology or theory, are honest and well-intentioned. They are not designed to detect clever, systematic cheating."

It is true that institutions and funding agencies often are ill-prepared to deal with allegations or evidence of wrongdoing involving violations of the scientific method. Dealing with such violations are primarily the responsibility of the institutions and they, as a matter of good management and administration, should be encouraged to establish mechanisms for dealing with these matters promptly, fairly, and effectively. Delays in appointing ad hoc committees and slowness in acting are inimical to sound administration and sound science. Since falsification of data is unethical, and since human research subjects should not be exposed to unethical research, perhaps a requirement for inclusion of a statement in the general assurances of protection of human research subjects that the institution has in place a mechanism for dealing with such violations of the scientific method would be the encouragement referred to above. This emphasis upon the institutions' responsibilities would be appropriate and would parallel the institutions' ethical responsibilities for protecting subjects of human research. No system will detect infallibly the clever systematic cheater. Generally, these cheats are discovered as the result of complaints by "whistleblowers" or accidentally by unusually alert superiors.

6. "—to enable the funding agencies to deal with the increased number of cases of alleged or actual misconduct."

Is the apparent "increased number of cases of alleged or actual misconduct" real or is it the product of better communication and reporting in the network?

7. "—from individuals or institutions under investigation or subject to post-investigational sanctions."

   The implication from the juxtaposition of "individuals or institutions under investigation or subject to post-investigational sanctions" gives one an ominous feeling that investigation is tantamount to guilt or sanctions. There is no statement as to how this information is to be used. There is no question of the need for better internal communication within NIH. But protection of due process and privacy for the accused but innocent requires careful and skillful consideration.

8. "General Policies and Principles—a brief statement of policy, intended to underscore the commitment to integrity in all research that is funded, conducted, or regulated by the PHS."

Commitment to integrity is not unique to NIH but is a universal principle in science. A lack of integrity is unethical conduct and a most serious violation of the scientific method. It would not be amiss for NIH to review the universal principles and to indicate what policies it will follow in helping to assure that the principles are not violated.

9. "It emphasizes the need to protect the rights of accused individuals and 'whistleblowers' and to provide an adequate public record of the agencies' actions without violating the privacy of individuals."

The protection of privacy of individuals and the development of an adequate public record at first glance do not seem to be compatible. There is no adequate repair of breach of privacy and a public record is exactly that—public. The NIH would be well advised to approach this matter with extreme caution.

10. "—embodies many of the same principles enumerated in the extramural document."

Since principles are principles, one would certainly hope that what is good for the extramural goose would be good for the intramural gander. After all, extramural investigators bear to employers, the institutions, the same employer-employee relationship as intramural investigators do to the NIH.

11. "Interagency Collaboration and Communication—establishes mechanisms for ongoing consultation on matters of policy and for the collaboration on specific investigations of concern to more than one PHS agency."

Interagency collaboration and communication presents a broader arena within which protection of the privacy of individuals must be given every serious consideration.

12. "The scientific journals have similarly begun to consider whether changes in editorial policies may be needed."

NIH should have serious second thoughts before even contemplating any kind of interference with the freedom of the scientific press. To manipulate the daily press is serious enough, but the necessity for freedom of the scientific press is still greater.

13. "Especially gratifying has been the response of those who have been asked to lend their expertise to agency investigations."

"The response of those who have been asked to lend their expertise to agency investigations" is consistent with the principle of peer review and should not be surprising. One should not expect a medal for doing one's duty. One would hope that this experience would encourage NIH to make greater use of those governed by regulations in preparing drafts of regulations—a sort of governing with the consent of the governed.

The overall problem of integrity in research is one of individual values, how to impart these values to those entering into training in the scientific method and how to preserve these values throughout a career as a research investigator. This should be a matter of concern to scientific societies and to institutions. The "publish or perish" policy is in very serious need of revision to one of *quality* of publications.

In summary, the topics addressed by Dr. Malone can be condensed to:

1. Detection of real or apparent problems which are breaches of the scientific method.
2. The determination as to whether a real problem exists.
3. The imposition of administrative actions prior to completion of an investigation.
4. Procedures for investigation of alleged or real problems.
5. Administrative action following completion of an investigation.

In determining how and what is to be done in the preservation of integrity in research, there are certain policy considerations to be taken into account:

1. Protect the privacy and other rights of all concerned. *The PHS must be accountable for any findings or actions that may emerge from its investigations.*
2. PHS must work diligently to continue the trust relationship with the life sciences which has evolved over the years of partnership.
3. Misconduct in science is not just a federal problem nor is there only a federal solution.
4. The institutions have the responsibility to establish an environment that encourages free inquiry as well as high standards of conduct.
5. Major emphasis must be placed on the prompt and equitable resolution of issues at the institutional level.
6. Organized science (scientific societies, the American Association of Medical Colleges, the Association of American Universities, the National Academy of Sciences and others) has a continuing responsibility for assisting the partners—the institutions and the federal government—in maintaining the highest standards of the scientific method.

In relationship to academic freedom, freedom of inquiry, and other related matters:

1. Institutions reserve the right to decide what kind of research will be conducted in their facilities.
2. Public policy has supplemented professional standards with a greater definition of license.

There are certain indicated action items:

1. Place greater and continuing emphasis on the necessity for the scientific community to police itself.

2. Encourage institutions to implement, or if necessary, to initiate and implement, a mechanism which responds rapidly and equitably to allegations of violations of the scientific method.
3. Encourage scientific societies, institutions, etc., to inculcate in students, faculties, and other research investigators the high standards of personal integrity required to carry out research using the scientific method.
4. Protect, at all cost, the intramural and extramural scientific communities from politicization. The lessons of Lysenkoism need not be relearned in a new environment.

32. FOSTERING INTEGRITY IN RESEARCH: A FEDERAL PERSPECTIVE

Michele Applegate

I want to underline the collective responsibility for integrity in research which is the theme of this session. Clearly, the federal government, educational institutions, individual investigators, scientific journals and professional societies all have a role in creating an environment of integrity which is essential to public support for science. My comments on this subject reflect my personal views, as someone who has been involved in development of the Public Health Service (PHS) policy in this area.

To begin, I want to note my reservations about Federal policy development in this area. Clearly, we have a great challenge in trying to develop policies and procedures which protect the government's interests, but which also do not inappropriately interfere with the rights, responsibilities and relationships of trust with grantee institutions and the scientific community. Unfortunately, we are at a point when a structured, formal response to these issues is necessary. While the number of illustrious cases of misconduct has been very small, they have captured the attention of the public and the Congress. In fact, we are expecting legislative action shortly which will require us to establish procedures for responding to allegations of scientific fraud and violations of the rights of human subjects.

I hope that we can respond to this situation by developing guidance for agency staff and awardee institutions that reflects the values of science and which provides for a cooperative approach to this problem.

Boundaries of Misconduct in Science

In developing and implementing policy on misconduct, we need to be concerned with the boundaries of misconduct issues and how we should judge when misconduct has taken place.

The PHS has defined misconduct as covering three general types of activities (Public Health Service, 1983):

1. The violation by an investigator or institution of federal laws, regulations, or policies governing research or research training conducted,

funded or regulated by the Department of Health and Human Services, for example, mismanagement of Federal funds or material failure to comply with requirements governing the protection of human subjects or the welfare of laboratory animals.

2. Breaches of professional ethics that raise serious questions about an investigator's or institution's scientific or fiscal integrity, and
3. Serious failures to comply with other specific terms or conditions of an award.

While I believe this is the most straightforward statement we can make right now about the boundaries of our misconduct concerns, individual cases can present difficulties in terms of determining the appropriate scope and conclusions of an investigation. This issue seems most challenging in regard to alleged breaches of professional ethics. For example, to what extent is sloppiness in research a serious breach of professional ethics? I am sure there is a consensus that charges of fabrication and falsification of data must be investigated. However, is it misconduct when an investigator has failed to calculate an important statistic? Or does not pursue negative findings? Or does not have complete research records? Similarly, is it an issue of misconduct in science when one investigator alleges that another has reached inappropriate conclusions from the data she or he collected?

In my view, such issues typically can be resolved only in the context of specific cases. Our focus should be on the question of whether there is reasonable evidence of dishonesty, serious malfeasance or what Dr. Donald Frederickson (former Director, NIH) referred to as "violations of the scientific ethic" (Memorandum, 1980).

Conversely, it is also important that investigators, sponsoring institutions, and the public at large understand that misconduct procedures are *not* intended to deal with differences of opinion and of scientific judgment, which are part of the everyday business of science. Scientific disputes should be resolved through the normal channels of debating ideas and findings with colleagues, the refereed journal process, and perhaps even through professional organizations. Members of the various research professions may wish to give some thought to whether and how they might improve mechanisms for resolution of conflicting scientific judgments and conclusions.

Reporting of Allegations and Conduct of Investigations

Turning to the issue of how misconduct allegations are reported and handled, I want to highlight some key principles which I believe should be observed by the federal government, scientific institutions and others involved in such matters:

1. Above all, a fair and equitable process must be followed.

2. An atmosphere must be created where persons are encouraged to report allegations promptly, without fear of reprisal.
3. The person making an allegation has a responsibility to provide a reasonable basis for the charges he or she makes.
4. There must be an opportunity for the subject of an investigation to know the charges against him or her and respond to these.
5. Confidentiality should be observed to the maximum extent possible, in order to protect the rights of the subject of an investigation, and where requested, the person making allegations.
6. Investigations should be carried out by persons who clearly can act with objectivity in the case.
7. Where there is a finding of misconduct, appropriate sanctions should be applied; conversely, where allegations are not substantiated, steps should be taken as needed to restore the researcher's reputation.

Formal procedures embodying these principles are needed to protect the rights and interests of all involved parties, as well as to maintain public trust in the integrity of science. In general, the procedures PHS is developing for extramural programs reflect the position that matters of misconduct are best handled in a fact-finding, rather than adversarial, manner. This model seems to us the best suited to resolving the difficult types of professional judgment in this arena, and to fostering cooperation and prompt action by the various parties involved. I would add that we are interested in providing maximum opportunity for local institutions to deal with allegations of misconduct by their faculty or employees. However, it is also important to note that the interests of institutions and the federal government may not always be identical and may therefore require cooperative or possible separate responses to allegations.

While the Government and representatives of educational institutions (e.g., AAMC and AAU) have made some useful progress in developing appropriate procedures for preventing or dealing with misconduct, clearly further efforts are needed at all levels. I would encourage those of you attending this session to join in the debate about these issues and to help to refine the evolving strategies for fostering integrity in science.

The opinions expressed in this paper are those of the author and do not necessarily represent the views of the Alcohol, Drug Abuse and Mental Health Administration

REFERENCES

Memorandum: Rogues in science: The limitations of procedural safeguards. *Information*, August 7, 1980.

Public Health Services, General policies for handling misconduct in science, January 25, 1983.

33. FOSTERING INTEGRITY IN RESEARCH—NIH RESPONSE

Mary L. Miers

The Public Health Service (PHS) initiatives described earlier are largely an outgrowth of recent NIH experience. As the principal research funding agency, NIH has had the dubious honor of confronting the lion's share of the problems associated with detecting and dealing with misconduct in funded research programs. I would like to share some of the perspectives we have gained in the past year or two.

First, I should emphasize that we do regard the canons of the scientific method and the integrity of individual investigators as the most important factors in fostering integrity in research. The academic and research institutes have traditionally been committed unequivocally to high standards of professionalism whether or not Federal funds are involved. This includes, but is certainly not limited to, the observance of applicable laws, regulations and terms of awards.

I cannot emphasize too strongly that the recent efforts to improve PHS policies and procedures do not signify a lack of confidence in the extramural research community, although I think that there is general agreement that, like PHS, many institutions have not been fully prepared to deal with some cases that have surfaced in recent years. Our initiatives were driven primarily by the recognition that the guidance available to our own staff and awardees has been woefully inadequate. We continue to rely on and appreciate the efforts of individual researchers, mentors, and administrators who recognize and exercise their responsibilities for the well-being of the research enterprise and the stewardship of Federal funds.

Although we are still feeling our way to some extent, we at NIH believe that we have made considerable progress in the past few years. We have completed a number of difficult and time-consuming investigations, for the most part with the complete cooperation of the institutions and individuals involved. When misconduct has been judged to have occurred, we have attempted to impose sanctions commensurate with the infraction. When ongoing or pending awards have been involved, we have worked with awardees to try to protect the public's investment without compromising individual reputations or disrupting ongoing projects. In cases in which the subject of the investigation has disagreed with our findings, we have made every effort to develop a public record that accurately portrays all points of view. And we have developed an orderly and equitable process for preparing an investigative report, soliciting comments of the affected parties and revising as needed, arranging for impartial review by senior agency staff, and making recommendations to appropriate decision makers.

We certainly don't have all the answers. Many allegations are simply very difficult to investigate; some seem impossible to resolve fully. What appears to be deliberate misrepresentation to one person may simply be poor methodology in the eyes of another. We provide an opportunity to comment on draft investigative reports as a matter of simple equity, but it can be used to prolong or complicate an investigation unnecessarily. Protecting the rights of informants and restoring the reputation of those who have been wrongly accused continue to present major challenges to us as well as to the research institutions.

I would like to conclude by reiterating that integrity in research is indeed our joint problem and responsibility. I am personally convinced that recent increases in reporting are attributable less to changes in behavior than to the perception that the institutions and funding agencies want to know and are prepared to act. This perception, in turn, may serve as the most effective deterrent to misconduct in science.

The public patrons of science long have admired its commitments to rigor and objectivity. They have every right to expect us to uphold our time-honored code of conduct.